# THE BISMARCK SEA
# RAN RED

**J. ARBON and CHRIS CHRISTENSEN**

# Preface

As far as we know, this unbelievable, but true, WW II aerial combat experience has never been told.

Somewhere out in the boondocks of the forbidden land of New Guinea, about three miles west of Buna, where the giant bats wing their way south in the dusk of evening, and millions of birds scream and quarrel, stands a marble shaft. Now smothered in the tangled growth of the rain forest of 37 years, it has a message for all the world. A message that needs to be told.

Inscribed on the sides of this stone monument on bronze tablets are the names of the young Americans who fell in this "green hell" for a cause that only God can adjudicate. Many thousands of Yankee kids found themselves over there in the war fighting an enemy in a hostile jungle totally alien from any war that had ever been fought before. The foe was so strongly entrenched in the jungle that it was impossible to get at them except through the air. But to attack them from the air meant a whole new approach in aerial warfare.

Our B-25's that carried death and destruction to the enemy, became the most devastating fighting machines ever developed. Our foe had no effective defense against them. They could destroy some of us, but they could not stop us. Their harbors and bases would result to smoking ruins, and their ships would wind up on the bottom of the sea.

We had come to get the job done, to finish it and get back home. But for thousands life was cut too short. In this story I am attempting to relive for you some of the drama and choking fear that every one of us as combat crew members of the Grim Reaper outfit had to suffer at the time. Accordingly, I have written this as I so vividly remember it, mostly in the present tense.

By the grace of God, I was in the thick of it at the beginning of the war when the war was the toughest. Two years of my life are stamped very vividly in my mind, to the extent that I can, after 37 years, recall almost every detail.

Two years of American history, that, in the busy marts of human activity, has gone with the wind. But it did happen, and they were, so their lives were not given in vain. All those young lives were cut short by the bullets of the enemy. Has their loss been our gain?

As one whose name did not get on the stone memorial in the New Guinea jungle, I now tell their story. It is mostly about the smashing firepower of the converted B-25, and the kids who manned them, and their desire to "get it over with", and get back to the States.

This book is dedicated to General Kenney's "kids" who lost their lives flying the super destructive B-25 skip bomber-strafers out of New Guinea during the early part of WW II, and whose names are inscribed on the monument we built in the jungle at Buna, New Guinea.

# TABLE OF CONTENTS

# CHAPTER 1

## WEST TO AUSTRALIA

Our radio waves crackled with war talk. It was in 1940. The screaming threats of Adolph Hitler, beamed to the world from Germany, were front page bold type in all newspapers. His sword rattling put Washington on the alert.

There were rumblings from the Orient also. The technical advances in weaponry, and know how to make war was giving the aggressive have-not nations a new impetus and confidence in a demand for more territory and resources. With new modern arms they thought to gain a way to terrorize the peace loving nations into submission. The race for arms went to the aggressive nations. To rain war from the skies was their chief device to strike the people with terror.

Strange words and ideas began to seep into our vocabulary which formerly were used by only the military. The military, who for a long time had not received much attention in the States, now took on status. People even began to salute the flag.

The United States, the most affluent and potentially powerful nation in the world, was not in a position to remain aloof from crises that seemed to be developing among the industrial nations. It was plain that America had to stand up to these aggressors.

"In defense", America began to mobilize.

The words of President Roosevelt, "ah hate wah" did not deter America's escalating preparations for war. With these

1

preparations the great depression was over. People were eager and excited about the new jobs and good wages that were now being offered. The social and economic climate in America was given a great impetus. War clouds in Europe got thicker and blacker. Rumblings also came from the Orient. Here was another nation to be heard from. Japan needed more space, more of the earth's natural resources for her people. Another nation without was on the march.

The scare of all-out war was in the air. The threat of modern war was a fearful thing. We did not know how destructive the new, never tried weapons would be until they were tried. But they had been tried in Spain with dire results. Warmongers thought that their psychological war would bring them quick and easy victory. America was being inexorably sucked into the vortex.

From the time during the depression, when it seemed there were too many men, suddenly America needed more manpower. The call went out for volunteers for the now building armed forces. Not to go to war, but to prevent us from having to go to war, was the cry. We would show the warmongers we were ready, and that they better not start anything.

The first call was for one year. Get in your stint for Uncle Sam and then you can be free from any further military service.

I was prime draft material. This volunteering business seemed just the thing for me. So I enlisted in the Army Air Corps. That was where the glamour was. It would be a lark. One year and I would be home and be free to live my life. But like so many wars in the past it didn't seem serious then. No nation dare come against the might of America. It would soon be over.

I soon discovered that enlistment wasn't a lark either. Basic training taught me the Army meant business. I'd better take this seriously.

After graduating from Curtis Wright Tech I was assigned to the 7th Bombardment Group. We got the word we were being shipped out and our destination was "PLUM" which was a coded word for Clark Field in the Philippines. I told my mother on my last trip home that we were going to fight the Japs. This she did not believe. It did seem remote at the time. This was a month before Pearl Harbor. Our farewell was so full of uncertainties, it was pretty hard to take. Like thousands of others in the same situation, I left the country reluctantly. How did we ever get in this mess?

There was an uncanny, inexplicable feeling in our outfit that war was inevitable. There could be no other explanation. Our seven ship convoy was just three days out of Pearl Harbor when the Japs stabbed us in the back. The news we heard of the sneak attack was amplified over the loud speaker system. We could not believe it. We had just left Pearl. It must be a joke, a propaganda trick of the Japanese. It couldn't be true. It was two weeks before we admitted to ourselves that it was really true.

The 7th Bombardment Group had just recently received brand new B-17's. Those big planes were being flown from Hamilton Field to Hickam Field in Hawaii. They were landing when the Japs hit. All those big beautiful planes were destroyed.

This was war and sooner than we thought. New orders came from Washington. "PLUM" was canceled and we were heading for Australia. This was something we could not understand. We expected we would be right in the thick of the fight. We could have helped those guys trapped over there

3

in the Philippines. We were six ships loaded to the hilt with men and supplies and with a destroyer escort. Our mission was to fight Japs. We knew it all the time. Why did we turn away? We could not understand.

The enemy knew about us. Of that we did not doubt. Their spies in Hawaii had seen our ships leave Pearl. So the war was on. We were alerted for an attack on our convoy. We knew the enemy could wipe us out if they found us.

Submarines were our big worry. The chance of being torpedoed was a sobering prospect.

Tokyo Rose, the voice of Nippon to the American Armed Forces, even reported that our ship, the Republic, had been sunk. She repeated the news many times to make it more convincing. The only people she didn't convince were us, who were on board. But the news didn't make us feel a bit more secure. There was one thing for sure—they knew we were there.

The trip to Australia was a nightmare for us. Thirty two long hot hellish days we spent trying to exist on those over-crowded transports. There was always the gnawing fear of attack. The attack alarm would awaken us in the middle of the night or any other unexpected time. We would scramble to our abandon ship positions on deck and wait and watch. We would crowd the rail to scan the sea for the tell-tale sign of an approaching torpedo, waiting for the explosion, which luckily never came but was hell in the suspension. This was lived over and over again. What we did see were flying fish, porpoises, whales, and those dorsal fins of the ever present lurking sharks. Those devils of the sea were hungry for anything and we knew their intentions if we ever had to take to the water. They would follow in our wake ready to devour anything that might be thrown or would fall overboard.

4

We had strict orders not to throw anything into the sea. Anything left floating on the sea would be a dead giveaway for any searching sub. All they would have to do would be to follow our trail to find us.

We trailed a zigzag course now, trying our best to avoid any subs. This slowed our time and the monotony of our journey. This was not to our liking, but was part of war strategy.

We were a bunch of landlubbers and the sea was not our first love. Almost as soon as we set foot on board most of us contracted the old usual landlubbers malady called seasickness. Sick? We were the sickest bunch of humans that ever rode the rails of any ship. Agony? This agony can be almost akin to death, especially when vomiting from an already emptied stomach. Garbage cans we used for repositories, when there was no room at the rails.

And seasickness can be catching, especially by the bilious smell of it. There was no escape. The nauseating odor of vomit filled the entire ship. And the sight of some mothers son retching over a garbage can didn't help to keep your own breakfast down.

But no one died of seasickness, really. They just wished they were dead. And then, when we finally began to get our sea legs, it was hard not to get a relapse on the food they gave us. It was dried and powdered, and beans every morning for breakfast.

But we sailed on and mostly leaving a clean sea behind. The ship we were on had been christened the Republic. This was a misnomer. She was German built and had been taken over by the U.S. as part of reparations from World War I. She had few refinements and no conveniences. She was carrying enough human freight to fill all her space. No diversion was possible. Wherever a man stood it was the wrong place. "Move away buddy, you can't stand here", was the eternal cry from the Navy crewmen who had the job of keeping the big tub in some sort of ship-shape.

Talk became our only escape from the dead monotony and misery. It was a way to forget. To talk and exchange experiences and stories was a way out of what we imagined was in store for us. Some of the kids had the gift of telling stories and jokes. These kids always had an audience. You guessed it. Most of the conversation was about girls and some of the talk was pretty raw.

And there was the American freedom in griping. Why were we here? There must be a reason. This was made the butt of our jokes and as a means of letting off steam. Why did the Japs do this to us? Who do they think they are? Do they not know that we are superior to them? We can wipe them off the face of the earth in time. One thing they failed to consider was that what they did at Pearl galvanized the whole nation of America to united action. We all agreed that Japan was in for a licking. We were there to hand out the first blows.

But on a man to man basis it was home that we talked about. We soon gathered that we were all proud of our homeland, and that we would go to war with those little yellow Asian monkeys.

We got close to each other. We made friends and told of our private feelings concerning the stab in the back the little country of Japan is guilty of. We learned to know each other. I knew our friendship would be broken, and we would perhaps never see each other again. But while it lasted it was real. Most of us believed we would meet again somewhere.

Ard would go to India. Juel would go to China after he married an Aussie sheila. Smitty would go to Java. Meza would go to India also. Others would go to China. Some would go to Darwin, and Alice Springs, and Amberly Field, and some went to New Guinea where I went. But most of us went to Java, China, and India.

Crossing the equator was ritual. When the Southern Cross replaced Polaris, we had to be initiated, every last one of us. This was protocol for the Navy. There must have been between four and five thousand of us on that old tub. And every last one of us had to be whacked on the butt with a paddle. We had to crawl through a huge pipe sprayed full of salt water. We sat in a chair while the Navy poured tar and oil on us. Then they tipped the chair while the Navy poured boiling salt water on us. Our heads were shaved and we were whacked and re-whacked 'til the tears came. After it was all over we were changed from pollywogs to shellbacks and they gave us a diploma to prove it. The diploma is now our passport and assurance policy that we'd never again have to do homage to Neptune.

It took two days to clean up the ship and us. But tough as it was it was a diversion and we enjoyed it. It was better than being bored and seasick.

Land? How we longed to get back on the good earth. Was there any such thing as land out in this huge ocean? There must be land somewhere in these thousands of miles of tossing, heaving water. On this rolling, smelly, bilious boat, it was a constant struggle just to keep one's balance and keep out of the way. Few of us had the strength to keep our head up or our breakfast down.

Then we sighted it. Land. It was a sight to behold. The Fiji Islands. Could anything be so beautiful? This must be the lush, green, tropical land of the South Pacific. This was a part of the land we had come to defend, and which we would be so accustomed to see and live in in the next few years.

It was a sight unbelievable. What a pretty land. But it was no land for us. There would be no shore leave for us here. All we saw of the islands was what we could see from the ship. It was only a glimpse over someone's shoulder. One of us got to go ashore. One of our buddies died of sunburn and the general hell we all had to endure. He was our first casualty and they left him on Fiji.

But we did get to see some of the natives. True to South Sea courtesy and curiosity, the natives came out to our ship in their boats to give us a greeting. With their immense hairdo's and mini skirts, it was not hard to see where some of the American styles originated.

The nights were stifling below decks. There were too many bodies and not enough air. So we would go topside where the air was free of the stench of puke. But nowhere could we find a cool place. Maybe there would be a breeze. But this night there was no breath of air stirring. The sea was dead calm. The water was like glass. I walked the deck and watched the eeriness of the night in the South Seas. Southern stars do shine bright like in the movies, and the Southern Cross is beautiful in the clear sky. Flashes of light came from the water, stirred up in our wake. And occasionally a flash would come out from the sea as a fish would disturb the surface. This was the curious phosphorescent light that comes from the phosphorous in the water.

There was an eery still in the night. Then came a cooling breath of air. It started like a whisper, steady, refreshing.

Something began to stir out there in the night. As the air got cooler and the night wore on the breeze became a wind. The glazened sea began to ruffle. By morning we had a steady blowing wind which rose the waves higher and higher to white caps and white water. We were in for a blow. The sun rose out of the sea in a mist. Cumulus clouds began to appear while the wind built up and up as the water began to boil.

Are we heading into a typhoon? This old tub won't take a thyphoon. The word goes round that this will not be a thyphoon, just a stiff storm. But typhoon or storm, this is bad enough. The wind rose to 70 miles per hour bow up bow down, and the old ship plowed through the swells. Now the troops begin to heave again. Some are now chasing garbage cans which are sliding across the deck. You can't throw up over the side if you are not on the leeward side, and only a few can line the leeward side. About noon the storm builds to its maximum and then tapers off some. But the wind held to about 65 miles per hour to about 1800 hours, then eased off during the wee hours. The next morning it tapered down and by nightfall it was back to normal again.

Our convoy is now 28 days out of Frisco and off the starboard beam on the far horizon is a black line that we learned was New Caledonia. A speck on the water line she is, but it is New Caledonia. This means we are only two or three days out of Australia. Wouldn't it be great to walk off this old boat and into the jungle and look for fresh fruit? Fresh fruit? What is that?

No person aboard ship except the crew knows where we are going to land in Australia, but I saw a chart, and if New Caledonia is to starboard we are heading for Brisbane which is the largest city on the northeast coast of the land down under. The people there are not going to believe that we came to help so soon. We will be the first Yanks to ever come to Australia but for visiting warships in peacetime.

The storm is finished and the Navy crews are hosing down the decks with sea water. We are now about two days off the Australian coast and then we sight an airplane high in the sky near the sun. You can bet this catches the attention of everyone on board. Is it friendly or enemy? It heads our way and circles. It is in a dive and headed for us. It must be Japanese. An Aussie plane would not dive on us. Then it comes closer and we can read their Aussie round insignia. Later we learned it was a Beaufighter. It circled our convoy at a wide angle, then it came closer and closer. What a sight for sore eyes. We feast our attention on that harbinger of friends and the new land. It circles low, dips its wings, and heads north into the blue. The next day we awaken to see land. It is the coast of Australia. When the sun burns off the haze we see clearly and we are quite close to shore. The coastline is low. No mountains. We see a town or city. It must be Brisbane. As we move closer I can see the entrance to a harbor. We still are not sure where we are. Boy, that is the most welcomed sight I have ever seen. There may be many people here to meet us if the pilot who spotted us reported us.

But maybe we will anchor out. Our commanding officer may not even let us go ashore. They may send us directly to New Guinea where the war is.

Our ship slowly eases up to the dock without the aid of a tug. There are no crowds there to greet us. What's the matter with the Aussies? Don't they know the Yanks have come?

The good word comes. We can go ashore if we will keep our mouths shut. Who wouldn't? We have nothing to talk about. We know no military secrets. The military police and shore patrol will be walking the streets and checking their bars. Anyone who gets drunk will be toted back to the ship. That should be incentive enough.

The Yanks are here. The word spreads and the people come swarming into the city to see their liberators. Tens of thousands of Aussies fill the streets. And what a welcome! We found the people down under real after all. They came to see the Yanks. They had never seen a Yank before.

# CHAPTER 2

## THE GRATEFUL AUSSIES

The Aussies were running scared when we got there. The yellow peril was right on their doorstep. Every newscast told of the inevitable conquest by the Japanese war machine as it took island after island on its way south. It seemed there was no stopping them. It was evident that Australia was their big objective.

In any war of conquest, it seems beauty and booty is the prize. For the Japanese soldiers to take over their land was terrorizing to all the Aussies, especially the girls. When we landed at Brisbane we were like a gift of the gods to them. When the news got out that we were really there, the people flocked to see us. They came by the thousands. The psyche of our arrival was or came as great relief to the frenzy of fear that had been haunting them. And after the 32 days of hell on the sea, we were as happy to be there as they were to have us, no matter what else might be in store for us.

The streets were lined with pretty young girls—eager and waiting. We all had our pick and it was a stupid G.I. who grabbed the first one in sight when there was so many to choose from. We were already their heroes and we hadn't been to war yet. At the time we could not have helped defend their land because our weapons on the way over had been destroyed at Hickam Field.

It was not hard to see that this business of war might have its compensations. From the stern realities of war we

12

had found a Shangrila. The balmy breezes of the land down under were freighted with romance. These were people just like back home, but for their accent. The femes were tall blond and beautiful, showing an ancestry common to our own. We took to them as long lost cousins. There was no formality in getting acquainted. Would we not be their saviors? American movies and the media had created the image for us. We were the Yanks and as far as they were concerned, that was enough. They swarmed over us. "Buy ya a drink, maitee? Wanna meet me sister maitee?" So many girls and few men. Where are the Aussie men? It didn't take long to learn that the Aussie men were out of the country fighting the war for England. Most were in Europe and Africa and some were in New Guinea trying to stop the Jap advance. It was not hard to take their places in the hearts of the Aussie girls. They were for the taking, but nothing comes free in this world, and we found too often that they took us.

There was this cute little blonde who came after me. She followed me on the street until I could not shake her. I finally turned to her and introduced myself. From that time on I was unable to shake her. Not boasting, but I was a Yank, and that was enough. Her name was Monica and, anyway, she made me feel special. She told me that she would give up all of Australia for me. That was impressive, but not impressive in enough ways to sway me to find a way to get her to the States. That's what she wanted. However, there was no future in that for either of us. I probably would not get back to the States myself.

Some of the Yanks got caught in the tender trap, and got led to the alter. They thought it was a good move at the time, but in most cases it was a stupid mistake. There was

13

no settling down for them. They were soon shipped out never to return. Other Yanks came in to take over the wives and the girlfriends. It became a cycle. There was nothing in it but disappointment and heartbreak. But that is the way of war.

The 88th Reconnaissance Squadron with the 7th Bombardment Group moved to the Ascot race track and set up camp. This delighted us. This meant that we were going to stay awhile. Could this last long? It was too good to be true. We all knew that, but while it lasted, we enjoyed it.

Our duties were minimal. Drill and inspection and then we went to town. The girls always were waiting for us. We needed very little money. The Aussies would not let us spend our money in the beginning. The merchants even gave us special prices. A meal in a restaurant cost a few cents or Australian shillings.

But it wasn't long until inflation struck. The Aussie merchants could not resist all that American money floating around. They jacked up their prices and we knew we were being taken. Prices went up and away went our money. How could they do this to us? We had come over here to save them.

We hung on every newscast. The war news was all bad. The Nips were taking every island they wanted. They had just taken Milne Bay on the southeast coast of New Guinea and close to Port Moresby. They could now control nearly a whole of the second largest island. And we are helpless to stop them because we have nothing to fight with. The word from here is that all war materiels are going to Europe.

If we had our airplanes we could strike a blow at them from Port Moresby. From there we could hit all their bases in southern New Guinea, New Britain, and New Ireland. The names of all their bases will someday soon become stamped in my memory. These places will be few of our targets in the titanic struggle for the superior advantage in the air that we will finally get when we receive our B-25's.

We learn there is an Aussie infantry regiment moving through the jungle up the coast of New Guinea toward Milne Bay. We are hoping they will take it and begin pushing the Japs back. But one regiment is hardly enough force to re-take this strong enemy base. The Aussies are stubborn fighters and we are hoping they will hold out long enough so we can get there to help them.

The war records of the Aussies is a proud thing, and to the world they stand in high esteem. Like the Americans they have learned self-reliance. This has put them in good stead when they have had to face great odds. They are not a military people, but when the need comes the people can muster a citizen's army that will not flinch in the face of any danger.

Because they are a part of the British commonwealth, the mother country has given them some pretty tough assignments far from their native land. In World War I, they played a vital role in stopping the German advance in France. Now in World War II, under great odds they acquired the nickname of the "Rats of Tobruk" in stopping the Germans again in Africa. Now they are fighting for their homeland in the steaming jungles of New Guinea, to try to stop the advance of the Japanese, and again under great odds. They will never give up, of that we can be sure.

We had come to help them, but we were not anxious to get there. We talked to some of the Aussies who had been to New Guinea. They said it was a hellhole of heat, vermin,

15

malaria, and dengue fever.

We moved our camp to Amberly Field, near a little town called Ipswich, about 60 miles inland from Brisbane. We were the happiest guys on the earth. This meant we were going to be in Australia a while longer, and at the time New Guinea seemed remote.

Like Brisbane the girls came running. The people of Ipswich had never seen a Yank or an American tourist before either, and they too presented the town to us. If a Yank was with an Aussie he couldn't spend a dime or a tupence. To meet the girls we would just walk down a street. They would walk right up and start talking in their clipped Australian dialect. We liked that, and this was one of the attractions they had for us. And they seemed to like the way we talked too.

However, Brisbane was more fun. It was a bigger city and there was more to do there. It was no problem to get there. There was a funny train that ran between the two cities with an antique locomotive and a high screetching whistle. Many times we rode this little train and each time it was like riding the little train at Liberty Park when I was a kid. Especially when it was loaded with Yanks and girls that always seemed to have something to do in Brisbane, when we "went to town".

Amberly Field seems like home to me. I am semi-permanently stationed here. Many different Air Corps organizations are coming and going while I am here, but I am staying. I can't understand this. What does this fouled up Air Corps organization have in mind for me? Or do they have anything in mind? What am I griping about? I've really got it made. I'm assigned to each group a short time while it is here, and when it moves up north, I'm attached to another Air Corps messed up organization. What a set up. I have no duties so I go to town. This is the good life. I didn't know the Air Corps could ever be like this.

So, I make the best of a good thing and take train trips to other towns for diversion. These towns are something out of the years of ox carts in the old west. Even in the small towns Aussies line up for their beer in the late afternoon to drink all they can while the pubs are open. The Aussies love their beer. They line up in long queues waiting for the pubs to open. The shortage of beer seems to whet their appetite. They want even more. They guzzle their beer as fast as they can, trying to outdrink each other. The Aussie beer has more kick in it than our Stateside beer. It didn't take them long to get on their way to being fighting mad. It was always a lively time around the pubs an hour or two after they opened, and the steam from the beer began to seep into the brains of the Aussies a little at a time. There was much oratory, and arguments, and some fighting. Women of course were the main subjects, then came talk of the Jap threat.

Travel for civilians in 1942 was mostly by train. There was no gasoline, so the enterprising Aussies converted their cars to burn charcoal. But their little trains were fun to ride. There was always someone to meet on the train, especially girls.

For a Yank, the land down under is turned around. Shadows point south, and to find the sun you have to look north. Unless it is December and then the sun can be straight up. Can it be hot? The north of the country is where the heat is, and it is hard to get used to a tropical land being in the north.

If Australia is an island it surely is a big one. It is as big

17

as the whole country of America. It is divided into six states which are all about the size of Alaska. But there's proof that it is an island. The kind of flora and fauna found there is found nowhere in the world. These are unique making it seem like a world apart.

There is a species of four legged animal there that stands erect like a human. It eats sitting on its tail and hind legs. It can run up to 30 miles an hour in great leaps through the air making three point landings. It holds the worlds broad jump record and stands seven feet tall when it straightens up. It has ears like a mule and chews like a deer. They are a variety of sizes from the little rat size roo to the big seven footers.

Because of their jumping tactics nature has provided them with a carrying pouch for their babies. This pouch can shut zipper tight and open to allow junior fresh air and freedom if he desires. He is born tiny and hairless. When he is growing up he has a nipple for food within reach of his pouch.

Also, you will find an animal that lays an egg like a hen. And there is the beautiful and facinating little koala bear. These animals if captured when young make perfect pets, and we had one for our mascot, and it used to ride on the back of our squadron dog.

The native inhabitants of Australia are in a way different also. They have no known relatives anywhere in the world. They look similar to African natives and are coal black when mature, but some are born with light skin and are blonde until they get older. They live in bands or tribes like the American natives and travel over the land, from its lush rainforests, to the most forbidding desert area. Many of them still hold to their primitive ways and are hunters, but others have moved to the cities and have taken to the ways of the white man.

The eucalyptus tree comes in 32 varieties and is also different and strictly Australian. It is hardwood and burns with a sweet odor, and is both pleasing and medicinal. They are now growing in many parts of the world, including a large variety in California. You may know when you see one that it orginally came from down under.

Two of my friends and I went hunting kangaroos. We rode the train as far as we could go and then started walking. We had our 30 caliber Girand semi-automatic rifles which gave us plenty of fire power for any game we might scare up. All the area was wide open with tiny groves of eucalyptus trees. We decided to split up. Soon I could spot several roos hopping away but too far for my gun. Then I scared up two kangaroo rats. They were too small for my meat. Suddenly two big roos flushed from cover right under my feet. The wicked Girand gave them no quarter. One of them went down while I let the other one go. This was too easy. With a Girand all you have to do is pull and pull until you find the mark. I killed five more in the same way and felt ashamed. It wasn't sportsmanship. We let them lay and went back to base. I never shot another roo, although there were thousands in the bush. I might say that I came to kill, but not kangaroos.

This waiting for airplanes was getting on my nerves. A few A-17 Douglas Dauntless two man Navy dive bombers survived the trip with our convoy. They are now idly sitting on the Amberly Field dispersal area. They are just waiting for someone to fly them. These old planes are obsolete, but perhaps they are better than nothing. We kept eyeing those old planes. They are no match for the Jap zero, but they are all we have. Maybe we could fix them up. Well, there is nothing else to do.

I wanted to get into the war. This was the stupid youth in me, but I was tired of nothing to do. We got it through the grapevine that all the war materiels were being sent to Europe and we would have to wait until they knocked Hitler out of the war.

Then I ask myself what I am beefing about. I could be rotting in the jungles of New Guinea. Instead I have the run of unspoiled Australia. I am complaining?

Rumors. There's no time like wartime and also no place like the Army for rumors. When we don't get any word from the top brass we have rumors. Scuttlebut has it that there is danger of a Jap invasion from the Coral Sea and the north coast of Australia. We are told to wear our side arms at all times. Those little Nips are crafty. They could infiltrate without us knowing it. So we wore our side arms. The Aussies noticed this and some of us were confronted by the Aussies. They were scared and wanted to buy guns from us. We could not sell guns to them of course, but one couldn't blame them for trying.

The Japs did not invade. Not because they didn't have the means to do it, but because, at the time they were overextended in territory. At the time their empire extended from Japan to Alaska, China, most of Indonesia, the Philippines, a big part of the Solomons, New Britain, New Ireland, a big part of New Guinea, and many other islands. A logical reason as to why they didn't take more was that they had too much already.

My wartime buddy, big George F. Juel went to the altar. He would rather fight than eat, but a little Aussie sheila tamed him. She led him to the altar as meek as a lamb. But

20

after the wedding he broke loose. The party lasted all night and the grog ran like rainwater. The new couple was riding on cloud nine until ten days later when an order was cut and big George was shipped out. I never saw him again.

I wanted to get into the war. I was bored to be useless. Weapons were still not coming in from the States. I went down to the Brisbane docks to watch for airplanes being unloaded. There were none. It seemed we would never get any airplanes.

Then we heard that MacArthur was coming to Brisbane from the Philippines which seemed to be good news. Now we might get some airplanes and get ready to attack the Japs. He would put some pressure on Washington and get us some planes.

But bad news follows good. There were some men at Amberly now who had been with MacArthur in the Philippines. They were eager to talk. One of them became my confidential friend. He told me he hated "glory Mac" with a passion. He said he was going to shoot "glory Mac" when he got his chance. "MacArthur considers himself a God and someone must stop him." He said "glory Mac" was hated by the troops more than any general ever, and he told of some of the stupid things "glory Mac" had done. "And the people back home believe he is a great hero. 'I shall return,' the great general said, as if he was the whole show, with no regard for the millions of service men who were to do the dirty work to make it possible for the great God to return".

"Well "glory Mac" was never shot and it was because the "great general" was afraid to show his head out of his hole", my friend said. "That is why they also called him "dougout Doug".

But there was a bright side to the story. A general named

21

George Kenney came to Brisbane to organize the 5th Air Force. His headquarters is to be in the Lennon Hotel. I shall never forget the Lennon Hotel because that is where I was ordered to report to be decorated by our esteemed General Kenney when the war was over for me.

Rumor spread that General Kenney was some kind of general. That he was a regular guy in a generals uniform who would not order his men to do anything that he would not do himself. And time proved this to be true. Soon we heard some reports that the General was flying over Papau without fighter escort. We supposed he was planning his strategy and getting the layout of the Papuan campaign first hand. MacArthur made a similar trip over Southern New Guinea. He had ten Army Air Corps pursuit planes escorting him. We saw a huge picture on the front page of the newspaper in Brisbane showing "glory Mac" looking the situation over from the waist gun position of a B-17, as if he was up there fighting Japs. General "Ike" pretty well put him in his place when he told the country that "MacArthur was an actor, the best actor I have ever served under."

The Aussies in New Guinea, with the help of a few Yanks have attacked and re-taken the seaport base of Milne Bay. This is the first time in the Southwest Pacific for our troops to hit the enemy in a ground offensive. It was a very tough battle. They not only had to beat the Jap, they also had to fight malaria, heat, lack of supplies, dengue fever, and rain.

The call came for volunteers to work on the old A-17 dive bombers that have been sitting in the boondocks at Amberly gathering rust. Smart guys in the Army never volunteer. Well, I'm just sick and tired of doing nothing, so I volunteer.

Are we really going to attack the Japs with that little

handful of obsolete crates? Well that seems to be on someone's mind. This is insane. These airplanes must have come out of WW I. So I pitched in to help make the old relics flyable. They have open cockpits and only four little 30 caliber machine guns—two for the gunner and two for the pilot.

After days of work, we finally get eight of them ready to fly. I'm invited by one pilot to make a few practice dive bombing runs. We practice bombing with duds day after day until, much to our surprise, we get pretty good. There is one good thing about those old dive bombers. They are accurate.

They are accurate dive bombers but they are no match for the Japanese Zero. We will have to stay away from them. The Zero is a better plane. It is much faster and more maneuverable. These planes have poor defense also. The guns are too small and there are not enough guns. The two 30 caliber guns that are fixed and fire forward do not have enough firepower and the two 30's aft of the pilot are not enough either. The gunners seat has a 360 degree railing and these guns do fire in a complete circle, but vertically they can only be fired about 60 degrees. We would not have a chance against the Jap Zero.

The dive flaps that slow the plane down in a dive gave us some trouble, but after some experiments we were able to solve that problem. To compete with the Zero we had another weakness. I learned that the Zero had a very high ceiling. The A-17 does not have a supercharger so it has a low ceiling. But the big problem with this airplane will be its slowness and lack of agility. This we would have to live with—or die. The Jap Zero, we have heard, is so fast you can hardly swing your guns fast enough to follow it.

Doolittle's B-25's have just made a daring raid on Tokyo from an aircraft carrier. This unbelievable feat electrified our troops. It is a coincidence that this should happen just as we are about to try to do something similar. What we will try to do will not have any impact out there in the world however, because we will have no publicity. But the fact that Doolittle could do this is an omen to the Japanese people. His great accomplishment was more psychological however, than real. Maybe though, if they can do it, we can too. Because the Japs have never been attacked by the Air Corps in the Southwest Pacific, this would really be a surprise for them. Seven days a week we trained and we lost one of our airplanes. Its engine caught fire and the engine fire extinguisher malfunctioned. There was nothing to do but bail out, so the gunner jumped out without his chute on. He was not in his chute so he just grabbed it as he threw himself out. He managed to put it on as he was falling and he landed o.k. The pilot made his bailout safely also.

As far as the Japs are concerned they have little to worry about from the Air Corps. But if we can get to New Guinea with these old airplanes maybe we can shake them up a little bit. We will also be the first to offend them here.

# CHAPTER 3

## NORTH TO NEW GUINEA

After several days of dry bombing runs we all felt we were as ready as we would ever be to attack the enemy. By this time we were pretty well familiar with all the whims and foibles of these Douglas Dauntless Navy dive bombers. Flying the old crates at best was a crazy undertaking. But to do or die might be better than doing nothing.

We were to fly to Port Moresby, which is located on the southern coast of New Guinea and set up our base camp. This was not far from the Jap base of Buna, which was our objective, but it was on the other side of the Owen Stanley Mountains. These mountains rose up to 13,000 feet, and our planes would ceiling at 12,000 feet. We hoped to find a pass through the mountains.

Our plans were to hit and run, and we had to depend on a lot of luck and maybe answer to our prayers. We hoped this would be a sneak attack. If we could foul up their runways and hit their planes on the ground our chances of getting back to our base would be better.

We were working in cooperation with the Royal Australian Air Force (RAAF). On our way we would be fueled at Rockhampton and Townsville. We would mess with the Aussies and they would gas the airplanes. They would also fill our bomb racks when we got to Port Moresby. Our ammo containers would be filled at Amberly before we left. Our bunks would be under the wings of our airplanes on the ground.

Seven planes were ready to go. For our gear we had air mattresses, water canteens, k-rations, atabrine for the prevention of malaria, mosquito nets, and tools.

We left Amberly Field without any fanfare. We pointed north flying in a "V" formation at 9,000 feet. The weather was good with a few rain clouds in the west. Upon landing at Rockhamton the RAAF met us and escorted us to their mess hall in lorries. They had out the welcome mat and gave us the best they had—greasy mutton. I did better than most of the kids on the fare so popular with the Aussies. My father always had a few sheep on the farm and I learned to like mutton. But for us cow chowers we had to like it or else. To an Aussie, mutton was a good dish and the best they had. They treated us as if we were royalty, and their facilities were clean and neat.

When we got back to the airfield they had fueled our planes and they were ready for takeoff. We followed each other into the sky, made our formation, and headed north again for Townsville. This town was to be an important place in my war experience. In about two months when this experience was over I would be going again to school there. If I had known it then, this would have been a great relief to me, knowing that I would get back from this dangerous trip. To go to school again meant some new and different assignment and experience for me.

Townsville was overnight for us. The RAAF was prepared and gave us another Aussie royal welcome. They took us to their billets, as they called them, and gave us the key. They were as clean as a pin, neat, and tidy.

It got warmer as we went north. We were getting into the tropics.

The showers the Aussies provided were more than

welcome and we were ready for mess. Again we were treated to the best they had—greasy mutton. Australia is a beef country also, but they like their mutton, tea, and beer. It may be that they inherited this from their British culture. This you better accept without any complaint when you are their guests.

They took us to see the town. We wore our A-2 jackets and our hats bent with the well known 50 mission crush. As we walked down the street together the Aussie civilians stared at us with their mouths agape. They couldn't make us out. To them we were from another world. We made an enviable impression.

As usual the Aussies were waiting for the beer and lined at the pubs. We joined one line and an Aussie asked who we were. "Where ya frum maitees?" We answered, "Yanks from America." We were kinda proud to say that. "Yanks is it," the pubkeeper said. "Well, drink all ya want, your money's no good here." They came near us and plied us with questions. "Where ya goin' maitee?" We couldn't tell them, hoping to keep our mission secret. "Just passing through. We are on a training mission."

The Aussies have a saying that we heard so many times. "Good on you Yank, ya shoulda been a digger." A digger was an Aussie infantry soldier. They are a proud people and not too keen on the English. They prefer the United States.

One thing they really liked was our 45 caliber automatic pistols and our leather A-2 jackets. They always wanted to buy them or make a trade. They wanted our small 30 caliber rifles too, which we called carbines. We could not make any trades with our guns, but we always would trade our A-2 jackets for their flying boots. Their flying boots were attractive and were a status symbol. They were sheepskin lined, calf length, and looked very sharp with our cut-off suntan shorts. I brought three pair of those Aussie boots back to the States with me.

That evening when we went back to our billets we were all wearing those new sharp boots. Who needs jackets in this hot place anyway?

It was time to go back to our billets, said our squadron commander. Tomorrow was a big day, and besides, some had had too much of that unbelievably good Aussie beer. If you want to be pitched in a hurry try drinking that stuff. It has a brew all its own. The Captain was right, we couldn't face tomorrow with a hangover. Anyway, this was not my vice because I did not have a hankering for it.

New orders came to change our course. We were to fly to Cooktown because it was closer to Port Moresby and would take less gas to fly to Port Moresby across the Coral Sea.

Sooner than we thought it was breakfast on mutton chops and coffee. Then we went to check our airplanes. One had a RPM drop when switched to magneto, so some of us went to work on it. In a few minutes she was purring like a kitten. Now it was off for Cooktown. As we winged again north along the coast the towns seemed to get smaller and smaller. Our chart told us that when Cooktown came up we would be almost to the terminal city on this side of Australia. From Cooktown we would fly across water all the way to the place the Aussies called green hell.

We sight the Great Barrier Reef. It is only about ten miles to sea, and it is a sight to behold. We fly over the city of Cairns which will be the sight of many memories for me. It is to Cairns that many of us will go on combat leave during our fighting to come in the future. Sydney and Mackay will also be favorite vacation spots for combat crews only. Ground crews will get no leave.

√ Our welcome at Cooktown is cordial with the usual Aussie fare—greasy mutton. Tonight there will be no going to town because tomorrow is the big day when we will fly over the Coral Sea to Port Moresby, New Guinea.

In the morning the planes checked out o.k. Each plane was topped off with a full load of gas. Soon we are out over the beautiful Great Barrier Reef. The crystal clear water is full of coral and an aqua shade, and the coral can be seen under the water as well as above. The reef is visible for 30 miles in each direction. The great reef is inspirational and worth the trip here. It is the longest coral formation in the world, and extends in broken chains for 1250 miles along the northeast coast of Australia. A shallow lagoon lies between shore and the reef for its entire length. A deep water channel lies next to the shore. This permits a variety of boats to navigate along the picturesque shoreline. It seem incredible that something so awe inspiring could be the scene of so ghastly a thing as the war we are about to become involved in. At this time our trip here seems so unreal. The reality of it is hard to comprehend.

We gain altitude and see divers in the lagoon and a few boats anchored in the crystal clear water. I think of the many kinds of fish and shark in the waters below and the venomous sea snakes that live among the coral. We carry shark repellent, but do not have much faith in it. There are more enemies than one in the sea below. Our lives are now totally dependent on the steady exhaust of our single engines. Port Moresby is going to be a welcome sight.

We climb to 10,000 feet and it gets chilly. I miss my A-2 jacket but would still rather go without one for a while to have these boots. I lean forward and yell to my pilot. "I want to see our heading." The compass reads 46 degrees magnetic which is our correct course with no cross wind. Should a cross wind arise we would have to drop down to water level to check the direction of the waves and then compensate for the wind.

I yell again, "Do you think we will see any Jap ships?" My pilot shakes his head. This would mean the enemy would know of our coming. In the near future the Battle of the Coral Sea will be fought not far from where we are.

A rain squall looms ahead and our squadron commander decides to go around it. This is good because our planes are open cockpit. Our heading now is 66 degrees and we fly this for 9 minutes to get around the squall. We turn and fly 26 degrees for 9 minutes to get back on course. Then we turn back to 46 degrees and we are back then to our course, and around the squall.

Far below we spot a ship. This could cause a problem not knowing if it is Japanese. It has a few booms topside which makes it a freighter. We see that it is not heading directly from where we are heading so it must have come from around the tip of Australia and the Timor Sea. We are too far away to see its flags and there is nothing we can do about it anyway, so we continue on our way.

Two hours have passed since we left Cooktown. The Great Reef is out of sight and there is nothing but water in all directions. I didn't realize the distance would be so vast. It isn't a very solid feeling way out here. If an engine stops the airplane would sink like a rock and we have no means of rescue.

Three hours and still no sign of land. Two thirds of our gas is gone, and it time for concern. Then far to the north, through a haze, low on the water, a dark line appears. It gets longer and higher. It is land. It must be New Guinea because there is no other land out here.

In 15 minutes we start our descent and the cool air gets hot. Port Moresby is dead ahead and we are right on target. One by one we line up with the RAAF strip and make our landings. We breathe a sigh of relief mingled with dread. It's hard to believe that this is Port Moresby, the green hell in New Guinea.

Hot? Man is it hot! Do people really exist and live in this heat? We shed our clothes down to shorts and start swatting mosquitos and persistent flies. They zoom in for the attack. Our anti-mosquito ointment only bluffs a few of the cowardly ones. There is no reception to meet us. We start drinking water and take our atabrine.

Soon two lorries arrive and take us to the mess hall. The RAAF shows us their camp, showers, latrine, and mess hall. We all immediately jump into their showers to wash off the sweat. Then it was to the mess hall for more greasy mutton.

They asked us what we were going to do with our little open cockpit airplanes. We told them we had no other airplanes and we considered those airplanes better than nothing, and we were here to attack the Japs with them. "Well good on you Yanks," one Aussie said. He said they wished us luck and it was going to take a lot of guts to attack the Japs with those old airplanes. They also told us how good the Jap fighters were, and that didn't boost our morale any.

Their mess hall is a screened in tent. Their screen is supposed to keep the insects out. But it seems there are as many flies inside as out. They are mean and persistent. You swat them off and they are back before you can take a bite of your food. It takes some doing to get any food without flies.

The Aussies don't have much to fight with either. What few planes they have are Whiraways. They are home built and are about like our A-17. They have about given up trying to bomb the Jap bases. Their losses are too high. They have been to Buna, Gona, Dobadura, Morabe, Lae, and other Jap bases on the other side of the big island.

I talked to a radio operator here who told me that the Aussies have spotters along the east coast of New Guinea from Buna north. The Aussies know what the Japs are doing. These spotters have short wave radio transmitters and receivers, and they broadcast all troop movements, and ship and aircraft activities. He also told me that the Aussies and Yanks who re-took Milne Bay are now moving toward Buna, hacking their way through the terrible jungle. But they are having a hard time with malaria and dengue fever. "Why don't they go along the beach?" I asked stupidly. "They are forced to go through the jungle," he told me, "because the Japs would spot them on the beach."

I had work to do on my plane, so I had a driver take me to the flight line. I dug out my tools and performed a 50 hour inspection on it to put it in the best of condition for our mission tomorrow. There were a couple of oil leaks and a broken dzus fastener. Aside from that she was in good shape. An Aussie gas truck came up and we filled her up with gas and oil. I checked the machine guns, and then, but for the bombs, we were ready to leave. The Aussies would load the bombs that night.

The Aussies use the New Guinea natives to do their dirty work such as kitchen police and clean up work. These natives are something else. It is nothing for them to go naked. Some of the older women let their busts hang down so far they look like ropes. Some hang all the way to their navels. To us of another culture we look at them and wonder. We wonder how it is possible for them to survive the fly and mosquito attacks with no clothes. The Aussies at mess told us that some of the natives in the interior are still head hunters.

The natives near the Jap bases are helping them. They can't be blamed, because those people know little of the war. They don't know about the sneak attack on Pearl, Hickam, or the other Hawaiian bases. And even if they did they probably could not understand.

That evening after the mutton and flies, we were invited to a sort of beer party. The RAAF tried to put themselves out to please us. They had a small group who played popular tunes. We enjoyed this mostly because we had not dreamed of music in the forbidden jungle. One of their officers sang "Waltzing Matilda," and that was a favorite with all of us. Then someone in our group sang "Sherilee" which brought a few wet eyes. It was their attempt to get our thoughts off what might happen to us tomorrow. We enjoyed it, but the mosquitos drove us out. It was time to set up our defenses against the mosquitos. We went to our airplanes, inflated our mattresses, and rigged our mosquito nets. Warning had been given us about air raids. True to the warning, we had just got settled under our nets when the air raid siren sounded. We took off for our fox holes and scanned the skies. It was our first "baptism by fire".

The Jap bombers are about 20,000 feet. The Aussies pick them up in their searchlights and begin their bombardment with their ack-ack guns. The puffs of black smoke are exploding below the bombers. The Aussies are not doing so well. Their shells are not reaching high enough.

The enemy planes are heading for the downtown area of

Moresby. Then we hear the BAROOM of the bombs exploding on the town. The planes then turn and head north. The searchlights go out and everything quiets down to the constant hum of thousands of mosquito wings outside our nets.

The Aussies told us that the bombers came from Rabaul, their strongest base in the Southwest Pacific.

We are back under the mosquito nets. These mosquitos are something else. They buzz on the outside of the net by the tens of thousands, and if you touch the net with your elbow or knee they stab through the net with their sticker to suck blood. We would often wake up in the morning to find a knee or elbow ablaze with inflammation. They have a revenous appetite and are loaded with malaria.

I stayed awake most of the night because of their whining. And oh, was it hot! I thought about the cool summer nights in the mountains back home and wondered how everything was, and if the people back there knew how desperately we needed weapons here. I wondered if they knew, or cared, that we, in the morning, were going to attack the Japs with weapons far inferior to what they have.

I awoke and my knees and elbows were a mass of bites where the mosquitos had been able to reach through the net to get to me. I don't know how much blood they got, but I hoped I had enough left to face the ordeal we had to face that day. I felt as though I had been cheated and robbed, and even forgot to take my atabrine.

At mess a sergeant stands at the head of the chow line to visually check to make all of us take the atabrine pills. They turn one green or yellow like juandice. After taking them for a while we look like a Jap.

It is time to fly that mission. We are in a good mood,

everyone is eager to go in spite of the fact that we know the odds. But most are bluffing. Nobody is a coward when everyone is nearby.

After chow we gather around one of our planes for a final briefing. Our target will be Buna, the closest Jap base. It is a hard place to get to with these planes. It is because we have to climb over those high mountains. We plan to find the pass the Aussies told us about if we can. It will be a problem, as the peaks are nearly always shrouded with clouds. But we have a good chart that shows the location of the pass, and it shows the height of all the peaks and where located.

The Aussies have flown over this mountain many times and they know it can be done. Today is clear so the weather is with us. We are to dive bomb Buna in the conventional manner to make two attacks, then hightail it back here. The engines are warm and we top off the tanks and take off. Visibility is about 20 miles in all directions, but already the rain clouds are looming ahead. We make our formation and climb as fast as possible pointed toward the peaks. "All pilots and gunners check your equipment and guns," came over the command set. My tracers smash into a tree while we skim at treetop level. There is no other target near by. We are climbing steadily and the peaks in the distance grow in size as the rain clouds get close.

Approaching these mountains was a fearful thing the first time. This was a hazard that seemed worse than the mission ahead. We didn't relish the idea of crashing into a stone wall on a lonely peak. Getting over the mountains was a real test with these old airplanes.

The clouds covered the peaks completely. It was impossible to find the pass. We didn't have enough gas to fly around them. We would have to fly almost to Milne Bay to get around those mountains. We were forced to turn tail and go back to Moresby.

What a hell of a deal. Here we are all on the apex of fear and primed for our first combat mission against the Japs, and we are forced to turn back because those old planes are too weak to climb over the mountains. There was a consolation however. We would all be alive in the morning. We all landed safely at Moresby, a letdown to the Aussies, and were back with the mosquitos and heat. Flying at least gave us a break from the steaming heat of the jungle and when up there the flies and mosquitos can not get to you.

There was nothing but disappointment for us and the Aussies when we got back. They gave us a ride to a nearby stream and we soaked in the tepid water. This was a sad mistake for me. I contracted what we called jungle rot. It is a fungus that lives in the water there. My fingers, hands, and feet were never free of it again.

That night we had another visit from the Jap Air Force. They must have known we were at the Moresby air strip because this time their bombs all fell in the area where our airplanes were parked. In desperation we grabbed our helmets and jumped into our foxholes. The bombs smashed nearby in our dispersal area and dirt and shrapnel flew like hailstones. One Aussie Beaufighter was badly damaged, but our planes escaped serious injury. Some of our men were a bit shook up, but no one was hurt. The Aussie ack-ack gunners missed them again and the Jap planes banked off and headed for Rabaul.

How do we know they came from Rabaul? Now we have three B-17 aircraft from the 19th Bomb Group that were saved from the Philippines, and they have been flying reconaissance over some of the Jap bases. They take pictures, and also the Aussie spotters are watching them.

Rabaul is the most dreaded word in our language. It is a place we know we will have to attack someday. Unknown to us before this time Rabaul is a small city on the big Jap island of New Britain with a very large harbor. It is Japan's strongest and most fortified base in the Southwest Pacific. The B-17's have taken a lot of photos and they show the harbor almost always full of ships. They are mostly warships including carriers, cruisers, destroyers, submarines, freighters, troopships, tankers, and many lesser ships. Sometimes there are as many as 50 ships in the harbor. There are many airstrips around Rabaul all loaded with fighters and bombers. There are 367 anti-aircraft guns. It is called the Japanese Rock of Gibraltar of the Pacific, and we are destined to strike it from mast height and treetop altitude, day in and day out until it is not there anymore. We will literally wipe it off the map. We'll smash it so completely that it will be only rubble. Our Infantry won't even land there.

At the time of the aborted mission, we did not know it, but it would have been a blessing to us had all our airplanes been destroyed in that bombing raid. If they had destroyed them most of the crews would be alive today.

Dawn finds us up and ready to take off as soon as we have chow. We preflight the planes, top off the gas tanks, and take off. Then we form our formation and start climbing the long climb to get over those mountains. There is supposed to be a pass just starboard of a direct route to Buna. At 12,000 feet we see a clearing dead ahead with clouds on either side. We know there are peaks behind the clouds. We climb to 12,200 feet and fly through the pass. On the other side we bank to port and begin to descend. Our engines are very sluggish at this altitude, but as we get lower they begin picking up power. We know our planes are all right to make the attack now, or they are as good as they will ever be. We check our guns on our own as the radio cannot be used here in enemy occupied territory.

One of our planes went back and we do not know why. Was it fear that turned them back or did they have mechanical trouble? Later we learned their oil pressure went down. Now we have a force of only six old airplanes to do a job we believe requires 100 airplanes. And we won't be able to surprise them. Their radar has already picked us up and their fighters will be in the air waiting for us. We will not catch their aircraft on the ground.

We level off at 9,000 feet and maintain our maxium speed. The Buna airstrip is visible now and I'm shaking with fear. They know we are up here now so we can use the radio and some one yells, "Zeros below us." I look down and see a dozen pairs of shining wings. They are climbing to attack us. We are almost over the strip and I check my guns again. Our lead plane banks to dive, and the second plane also banks for their dive, and we begin our dive. I see no airplanes on the runway. We are diving on a camouflaged building, and ack-ack begins to burst near our airplane. The concussion jolts us as we let go the bomb and the dive flaps whistle, scream, and slow the airplane. An airplane below us is smoking. It's one of ours. It has been hit, and ack-ack-puffs are all around us. Then I hear it splatter on our air-plane as we drop another of our bombs. I'm looking for those fighters while the dive flaps slow us, and there's a Zero in a dive above us. We are its target and its lead and steel crash into our plane while I spray it with my guns. It is right on top of us and then it banks away as I try to follow it with a long burst. The Zero is gaining altitude for another pass at us. We drop down to the trees and head back toward the mountains. I see an A-17 go down and another one smoking. It crashed on their runway. About ten Zekes are visible above us which is a bad position for us. One dives on us and we dive for the treetops. The Zeke zooms past us and fills us with more holes and I fill him with some too, but no smoke. We are loaded with holes but are still flying. So far we have not been hit in a vital spot. We skim the trees so low we hit a branch. We can't attack the second time. We don't have a prayer. I look around for more Zeros but see none. So far our low altitude has saved us. I see another A-17 to our right being chased by a Zero at low altitude. In a second it goes down in smoke. They are slaughtering us.

We cling to the treetops and climb the foothills. The mountains loom ahead as we bank left to stay with the rising terrain. Up, up we go to a height of 12,000 feet and we are still on the treetops. Then we see the pass and through to a descent to safety leaving our buddies behind. We can do nothing to help them. It's a miracle we made it back.

After landing at Moresby we watch, wait and hope. We listen for the sound of engines but no other planes show up. We look at each other and ask, "How did we ever get back?" What fate made it possible?

## CHAPTER 4

## FIRST LOSING BATTLES

Fighting the Japs in 1942 in the Southwest Pacific was a losing battle with the weapons we had. We proved that those A-17's were not nearly as good as the Japanese Zeros. It was like Russian roulette with five of the six cylinders loaded.

My sleep that night after the first strike, what with the heat and excitement of the one sided battle still ringing through my mind, to say the least, brought me no pleasant dreams. When I opened my eyes the next morning I lay dazed in my sack. Something was haunting me, but for the moment I could not realize what it was. I was in New Guinea and had just gone through a day of infamy.

With my pilot, Bill Peterson, we rushed out to get a closer look at our plane. How we ever got over that 13,000 foot mountain was a lot more than we could believe. Two gas tanks were leaking and there were oil puddles covering the ground. Control cables were cut in a number of places along with electrical wires. The rudder, ailerons, and wings were full of holes, and the fuselage also. But neither Bill nor myself had a scratch. When I remember the Zeros attacking us from behind with their cannons and machine guns blazing, their bullets ripping into our plane, it seemed impossible that we could escape. There must have been two other things going for us.

And our buddies? Where were they this day? Five airplanes went down before the superior Japanese Zeros, and the anti-aircraft fire. It was something I will never forget. Why we did not go down too was probably the result of a fickle fate and the skillful handling of the plane by Lieutenant Peterson, and maybe I was a little help in being able to pour enough of our ammo into the Zeros to throw them off the mark so we could escape.

Five planes were lost, but by far the big loss was the ten eager kids who were in those airplanes. Those American kids, scared, every one of them. Volunteers, every one of them. It was our task to show the Nips just what those soft pleasure loving Yanks would do when the call came. We didn't do much, but we tried.

This was the first chance we had to get a blow at the Japs since Pearl. It may have not been much but it was a start. It will have a psychological effect on the enemy, but it might also give the ememy more confidence. It showed the spirit of these citizen soldiers and our willingness to sacrifice. They gave their all willingly, even though it seemed useless. Did they die in vain? Somebody had to be first. I think the names of those ten men who are missing in action should be emblazoned in the annals of history. Their story has never reached print and that is why we are telling it now.

Bill and I rested that day and discussed a next move. He decided to go back to Australia to try to get more of those A-17's ready for combat. I would stay at Moresby and work the damage out of the shot up plane. The failure of our first assult on the Japanese did very little to lessen our desire to get after them again.

He caught a ride on a Dutch Lockheed Lodestar back to Amberly. He told me he would be in touch by radio through the RAAF.

I needed help to repair the plane. I appealed to the commander of the RAAF for a man to do the sheetmetal work on the skin of the airplane. In no time a young Aussie reported with his tools.

What were we going to use for metal? There was none at the base. Then we remembered the Beaufighter in the boondocks that had been bombed in one of the air raids. This would be just what we needed. We ripped metal off the wreckage and he went to work on the holes. I began work on the mechanical end of it.

When I got into the repairing of the plane I found the extent of the damage that had been done. One of the control cables had been cut by a Jap bullet. This may be impossible to repair in New Guinea. Where would I get a replacement? I measured the cable and went back to the boondocks. I found one but it was slightly heavier and larger in diameter. I found I could make it fit with some modification. With more help from the Aussie rigging department, they cut it and swedged the end and I was in business.

We were making progress and who knows, this old plane might again be making a suicide trip to a Jap base. But I ran into bigger problems. A hole in an oil tank and several in the gasoline tanks had to be repaired. They needed welding and to weld them meant removing them which was a very big job. Maybe there was another way. In my sleep I came up with an idea.

We enlarged the holes and made them oval in shape. With scrap metal from the wrecked plane we made plates larger than the holes. Then with rubber from the tubes we made gaskets the same size as the plates. With a bolt through the center of each plate we inserted it all through each hole sideways, then turned them to fit on or cover the holes. Then with another plate on the exterior we tightened a nut to seal all the leaks.

We worked ten days and made all our parts. In another day our airplane was back in flying condition. We gave her a good scrubdown, a preflight inspection, and brought the form "1" up to date. The engine kicked off the first turn and she was ready to try her luck again. All she needed now was a couple of eager kids to fly her into combat and take their chances.

My young Aussie helper was named Leroy. In working together we had become friends. I renamed him Kilroy from "Kilroy was here." Kilroy told me about a rumor floating around. Gold was an exciting thing and it had been discovered a few miles from where we were in New Guinea. We had some free time now and the Aussies had no jurisdiction over me, and Kilroy had some free time too, so why not try our luck?

Yes, you might say we had a slight case of gold fever. If we were lucky, real lucky, and found a rich strike, and if we lived until the war was over, we would come back some day and go in the mining business. Our luck had been pretty good so far. Why not take advantage of it and see if we could stretch it a little further. We decided to go panning for gold.

We knew a lot less about prospecting than we did about airplanes, but it would certainly be a diversion. All we knew was what we could remember from western movies. Those old sourdoughs of the west always prospected for gold in the desert. Where we were going was no desert. It was impossible to travel overland. The jungle was like a green wall. Our only chance to go inland was to find a stream and use its bed as a trail. And we would have to limit ourselves to placer mining. We packed our duffle to get ready. Our load included mosquito nets, mess kits, k-rations, water, atabrine pills, a GI shovel, waterproof matches, a knife, and a rifle. My rifle was the regulation Army Girand. Kilroy's was a big Aussie job. There were some fearful looking creatures in the jungle, including headhunters, so we were told.

Kilroy knows the Aussie mess sergeant, and that will make it easy to get food. Early in the morning we raid the kitchen before anyone gets up. Then we are on our way just as the sun is coming up. Already it is hot as we head west hiking along the beach. We are looking for a stream and we don't know from Adam where one is. This is a beautiful land if you discount the bugs, mosquitos, snakes, humidity, and heat.

Our walking had taken us far from Moresby and it seemed we were all alone in a not so friendly world. Then far ahead we saw some people on the beach. Some were bathing and a few were lolling in the sand. What manner of men shall we meet? When they saw us they were stirred. They could not be Japs on this side of the island. When we got closer they became familiar and turned out to be natives. As they got near us they just stared at us. They had no weapons but they eyed our guns and showed us respect.

"Do you speak English?" I asked one. The man smiled and shook his head. I knew beforehand that in Papua alone, which is just half of New Guinea, over a hundred languages are spoken. And we couldn't speak one word of one language. So we were totally dependent on the signs to make ourselves understood. And about the only signs we could use were a wave and a smile. But this was all we needed to show we were friends. And this is how we said goodbye.

"Why do you call me Kilroy?" Leroy asked. I told him that Kilroy was a very famous person. "Wherever he goes he leaves a sign on a fence or a building or anyplace. The sign will always read "Kilroy was here". He is a little old man with a long nose hanging over a fence. This is an omen that the Yanks have been anyplace the sign is. You will find this sign almost everywhere in the world."

A black object appears far ahead in the sea. As we get nearer we can see that it is a sunken ship with its bow above the water line. At low tide most of the ship is above the water. It is not much to see, that old ship, except to think about how it had been sunk. I didn't know it at the time, but that old hulk is going to play a big part in my life and the lives of thousands of others in this man's war. We will use it for our skip bombing and strafing practice runs. It will serve a great purpose in teaching us what we have to know to destroy Jap ships and fortifications. When we get through there won't be much left of it, but we will have valuable know how on how to sink enemy ships which will spell the end of their invasion of the Pacific.

Walking along the beach was an experience. The sand washed white by the tide and ceaseless action of the waves would have been a famous resort beach anywhere else in the world. This is a tropical paradise but for the vermin and heat. Such a land I had never dreamed existed. It is such a contrast to my homeland in Utah where a rainstorm is an occasion. Here everything is a paradise for the abundant life. Copious rain under the heat of the equatorial sun with never a hint of killing frost. So much vegetation makes the jungle almost impenetrable to man. No roads, no cities, no civilization. Our only way to penetrate it was to find a stream and follow its course. To venture into this green, tangled web of life seemed more than foolhardy, but we were eager to try it and take our chances.

We came around a point in the curve of the beach. There we found it, our trail into where we wanted to go. It was a good sized stream maybe 20 feet wide and shallow. It was just right for wading and luck was with us. We rolled our pants up and started wading. The dense growth closed over our heads. This was really an adventure and we expected just about anything. Our invasion of the jungle was protested by a million birds in their brilliant plumage. Each of them seemed to be squawking at us to go. Mostly it was dark but the sun peeked through the foliage here and there. We were in a lost world at the least and we thought about the guys who were shot down and how impossible it would be to go more than a few yards in this growth.

Life is cheap here because it is so abundant. The foul, fetid smell of death is in every breath. Where there is so much life, there must be much death. Each species and individual was the victim of others. Vegetation takes possession of every inch of space. Insects crawl here and there and everywhere. Snakes and lizards crawl through the grass and wait for victims. There is a struggle for existence here that defies all description. This is the kind of life Darwin studied. His theory of evolution seems so real here.

We have come a long way and are tired and hungry. And we wonder about wild game. Could it be that some of those gorgeous birds would be fit fare for a couple of hungry prospectors? I wouldn't want to eat a crocodile, a tree kangaroo, or a python. But you better believe it, if we see a python we are ready to shoot it. We are on the lookout for some kind of tasty fowl or beast that would be a change from GI food. I eat K-rations only when I'm very hungry.

They taste like garbage if you are not starved.

We found a rock in the middle of the river which offered a seat and some protection from the snakes and sat down to eat our K-rations. I saw a fish in the stream which was good news. We then began panning for gold using our messkits for pans in the good old western fashion. Swishing the sand, gravel, and water around in the pan the right way is an art we soon learned. I found a small piece of what looked like gold right away and we thought we were going to be rich, but it was the only piece we found here. We swished it around and carefully poured off the water looking for color at the bottom of the pan. Nothing glistened again so we moved to another place. So far no fabulous bonanza. Oh well, we were just getting started. We kept going up stream, panning all the way and hoping the gold has washed this far down stream.

For about two hours we work every sand bar and possibility. There seems to be a special way to swish the sand and gravel. This throws out the sand and gravel and leaves the gold just lying in the bottom of the pan. What gold? No color, except the birds of paradise roosting in the trees. They gawk and squawk from every tree. The varied colored feathers of the male of the species is very bright. But there are no game birds—no ducks, pheasants, quail, or wild chickens. And we planned to live off the land?

"Are any of these birds good to eat?" asked Kilroy. "I don't know, shall we try one?"

I thought of the possibility of eating one of them just to see what they taste like. But it would be a shame to kill one of them, they are so beautiful. But there are thousands of them and one or two wouldn't make much difference.

We discovered fish in the stream. We did not think to

bring fishing gear, but we have our guns and I plan to kill a couple of them before dark. I can shoot them in the shallow water.

We find bloodsuckers in the stream, and have to watch our legs. They get on our flesh and soon burrow in. They attach themselves and to get them off you have to dig them out with a knife. So the trick is to find them quickly.

We work our way farther up the stream. In a little while we came to a fork in the river. Then we take the left hand fork for luck and continue to pan upstream. We are getting farther and farther away from Moresby. Then Kilroy finds two pieces of what looks like gold. It could be fools gold but fools gold or not it eggs us on the work faster and faster. Now we have a feeling that we will make a strike before dark. We move on and on and find only one more piece. The sun is behind the jagged peaks now and darkness comes quickly in this area and the dense jungle, so we must find a place to camp. This is not easy, but we soon cut a place in the bush by the stream for our mattresses and nets.

Kilroy went looking for dry wood and it was my job to shoot the fish. I climbed a tree to get a straight down shot at the fish. An angle shot would ricochet. I sat in the tree a few minutes and finally shot two nice fish. They looked like the ones I used to catch in our river back home. We fried them crisp. It was a real treat after all the powdered food and K-rations. We topped off our meal with a coconut found on the ground. There were some wild berries in the jungle that really looked good but I had never seen any like them and we did not dare eat them.

I had already picked up jungle rot beforehand so could not get it any worse, so we had our bath in the tepid water. The mosquitos attacked our bare skin so we stayed under most of the time to escape them. We used salt soap that I had brought from the old ship Republic.

The mosquitos had been eating us all day, but now in the evening they descended on our bare skin with all their relatives. Our big job now was to fence them out so we could get some sleep. We doused ourselves with mosquito stay-away and set to work improvising a shelter. How to keep the mosquitos and snakes out during the night was to build something out of what we had with us. I cut four stakes a little larger than my sack to make a rectangle. My next step was to cut four more shorter stakes for my corner posts. I drove them in the ground and fastened the rectangle to the top. I then inflated my mattress and laid it between the posts. Now I placed my net over the framework and packed the bottom with earth. This made a space all around the mattress between the net and the mattress so I would not touch the net and feed the skeeters.

Inside we were away from the flies and mosquitos, but not the heat. I slept in spite of it. Kilroy told me the birds squawked all night. But I worried about the snakes. Would they crawl to my net and through, or around. Apparently there is something about a net the snakes don't like. We had no problem with snakes.

Before daybreak we were both awake. I guess it was the loud squawking of the birds. It was a little cooler now and we planned our routine for the day. The first thing we would do is try the taste of a bird of paradise. If they tasted as good as they looked they ought to be fit for a king. Anyway they had it coming. We needed to get even for all the noise they had been making.

"Can you hit one in the head?" I asked my friend.

"Sure I can hit one in the head," he said.

We were both thinking about that big blunderbus of a rifle he had. If he hits it in the breast there wouldn't be anything left of it.

"I'll make the fire and the spit then, you'll shoot the bird." When he shot that rifle it was like a bomb going off. The jungle fell silent. He was pretty lucky too. He had hit it in the head.

We ripped off the feathers, cleaned it, and soon it was sizzling on the spit. Sinking our teeth in its brown and odorant flesh was something to remember. It didn't taste like quail or chicken, but it was much better than the GI food we were used to. We hoped to be out of the jungle before we had to kill another one.

We boiled some water and filled our canteen. The water was loaded with bacteria and we were not about to drink it without boiling it. Anyway, warm water was no novelty to us, and it was safe if it was boiled. No stream could run down that hill without picking up all the bacteria known to man and some that are not known. With our packing done and the fire out we began our panning again. We planned to work about three hours and then head back for the base. It started to rain, but the hot rain on our backs felt good and we kept on working, although the rain fell in torrents.

We said we were looking for gold, but we also were looking for adventure. This was an exploring expedition. We found no gold here, but we found many other things new to our previous experiences. There was no sign of civilization or primitive culture of any kind. We felt we were the first white men who had ever penetrated this part of the world. There were no signs of man in this idyll of nature. The natives on this huge island did not live in this area. The jungle was too wicked there. They lived in areas north and west of there in the high valleys. The jungle was not as thick there and was cooler at a higher altitude.

That day we saw many snakes and lizards. We also saw one turtle that would have made good soup, if we had a pot to cook it in. This was a botonist's zoologist's heaven. This was much more valuable than gold, but to our money oriented minds, we didn't see that. It was probably a good thing we didn't find gold there because it was no place for a white man to work. One would more than likely kill himself working feverishly in that heat and humidity.

We learned one thing about the jungle. There were no landmarks of any kind there. Without the stream to follow we would have never found a way out. At about 1000 hours we turned around, gave up our prospecting, and headed downstream toward the ocean and our way out. The way out was as unfamiliar as the way in. I would be flying above this jungle many times in the future, and hoped I would never be forced down in it. One would be helpless without a long knife for cutting, and if a man had a knife it would take an hour to hack through 20 feet of it. Many hundreds of Japanese and American flyers would be forced down in this maze of growth in the near future. This was one of the extra hazards we were up against in this Pacific war.

We got back to our base in time for the usual air raid, but too late for chow. We were raiding the kitchen when the siren began to scream. Their target tonight was our airplanes in the parking area which was some distance from the mess hall. There were 18 Nip bombers this time, and as soon as they laid their eggs they turned and pointed for Rabaul.

After the raid I lit out for the airstrip to see if they had destroyed my airplane that I had worked so hard on. It was o.k., so I checked the tie downs, rigged my net, and hit the sack under the wing.

We had the Norden bomb sight and thought there was none better, but the Japs had proven almost perfection with their bombsight. They must have stolen the Norden like they had stolen airplane and engine designs from us, because they hit the targets they aimed at. They were proving that now and they proved it in the near future when they wiped out every one of our new B-25's. We had them all parked in their revetments, covered with camouflage netting, and it was dark. It wasn't luck either because it was not the first time. They were accurate almost every time they dropped bombs on us. Apparently someone had leaked the know-how to make those bombsights, and it cost us plenty.

I had been waiting word from my pilot from Australia who said he would keep in touch with me via RAAF radio. Not one word had he sent. As I had no organization in New Guinea I decided to go back to Amberly Field. I needed a plane ride back to Australia so I contacted the Aussie operations officer and on the third day he had a lift for me. It was another Dutch Air Force Lockheed Lodestar. It was another long ride to Amberly, but it was cool and there were no mosquitos or flies. We flew at 12,000 feet and I sat in a metal bucket seat all the way. The wartime plane was not built for comfort.

When I got there eight of the A-17's were ready to fly back to New Guinea, and they were the last of the lot. Our plans were to fly the old crates back up there and attack the little men again just as we had done before. This was now old stuff to me and I was considered a vet. I pitched in with the maintenance to finish a few jobs in getting them ready. When we were ready to go there were ample engineer gunners so I was really surplus. I obtained permission to fly back to Moresby by Aussie Beaufighter.

This Beaufighter was a treat after the A-17. We stopped at Townsville and went to town for steak and eggs, then went to a milk bar for a last treat of ice cream. Ice cream was non existent in New Guinea and could be sold for any price. It was overnight at Townsville and then off for Moresby. I had a chance to see the reef again and this time without the worry of what might happen tomorrow.

My plane was still intact in spite of nightly air raids. The next day our A-17's flew in from Cooktown. The crews were eager to get at the Japs in spite of the fact they had somebody to tell them now about the odds against them. I told them what would happen but I guess most of them wanted to be heroes. I told them we were in for a clobbering, but they would not listen.

The new squadron commander called a meeting and I was interrogated by everyone about flying against the Jap Zero. I am no public speaker so I tried to answer their questions. I told them we should forget our airplanes are dive bombers. Dive bombers played a big part when Hitler attacked a defenseless people in France and other European countries because he had no opposition, but the A-17 is no match for the Zero and if we wanted to live we should sneak in on them at treetop altitude and surprise them. It was absolutely impossible to surprise them at high or even medium high altitude. They would have us on their radar screen 10 miles before we got there. And their Zeros would be up there waiting for us. If we came in at treetop level their radar could not pick us up. The most important thing to do was to stay in formation so the gunners could help each other when they attacked. The Zeros would come from behind so fast it would seem like we were hardly moving. They must have listened to my plea, for the news we heard on the radio told us they were going in over the trees.

We had ten airplanes including mine. There were plenty men to man them and the crews were eager to go. The squadron commander told me I was surplus, and because I had been there would I not go. "Sure I'll not go," I told him. I asked Kilroy if he had ever had a choice between life and death.

They warmed up their engines and I helped them top off their gas tanks. One by one they took off and headed northeast in formation toward the pass through the Owen Stanleys. I ran to the Aussie radio shack to listen to their conversation as they headed to their doom. On this side of the mountain they could use the command set because the Japs could not intercept them. But on the other side the radio was taboo unless the Japs had spotted them. The two way radio could be used on the way back too.

The chatter on the radio sounded familiar: "Make formation. This is your flight leader. We are going in over the treetops. Follow me." I heard what I wanted to hear—that they were going in on the treetops. Now, perhaps a few of them will come back.

Then there is radio silence and for us it is wait. It will be about two hours before they will broadcast again, so Kilroy and I go to the mess hall for some powdered eggs.

Then we hear the faint hum of engines. We scramble to the air strip and scan the skies. Two A-17's appear coming in from the east. And far behind them we see two more, and one is smoking badly. As the smoking plane rolls to a stop we all rush to help. The Aussie fire truck soon douses the fire. The gunner's face is in his lap and he does not move.

His cockpit is full of blood and the pilot is soaked in blood. The pilot is still alive and he is going to live, but the gunner is dead. Some of us lift the pilot out and then the gunner.

No more planes showed up. We lost 70% if the wrecked plane is counted. The other three planes were damaged also. The bloody plane was damaged beyond repair. The returned crewmen reported that they dropped all their bombs in the target area. They had come in low and had surprised the Japs. But the Zekes had come from another base somewhere and followed them and hit them from the rear. The gunners could not hold off the enemy fighters. All six of our A-17's in formation were shot down by the attacking Zeros. Those who came back were convinced that the Jap Zeros were superior to our planes. There was not much we could do about it. We had no other airplanes. Our B-17's could have done the job but they had been blown up at Hickam Field.

Port Moresby was vulnerable to Japanese bomber attack. That night we had another raid. This time it seemed to be in retaliation for our raid on Buna. We didn't know how much damage we did to Buna, but we must have shook them up a little. I was in the dispersal area, but they dropped all their bombs on the town of Port Moresby. We had work to do so it was hit the sack early.

The next morning Kilroy brought another man with him to work on our damaged planes. Everyone went to work including the pilots. Useless as it was, we wanted to get those old planes back in shape again and get back at the Japs. We repaired three planes with parts cannibalized from the A-17 that was all shot up with the blood in it. In two days we had three planes ready to fly again. These were the last of our planes and we wanted to make a good account.

On the third day after the last mission the three planes and crews were ready to hit the Nip base of Buna again. The crews who flew the last mission just automatically prepared to go. They now considered it their right to fly those flying coffins again. I did not want to die, and it seemed they didn't care, so we helped them with all the work in getting ready to go.

I had conceived an idea to make those planes a little safer. The Japs always attacked us by coming up from behind because they knew we had less speed. If we could build some kind of protection behind the pilot and gunner that would stop bullets and shrapnel, maybe we could save some lives. There was a big piece of armor way out in that wrecked Aussie plane. I had one of the Aussie welders cut it in three pieces. Then we installed a piece behind the gunners cockpit in each plane. We hoped this would do the job.

The three planes took off for the pass and never returned.

# CHAPTER 5
## BACK TO AUSTRALIA

The first three bombing missions by the Yanks against the Japs in New Guinea ended in a fiasco. Sixteen A-17's with 32 men flew out of Port Moresby to give the enemy a taste of American reprisal and only three of us got back. Twenty nine men had gone down somewhere in the jungle. Could any of them be rescued?

The wounded pilot had been sent to a hospital in Australia. My pilot had gone to Amberly. That left me the only Yank left at Moresby. I worried about those kids out in the jungle. I knew what it was like there. I figured there was at least a 50% chance of survival of a man in a plane hitting into the treetops at 150 miles an hour. This meant 13 or more kids were out there somewhere in the jungle trying to survive.

I appealed to the RAAF squadron commander at Moresby and asked him if we could try to rescue them. He told me that we could drop supplies and medication to them if we could find them, but the only way they could signal us would be with fire and smoke. And it would be next to impossible to create smoke from the time they saw us or heard us until we had left the area.

"Well sir," I said, "perhaps some of them may be on the beach south of Buna. We could fly at very low altitude and recognize them." He told me he would send a Beaufighter. I talked my way into going along. We stuffed food, water, and quinine into barracks bags insulated with wads of paper against the shock of dropping it. We flew over the Owen Stanley mountains and then hugged the treetops until we got to within about seven miles of Buna. Then we turned east until we came to the beach. We followed the beach for a while then flew back toward Buna. From the beach near Buna we flew back and forth deep into the rain forest then back to the beach, one pass about on the average of one mile. We watched for smoke but saw none. We saw no signs of man. After some 20 passes we decided it was useless and gave it up. I wonder how many of the kids below us, helpless, heard us and could not signal us. We could do no more, and we lifted back over the jagged mountains and back to Moresby. We dropped no supplies.

The war news looked bad. How can we win the war with no planes or weapons? We had tried and failed because of an inferior weapon. During all the time since we came to Australia, we had but one score in our favor. The Aussies and a few Yank infantry had re-taken Milne Bay. But the Japs bombed us without opposition or mercy at Moresby. Would we ever get planes from home so we could attack those egotistical little yellow men?

Again I am without anything to do. It is my duty to report back to Amberly Field and I plan to go. But first I would like to take one more crack at prospecting for gold. Kilroy is eager to go again, so we make preparations. This time we check an RAAF chart and find there is another stream farther down the coast about five miles on the other side of the stream we panned before. Kilroy has a friend who works in their motor pool who will drive us this time down the beach in a jeep. We have to know about the tide. Only at low tide can we drive down the beach. At 0730 hours in the morning the tide will be low.

Early the next morning we are rolling down the beach on wheels. We passed the stream where we had panned before, and in no time with this four wheel drive jeep, we were at the mouth of the other stream. This is a larger stream, which makes us happy. There might be more gold for us here. We unload our equipment and bid our pal farewell and begin to wade. We are back in the land of noisy birds. We pan every few yards in the same way with the swishing motion that we learned before. In about two hours I once more find a piece of something that looks exactly like gold. We thoroughly pan the area in an attempt to find more, but find nothing else.

At high noon, with the sun a little north of zenith and hot as hades, we find a clearing and have lunch. We could see fish in this river too which means a relief from K-rations. Most of our time is spent swatting mosquitos, flies, and other insects. We wet our shirts and put them back on to let what little evaporation we have cool us off a bit. Then we hit the stream again looking for gold. I guess we need an old prospector from California to show us how. We are not very good at it or else the gold isn't here. We are inclined to believe the latter.

Ever hear of a tree kangaroo? Well, you can find them in New Guinea. They are real roos in the jungle that live in a completely different environment from the Australian roo. I am sure they exist because we saw one that day. We did not see much of it because it vanished in the foliage quick as a cat, but we saw it. Then we saw a huge snake about 15 feet long that must have been a python. We saw only its body and tail. I wouldn't want to have that thing crawl in bed with me. But we saw no deer or big cats, or even small cats, or any of the wild dogs as the dingo in Australia.

At about 1700 hours we made camp. A lot of water had gone through our pans and we were a bit tired. I climbed a tree again and shot four fish and we had a real treat. They were not as good as the trout from the streams in the mountains in the north of Utah, but they were a delicacy to us. After chow it was time to rig our nets. Then a tepid bath in the stream and a dash under our nets. What a relief to get away from the swarming insects. I relaxed and thought again about the unbelievable fact that I was camping out in the savage jungles of New Guinea.

"Well Kilroy, what do you think? Do you insist we are going to find our fortune? We are now on our last leg and have one more chance in the morning and that's it." I get no reply. He is already konked out. I lay there listening to the sounds of the jungle. What is the turn of the cards going to bring to me now? I know I have been real lucky to be here at all. Already I have led a charmed life. I am grateful for my being here.

We had K-rations for breakfast and were on the job panning again up the stream. Our equipment was hampering our panning. Should we leave some of it and pick it up when we come back? I wanted to get rid of it but we decided against it because the green closing growth of the land would make it impossible to find again. This is a lost world and it would be easy to lose anything, or yourself, in its close monotonousness.

We worked about two hours more, then it was time to head back. We had at least 15 miles to walk and some of it was in the riverbed. We saw no signs of man. That close to a settled town, I was amazed that no one ever went there. I guess the people who lived there knew the jungle better than we did. That was why they never ventured into its dreary and forbidding vastness. That second trip of ours had about convinced us that we were not about to do it again either.

On the way back we gathered coconuts, milked them for their water and ate the meat. When we got back to the base the sack was all we could think about.

On the second day after our prospecting a B-17 landed at Moresby. I met the crew while they were tieing down the airplane. A B-17? I'd not seen one of them since leaving the Salt Lake Airdrome two years ago. It was like a friend all the way from home. Also, it was good news and a morale builder to see it. Those babies carried in destruction, quite a wallop. Once we got more of them and other airplanes, the Japs would know we were in the war.

This plane was saved from the Philippines. It was salvaged from the 19th Bombardment Group and they were using it for reconnaissance. Their co-pilot told me they were going back to Australia and that I could hitch a ride at least back to Townsville.

Our route was a great arc over enemy waters in the Coral Sea. I hadn't been in a B-17 in a long time and it was a treat to feel the bigness and security it offered. We did not meet any enemy resistance or see any enemy planes. We flew over the exact spot where the future sea battle called the Coral Sea Battle would take place.

Arriving at Townsville again I bid the crew good luck. They treated me like an old friend. It was a dream to go to town for a steak dinner, which was an impossibility in New Guinea, but it had been months since I had been paid, so going to town was out.

The RAAF gave me a bunk and I went to bed at an early hour in hopes that I could catch a hop to Amberly in the morning. But there was no military plane going south that day so I spent the day catching up on old news and writing home. I read all the old newspapers in the barracks. The old news was new news to me. Port Moresby was in need of a newspaper. My letters carried no return address as I was without an outfit as far as I knew.

On my third day at Townsville I caught the ride I had been waiting for. It was great to be back to Amberly. After my jungle experiences and all that went with it in the green hell of New Guinea, Amberly seemed like "home sweet home." There was an AAF Group there and I went to the headquarters and told them my story. A master sergeant searched through his records and located a list of the original names of the crewmen who went to New Guinea. My name was there and he said we heard that everyone had been on a list of killed in action. I told him that we were mostly missing in action. That three were alive for certain, one was dead, and all the rest were missing in action. I also told about our attempt to help those who went down. And I could not remember the name of the gunner who was killed.

The sergeant fixed me up with pay vouchers and a bunk and I went to Ipswich to see my old girl friend. As I suspected, she had a slew of boy friends by this time with all those Yanks at Amberly. However, she was glad to see me in good health, especially when she heard what a time I had. We went out on the town. When she found out I had a lot of back pay she was more than happy. If there was anything a foreign girl really loved it was a Yank with his pockets full of money. So she set the proverbial tender trap. But I was not about to be a sucker and get caught in the tender trap, and have a foreign girl hanging on. My chances of getting back to the States were a big question mark, and anyway her sights were probably zeroed in on GI insurance and veterans benefits. I knew the first thing she would want was a trip to the States, and then a trip back to Australia.

My future for the next few weeks is to stay at Amberly again with nothing to do. I am rated "casual" with no outfit, and am attached to each AAF organization coming through. This will be my status until the B-25's begin to arrive from the States. Then it will be up to New Guinea again with some real weapons. I am looking forward to that time. It will be a time at last when we will literally wipe the Japs off the face of the earth.

War news. The Japs sent an invasion convoy and took the island of Tulagi on May 4th, 1942. Their objective was to take our important base of Port Moresby. This put their air force within easy range of Australia. But now the Americans are going to have a say so in this. Admiral Nimitz organized a Naval operation to stop the Japs. His force was centered around the two famous carriers—the Lexington and the Yorktown. It was on May 4, the Yanks spotted the Jap fleet. A man I knew in the 7th Bomb Group sent the first radio message. Ninety three airplanes from U.S. carriers sank one Jap carrier. The Japs retaliated and sank one American destroyer and a tanker. The Yorktown and Lexington were both damaged and the Lexington eventually sank. This was the Battle of the Coral Sea and the Japanese were victorious tactically, but the Yanks gained a strategic victory in that they stopped plans of the Japs to take Moresby.

Now the stage was set for the Battle of Midway. This was one of the greatest naval victories in history. June 4, the two great naval forces of the United States and Japan came in contact near Midway island. Japan lost four carriers, two heavy cruisers, three destroyers and several auxiliary ships. The U.S. lost 92 officers and 215 men. This was one of the decisive battles in naval warfare, and a great victory for the U.S.

The Navy is doing o.k., but what are we doing? What can we do with nothing to do with? I am bored again had have no duties. So I begin to take short trips to the little Aussie towns and docks at Brisbane to watch for planes from the States. But there are no planes, so I tell myself that they are being unloaded north at Townsville or Rockhampton, or they are flying them here. But I know that only the heavy bombers and big transports have enough flying range to be ferried over. I am looking for medium bombers and fighters. These are what we in this area need.

On the short trips to the little towns away from all the American servicemen, who always go all out to spoil the area, I find myself respected and treated like a movie star. But this is not what I came over here for. I really am eager to get it over with so I can go home. In spite of the gloomy war news and our inability to fight the Japs, there is never a thought that we will not win the war. Back in '39 we used to brag about going to war with Germany, when Adolph was ranting and raving to the German people who were stupid enough to listen to him. People used to say we could win a war in two weeks. Well, it has been a year and a half now since the Japs stabbed us in the back and we still don't have a thing to fight with here in the Southwest Pacific. The people back home must be doing nothing. If we had anything here to fight with we could whip those little yellow bastards.

These days we worry about getting gasoline and food. Well, the Aussies had their problems too. In 1942 they could not get gasoline. The military took all the gasoline, so they rigged a charcoal burner mounted on the rear of their cars and converted the engines to burn the gas from burned charcoal. Many of the few cars you saw had this big contraption on the rear. They went chugging around without much power. A hill or some ruts would slow them down or stop them. They were not very efficient, but they would go, and that was something for 1942.

The Aussies were wild about American cigarettes. Cigarettes were a ready trade commodity and we took advantage of it. We were all issued one carton a week whether we used them or not. They were unknown brands like Piedmont and Cycle, but the brands did not make a plug to the Aussies. We used them in place of cash and traded them for just about anything they had. We would go out for dinner broke, but always with a carton of fags. The Aussie merchant was more eager to have the cigarettes than money. When I came back from New Guinea the last time I was issued a barracks bag and a half full of fags. I traded them for food, clothes, three pairs of those beautiful boots, jewelry, and a broken down motorcycle which I repaired.

Why cigarettes? The Aussies were as badly addicted on the weed as the Americans. And the American brands were more enticing because of the potency the Yank manufacturers put in the blend, and the sophistication that went with it.

At Amberly I met another Yank who was unattached and we were soon good friends. His name was Hartman and he had come out of the Philippines. How he got out was a story. He was stationed at Clark Field where our 7th Group was going. With the Jap invasion there, he had no way of getting out by air, and he did not want to hole up in the hills for the rest of the war, so he started walking south. He hitch hiked and caught rides on anything that had wheels or would float. He wore his uniform and the natives were kind to him. He caught rides on ox carts, wagons, trucks, and cars. He rode horseback and hitched rides on boats. The people gave him food and shelter a part of the time, and he sometimes lived off the land. Many nights he said he had to sleep out in the rain, but the rain was never cold. He confronted Japs on several occasions, but was always able to by-pass them. When he ran out of land he had to island hop. He said he would hang out at boat docks and wait for a boat that was going to another island farther south. He did not have any quinine or any medication for the prevention of malaria, but he did not get malaria. It took him six and one half months to make it to Australia. There he received all his back pay for all this time. He went out on the town for three weeks while spending it on Aussie women. Well, to each his own. He might have thought about all the hard days of the depression and saved some. He believed in living it up and wasn't this the way of the soldier? Why not, there may not be another day.

He did all this when he heard that Dugout Doug (MacArthur) had deserted his men during the Philippine campaign and gone to Australia. He said MacArthur took his maid and furniture with him and left ranking officers stranded.

Hartman and I went to town quite often to "give the women a break," as he said. He was a typical extravert. I was just the opposite. We got along however. He didn't have any trouble getting acquainted with the Aussie sheilas. He would butt right in and not wait for any formalities. I would let him do it and tag along and was happy to let him be the aggressor.

When the people back home finally sent us some airplanes to fight with, Hartman and the other few casuals, and myself went back north and flew combat together. We both survived 50 skip bombing and strafing missions, were on our way home, when he was killed. He climbed into a C-47 transport for the first leg of the unbelievable trip back home. His C-47 crashed on take off and all 53 veterans of 50 missions met their maker. This was one more of the times I missed it.

Such experiences are hard to understand. It seems there is no justice in warfare. The good kids always get killed first. To fly 50 suicide missions and get killed on the way home is not understandable. We did not have to fly. It was all voluntary. But there was always enough who were eager to do it because it was the only way to get out of the stinking jungle and sent back home. We were all sick of the unbearable jungle. It was like a sticky oven hot hades with no recreation and nothing to do in your spare time. We had no towns to go to, and most of the time it was impossible even to go to the beach because of Jap snipers. We hung around our tents a big part of the time scraping mildew off our boots, shoes and clothes. But General Kenney promised if we could survive 50 skip bombing, para frag, and strafing missions we could go home to stay. And every one of those missions was a step nearer to the day we could jump on that plane bound for the States. But any one of the 50 missions could have been the end as it was for most who flew.

Rumors are flying again that some airplanes are coming in from the States. Some of the Air Corps arrivals from the States at Amberly claim they have seen some B-17's, B-24's, and P-40's. I don't believe it, but it gives us something to talk about. Today marks the tenth month since I landed in Australia and still no planes.

The newspapers report the enemy air attacks on Port Moresby and Milne Bay have been stepped up. They have been bombing both bases at night with more planes than before. It looks like the Japs are going to make another try at taking Moresby. We've got to stop them in their drive for conquest. If we only had some B-17's. From Cooktown or Darwin we could bomb all their bases in southern New Guinea and on New Britain island. If we had medium bombers we could refuel at Moresby and bomb their bases with those too.

A B-24 landed at Amberly and shook up all the personnel. I got there fast, to try to transfer. I should have known they could not tell me a thing about where they were going or what their plans were. But it was so good to see a B-24 again. The crew told me that now there were a few B-25's at outback bases inland from Townsville. Maybe this was what I wanted. I rushed to the squadron I was attached to and asked the commanding officer if he would transfer me to one of those B-25 squadrons up there. He told me to bide my time until something came up. He asked my why I wanted to leave this paradise and go to some hole in the wall. I told him I was sick and tired of nothing to do.

Then more bad news. Jap infantry was crossing the Owen Stanley mountains on their way to Port Moresby overland. They got to within 30 miles of Moresby when the Aussies stopped them. However, we learned later that what really stopped their advance was the unpenetrable terrain, the humid heat, malaria, and dengue fever. The Aussie kids in the RAAF at Moresby strafed them with the few Whiraway's they had. I guess their planes made good strafers if they had no opposition. I'd bet the Zeros were not there to attack the Aussies.

The Aussies didn't have much to fight with. I flew in one of their Whiraways once. They were a light plane with little armor and not very much more than trainers. But those aussies were brave and did not hesitate to attack the superior Zero.

On August 7, 1942 the marines landed on the island of Guadalcanal. This was the second Yank ground offensive in the Southwest Pacific war. It was eight months since Pearl, Hickam, Wheeler, and the cowardly attacks by the little yellow monkeys from Asia. This offensive resulted in the most bloody in history, and Jap blood flowed there until February 1943. The stupid Japs on Guadalcanal committed suicide en masse. Tens of thousands of them charged the machine guns of the U.S. Marines to be cut down again and again until the bodies piled up so high it was impossible for the monkeys to climb above the dead. But they kept charging, and the Marines in their bunkers, kept mowing them down as if they were hay before a giant scythe. After Guadalcanal we could see that we were fighting fanatics. Little Asian monkeys who had been brainwashed to believe that it was an honor to die for their God.

The cowardly sneak attack by the Japs on December 7,1941 caught America flatfooted. It was like sneaking up on a man in an alley in the dark with a knife and stabbing him in the back. They sneaked in and attacked us and they knew they were more powerful at the time. But they did not reckon with the U.S. power of production. Slowly this was catching up with them. We needed planes badly in Australia, and finally, at last, they were beginning to arrive. It was only a matter of time until the productive might of America got into gear, and when it did, the islands stolen by the little yellow men were blasted into waste.

The Jap admiral who directed the cowardly attack on Oahu was right when he said while on his way back from the attack, "Maybe it was a mistake. Maybe we have just awakened a sleeping giant."

# CHAPTER 6
## FIRST B-25'S

It was a long road that had no turning and I finally came to mine.

Orders were pulled to transfer me to the 13th Squadron of the 3rd Bombardment Group who were presently stationed at Charters towers in the state of Queensland. Charters Towers? The name sounded for real but where was it? There was no Charters Towers on the map. The Aussies said it was out in the bush, somewhere east of Townsville. Why the Army Air Corps ever chose that godforsaken place for a base I'll never know. But later when I studied the location I could see it was strategic at that time.

However, my orders were the best news for me I'd had in a long wait. They told us we had a few B-25's there. There were 13 of us unassigned lost souls at Amberly. And we could not wait to get there and see those new planes. A new B-25 was coming to pick us up. My paradise and free life was over. My last night at Amberly was something to remember. We went out on the town, my shiela and I. And those last few hours were over all too soon. This was goodbye. A few tears were shed, but who could let the limit of time and sentiment stand in the way of the more important consideration of killing Japs?

A few winks of sleep and we were aboard a brand new B-25 heading north. She flew like a dream, but would she fight? This was what we all wanted to know. On her ability to do that, depended our lives and the outcome of the war.

We skim the tops of the eucalyptus trees, turn around to buzz Ipswich on the way out, and head for the boondocks. She'll do 300 easily. I look out the window to see the trees flash by and it seems like we are doing 1,000 miles per hour. The landscape is monotonous but for the huge anthills that I haven't seen in a long time. The anthills look like monoliths and are scattered among the eucalyptus trees. They look to be about twenty feet tall.

The interior of the airplane holds my whole interest. She has two 50 caliber gun turrets. They are operated electrically with a small triggerlike control and each turret has two 50 caliber machine guns. The turrets can be operated 360 degrees horizontally and the upper position, or turret has automatic cutouts or stops at the vertical stabilizers and rudders so they cannot be shot out. The upper gunner sits in a plastic dome and has an unobstructed view in all directions above horizontal. The lower gunner is the radio operator also and is supposed to be able to take care of everything below. I take a look through the lower turret sight. It has a telescopic sight that is like binoculars, but there is very little view. I see a big fault in this sight. The lower gunner has no view except thru this sight. How is he going to see the Zeros in that stupid sight? He must find the target not by any view he has, but by looking through that sight.

This is totally inadequate for meeting the speed and manueverability of the Jap Zeros. It's easy to see that they will come from below and the radio gunner will never see them. It is easy to see that whoever invented this stupid turret has never been in combat. These drawing artists must work on theory which too often turns into impractical dreams.

There is one more gun in the plastic cover in the nose of the airplane. It is a 30 caliber machine gun mounted through a socket and it is next to worthless. How in the world do we stop those Zeros with their machines guns and cannons with that little 30 caliber gun? The people who designed the armament for this airplane must be absolutely stupid.

Aside from these faults the airplane was a jewel. Those two big 2,000 horsepower engines caused plenty of vibration and noise but they turned out to be a life saver. However, it was the destiny of this airplane to be completely modified to meet the requirements we needed to annihilate the Japs. It was a waste of the taxpayers money to build them the way they originally came from the factory at North American Aviation.

The inside of the airplane from the top gunner aft was completely empty. The bomb bay was in the center of the fuselage between the navigator and all the radio equipment. There was a very small tunnel on the port side and above the bomb bay that became important to me. It was built for a small man and I am a big man, but many times I was forced to get through it.

The navigator sits behind the cockpit, while the bombardier sits in the nose. Both the navigator and the bombardier and all their equipment will be removed when we make the B-25 the most destructive air weapon in history. In the empty spaces, after the lower turret, the bombardier, the navigator, and all their equipment is removed, we will install guns guns guns.

We land at Charters Towers on a new corrigated portable metal runway that hums when we touch it with the tires. It is laid in interlinking sections and can easily be moved to a new location. The idea is to move these metal runways closer and closer to Japan as we smash the Japs into nothing.

Charters Towers is being built to a depot to supply Northern Australia and New Guinea with all Air Corps supplies. It is a hot dusty hell hole of a place with no town to go to but a 19th century village with one street and no pavement.

When I arrived the 13th Bomb Squadron had only three B-25's, but we were told more were coming. The 89th Squadron of the 3rd Group are slated to get Douglas A-20 Havoc's. The other squadrons of the 3rd Group will get B-25's. The 13th Squadron already has a reputation of one of the fightingest outfits in the Air Corps. It is an elite organization and when the war here in the Pacific is over it will rank right on top for combat missions flown and destruction to the enemy accomplished. The crewmen of the 13th will receive many presidential citations and commendations. The 13th Attack Squadron will someday be commended by General MacArthur and General Kenney and many combat crews will receive many high medals and citations.

Charters Towers, with its typically Anglo name was living in the past. This outback outpost seemed to have been bypassed by anything resembling sophistication in modern times. The streets were unpaved and it hadn't rained for months. The red dust was inches thick and the unpainted buildings were impregnated with it. On this flatland, the wind played a mournful tune around the street corners, and the awful dust it raised, ground in the teeth and settled on everything. The two blocks of businesses in the village long needed a stimulus to trade. A bonanza is being reaped now in Yankee dollars.

We from Amberly were too late for the girl fun however.

74

Those who came first had confiscated all who had been available. There was nothing to do unless you wanted to go to a local pub and drink some of that Aussie beer and you had to fight to get any. The Aussies were gone on the stuff. They'd gather round the pubs and make it just about impossible to get inside. A Yank not used to it couldn't drink much of the stuff unless he wanted to go back to the base drunk. Pubs were the thing for the Yanks in the outback in Australia but they were hard to get to because the line to get in formed hours before opening time and they were open only a couple hours a day.

The crews of the three B-25's we had were already assigned. This left us with few duties and we were still waiting for airplanes. To go to Charters Towers held no interest for us, so we were trapped. There were no buses or trains but we found a GI truck going to Townsville the next day. I wasn't anxious to go because I had been there before, but other guys wanted to go. So Strom, Hartman, Kerstetter and I hitched a ride. By air it was only a short hop, but by a truck over the long, rutty, dusty road it was an eternity. The truck raised clouds of dirty grime, and red dust that seeped through the aft end of the truck and covered us with fine powder. We planned to find a nice clean place to eat, but now we had to wash off the grime. We rented a room and showered off most of the outback dust and went to town. We found a favorite restaurant but it was not the same as when I was there before. The Yanks had been in town too long and the prices had gone out of sight as usual and the Yanks had spoiled the town. We ordered the best steak and eggs they had which was always the status dish in Australia.

I found the girls in Townsville had been spoiled by the Yanks too. They now played hard to get and were independent. The Americans had already lost their newness and glamour and we had not even begun to fight the war yet.

We went to a movie and a public dance. The dance was rowdy after booze was mixed with it. We'd had our kicks and enough of the wild life of Townsville so it was back to our hotel. The next day we hopped on the same truck and took the same old bumpy road back to Charters Towers. It was good to go and good to get back.

We still didn't have planes, and with very little to do and no recreation we felt like anything, even combat, would be welcome. At roll call one morning our first sergeant announced that more B-25's were coming in and when they arrived there would be a shortage of radio gunners. He told us he wanted volunteers to go to a radio operator and aerial gunnery school in Townsville. He said it was a one year course crammed into six weeks. "When you complete the course our airplanes will be here and you will go right into combat with a nice promotion," he said. Well, can you believe a man you do not know?

This sounded interesting and it offered a project, but did I need this additional training? I had been trained to be an aircraft crew chief and engineer. Why should I take this additional course? But I was bored again so I volunteered which was against all military advice. As soon as day broke the next morning we were all bouncing along that dusty road toward the city of Townsville with all our belongings.

This is a pretty good deal. We billet in new Aussie barracks which is a lot better to take than those tents back at Charters Towers. After a shower and shave we go to town. Now we can go to town every night if we want. But we soon find out different. Our time will all be filled and it will be cram, cram every day. This will be o.k. with me as it will keep most of us occupied and our minds off the worry of going into combat.

Townsville is now within bombing range of some of the Japanese bases, and almost to the minute every night a lone bomber comes out of the north to bomb the city. The air raid siren goes on and we watch the sky for fireworks. At the same time the searchlights go on and probe the sky for the airplane. Then we see the very bright lights flash on the wings of the bomber. The Aussie anti-aircraft gunners open up to make a thrilling show. The ack-ack gunners never seem to hit the airplane. The shells explode everywhere but where the bomber is. The Japs drop their bombs and we hear the baroom of the explosions, and the airplane turns and heads back toward Rabaul.

If the Aussies were smart they would black out the city and not use their searchlights. To turn on their lights only reveals the target to the Japs. If there were no lights at all an enemy plane could not find Townsville. The gunners can't hit the plane anyway. It's just a psychological bombing to harass the Aussies.

General Kenney has informed us that when we begin our big offensive our first objective will be to break the back of the Japanese air power. This means the first battles fought by the U.S. in this area will be in the air. This is not news to us. We have known that all along. The 5th and 13th Air Forces with a little aid from the RAAF will have to bear the brunt of the attack. There is no doubt that we will be among the first to attack the Japs en masse.

We won't get much help from the RAAF. They are a bunch of happy go lucky loveable guys always eager to do what they can, but not in a position to do much because they don't have a lot to do with. All they have of any military value is a few Beaufighters.

This school I'm attending is pressure. The Air Corps has a motivation that puts facts in a man's head faster than a school kid ever experienced. There is no love lost or permissive leniency. You better get with it buddy or else. The instructors are cramming electricity into us like there is no tomorrow. "You're gonna do six months of electricity in one week," an instructor tells us. There is electro magnets, flux, electrons, protons, silver conductors, copper conductors, induction, magnets, condensers, resistors, vacuum tubes—and what is electricity? Controlled electricity is electrons and protons flowing along a conductor.

"You're gonna learn the Morse code well enough to send and receive 22 words a minute," he said. "You're gonna practice it, sending and receiving, every day for six weeks, and at the end you will know it," We have a machine that will send the Morse Code over a headset system at any selected speed.

"You're gonna learn how to use the blinker system to send and receive coded messages at 10 words a minute. You're gonna learn the blinker code so well you can use a flashlight in an emergency," he tells us.

He tells us that we have to learn the communications systems and equipment on the airplane forward and backward, from the tuning units to the radio compass and the command set. "You are going to learn how to tune the liaison transmitter, which is a big job, with your eyes shut."

"You are also going to learn how to do some repairs in the field in case shrapnel hits your liaison set and proves it inoperative. And you are gonna learn how to use the code book so you can code and de-code messages. The code book is changed every day to confuse the Japs."

"And you're gonna learn how to shoot a fix or to "home" with the radio compass to get your location. When the six weeks is over you are going to be a radio operator and a radio operator navigator, and you will be the best damn radio operator navigators in the Pacific war. You're gonna learn how to operate the Gibson Girl (emergency transmitter) in case you are forced down and have to ditch or crash in the jungle, or your liaison set gets shot up."

"You're gonna learn the nomenclature and the parts of the 30 and 50 caliber air cooled machine guns. You're gonna learn those guns, I promise you, so well you'll be able to strip them down and reassemble them in the dark. And you're gonna learn how to fire those guns and hit a moving target at 400 miles an hour. You will learn how to maintain those guns to identify all the different types of ammo. Also you will know how to unjam a jammed gun with split second timing. Within six weeks you are going to be the best damned aerial gunners in the Pacific war," he concluded.

Wow! Who does he think we are? We are to be navigators too. I can see right now a lot of us are going to wash out. Well, I did not wash out, and I'm glad I didn't, because this was a life and death struggle, and if we are to whip those crafty little Japs this job has to be done. Later, our B-25's were converted to deadly gunships and the navigator of all airplanes was knocked out of a job and I had to be the navigator, the radio operator, as well as the lower gunner. The pilot became a bombardier also, and the co-pilot did nothing but sit there and wait for the pilot to take a bullet or a piece of shrapnel.

We had our work cut out for us. I never studied so hard

in my life. My formal schooling had been taken rather casually. I never flunked anything, but I didn't have much motivation to try hard. This assignment was something else and I didn't know I could do it. We did not go to town every night as we had been planning. Every night we had the regular air raids which meant blackouts. This shook people out of their usual nightly activities. The Japs were just proving to us that they could do as well as Jimmy Doolittle. Actually there was no real damage done in either case.

Sunday was our only free time. We went to the beach usually, and one Sunday we got into a gang fight with Aussie civilians. Some of us got our noses bloodied and our clothes got ruined. It started of course because of girls. Those Aussies are such nice blokes but they just got fed up with us taking their girls and I for one didn't blame them. The Aussie girls would let go an Aussie anytime for a Yank, and this time the Aussies had just enough beer to start something. Nobody won the fight but we found out how very good those Aussies were with their fists.

The Morse code was the hardest part of the school for me. Sending it was all right but taking it and copying it at 22 words a minute seemed impossible. One could not think in individual letters or numbers and get by at all. One had to copy and think a word at a time, not a letter at a time. I had to take the final speed exam three times before I made it.

The kids at the school would pounce on me for information concerning the Jap Zero and the ack-ack. They were scared to death and I didn't blame them. All I could tell them was how fast they were, how maneuverable, and that they were armed with a cannon. I told them they were good

80

fighters, but built very light without a trace of armor plate, and were built to be expendable. The Japs did not hold human life in high regard like we do and we heard they did not even carry parachutes. They had been known to shoot us in parachutes and in the water, and I suppose they did not want to give us the chance to do it to them.

The Jap Zero was very easy to shoot down if you could hit it. They were built like a feather and much easier to shoot down than any of our planes. Their defense was in their offense. They were so fast and maneuverable it was very difficult to hit them.

Our first encounter with the enemy in our B-25's taught us a lot of things. The most important was the uselessness of that lower power turret. And that little 30 caliber gun in the nose proved next to nothing. However, in time we junked both and made a flying battleship of the B-25.

It was a typical situation at the school. It was typical of the Air Corps to do nothing for months and then rush through a project and be forced to complete it in record time. The motto was wait and hurry up, or hurry up and wait. We all graduated except for four, then the C.O. gave us a pep talk, wished us luck in our future go at the Japs, and gave us our diplomas.

A large photo of the group was made for us and we headed back to Charters Towers. Years later I studied that picture and counted those who died. In the 13th Attack Squadron after we got ready and started attacking the Japs, our losses were 100% every three months among those who flew combat. This included new replacements from the States. We built a stone monument at our base at Buna and listed the names in metal of those who were killed or missing in action. The list grew so long it covered the whole monument, and we had been attacking only about 5 months at the time.

We had our last steak and eggs dinner and it was back on that bumpy old road to our base at Charters Towers. True to the word of our commanding officer the 13th now had 9 airplanes. I finally got my B-25 but was worried about that worthless turret I had inherited. Also, at school, we had fired the machine guns only one time and that was at a stationary target. We had not fired at those 400 mph targets we were told about. We were not the best damn gunners in the Pacific war. I was the only one who had ever fired at a moving target or the real thing. And we were going to face an enemy who probably had years of practice.

Well, I for one will get some practice as we fly to the targets and on the way back from the targets.

# CHAPTER 7

## FIRST B-25 ATTACKS

What is the psychology of war? Why do young men, when caught in the maw of war want to do all they can—to fight? Why do they want all the action they can get? Do they want to die? I say they want to live. It is the desire to continue living that drives them into the battles. Also it is the presence of others nearby that pushes one into it. Our fight with the Japs in a way, was a fight for survival. Not a war to die or be heroes, but a fight to live. Our only desire was to get it over with and get out of that stinkin' jungle and go home. We wanted to smash them so hard they could not retaliate. Our hope was that our government, the people back home would send us the airplanes and equipment that we had to have to get the job done. So far they had failed miserably. I had been over here so long now it seemed like an eternity and still we didn't have what we needed.

After many months of waiting and hoping we finally began to receive some of the things we had to have. General George Kenney, commander of the 5th Air Force had some C-47 transport planes, and we heard rumors that the Seabees and Army Engineers were being shuttled north to Port Moresby to build a big new airfield a little north and west of Moresby in the rain forest. Soon now, we hoped, we would be using this strip for a base camp to strike the Jap bases on the other side of the Owen Stanleys.

The combat crews of the 13th Squadron are called to the

briefing tent. Our operations officer explains that we are to fly some dry run practice missions, to fire at moving targets being towed behind airplanes. The moving targets will be towed about 1,000 yards back of the tow plane. The tow plane will pull the targets across our flight path at different angles and our gunners and bombardiers will take turns firing at the targets. He also tells us if we hit an airplane we will be court martialed. On the same mission on the way back, we will practice dropping bombs on a bullseye target on the ground.

This is great. Now at last we will get in some real practice. We'll have a better chance to beat the veteran Jap flyers with their Zeros of superior speed and maneuverability.

I am assigned to fly with the commander of the squadron whose name is Captain Connley, and right away I know we are going to get along. He is a hell of a nice guy and I hope to continue on with him. I will be the one who sends most of the radio messages and in the future when our airplanes are converted I'll probably do most of the radio navigation for the squadron. I am scared stiff for fear of making mistakes. I have had no experience at this time. Surely there is someone on combat status who has had some past experience. But I guess not.

Ten planes are going to fly this mission and our preparation is intense. Every man is in his position shuffling gear, toggling switches, adjusting controls, and getting acquainted with a hundred different systems in these new B-25's. This calls for teamwork and split second timing. Every man is a must in his duties. These planes are the best that modern technology and engineering skill can make except for the armament. But what about the scared young kids who are going to man them? This is our testing and we know it. All that's necessary now is for all the crew members to function with coolness.

But cool we are not. There is tension and excitement in the air. Even the planes seem to sense this. They are roaring, coughing, belching, and backfiring as the powerful engines are warmed up and the pilots jockey them into position for take off. Choking red dust fills the air whipped up by the blast from the whirling props. Can we make any purpose and order here in this excitement and seeming confusion? It'll take some cool heads to do it.

Every man has his orders. We spin into position for take off on the new steel runway. My ship is the first one to rocket down the strip. The Captain hits the brakes and the nose strut collapses and bounces back. He revs the powerful engines and holds the brakes. When he lets go the brakes we roll down the runway at an unheard of speed faster and faster as the 2,000 horsepower Wright Cyclone engines bite deeper and deeper into the wind and we rocket up over the trees.

The empenage section of the airplane is vibrating, shaking, and rattling to the stress and strain of the powerful surge of those fantastic engines. I switch to command and hear Connley's crisp voice: "Connley to flight. Connley to flight I'll circle at 5,000 feet, follow me."

We make formation at 5,000 feet and point toward the sun climbing steadily. This is more than thrilling to me after all those months in waiting. What a way to go to war. In all the wars ever fought in the past, no warriors ever went into battle in such a manner and with the hopes and fears we had on that August morning in 1942 out over the Great Barrier Reef in the Southwest Pacific. Our formation was beautiful and perfect.

"Connley to flight. We'll level over the reef at 10,000 and at 250 miles per hour."

The ocean hazes into the east and the tow plane appears coming up alongside. The target looks like an elongated white flag.

"Connley to flight. Connley to flight. Inform all gunners to fire with extreme caution. Hit the target. We want none of these precious planes hit or damaged. Anyone who hits a plane will be court martialed."

I'm stooped over the lower turret looking through this stupid telescopic sight. My view is much like looking through a long pipe from a dark room. The tow ship pulls ahead, makes a turn past us from below and to port, and I try to locate it in my sight. It is gone. I am too late. Then I hear Connley's voice. "Why didn't you fire?" "I couldn't find the target in my sight," I told him.

"Pilot to radio, we'll try it again."

"Roger."

This time I saw the tow plane at 2 o'clock through my window. Then I swung my turret and pointed the guns toward the tow plane, and I was able to pick up the target. I fired three medium bursts and could see my tracers tearing through the target with my telescopic lens. I could see tracers from other lower gunners too, ripping through the fabric of the target.

The tow plane made several other passes in many different angles and the upper gunners as well as the bombardiers riddled the target. Had that target been a Jap plane it would not have had a chance. But it wasn't a Jap plane. It did not move as fast and it didn't dodge around in the sky. But, at least now, we had a bit more confidence.

We banked to port and turned 180 degrees, a turn that pointed us back to the coast. About five miles north of our base in the bush, a big bullseye had been made on the ground. Without command we dropped our bombs (duds). The bombs were painted a bright yellow and I could see them fall all the way to the ground. They all hit near or in the target, but would they have hit the target if Jap fighters and flak had been all around us? We made two more bomb runs and then back to the base.

We parked our airplanes and rode to briefing in jeeps and trucks. The first thing the Captain said was: "Well, what the hell was on the minds of you radio gunners?"

"I could not find the target through that sight," came a voice.

"Why not?"

"When you look through that sight you don't have any peripheral vision. It's next to impossible to locate a target. Captain, have you looked through that sight?"

"No I haven't, let's take a look," said the Captain.

We all went to show the Captain the next to worthless sight. He told us he would take it up with the group commander, but for the present we would have to live with it.

That was the problem. We might have to die with it. We all knew now that our lives could be tied up with the functioning of that next to worthless scopesight.

Orders came on the second day after the two practices that we were going to fly our first B-25 combat mission in the morning. This was the big news we had been waiting for. Now we will find out what our new airplanes will do against the Japs and if our lower guns are as vulnerable as we feared.

All the radio gunners got together to discuss what to do

about the sight. We decided to all watch through our windows for fighters, to swing the turret in the direction of the fighters after we have spotted them before we try to see them through the sight. However, if the Zero comes in from the side or forward we'll not have enough time to do this because they come in so fast. We all agreed that this precaution was about the only thing we could do.

Our preparation for our first B-25 combat mission is thorough and intense. Tomorrow we will fly to Moresby and we must have all our equipment in order. We must have extra ammo, a 45 caliber automatic with shoulder holster, a mosquito net, a carbine, K-rations, atabrine pills, a knife, an air mattress, mess kits, and cigarettes for barter.

We are the 13th Bombardment Squadron and under the 3rd Bombardment Group. Some of the guys are superstitious about the 13th, but it doesn't make a plug to me. I feel we have as much chance for survival as anyone else. Our squadron insignia is the "Grim Reaper" which is a skeleton holding a scythe on a blue background. The Grim Reaper Squadron is destined to make its mark in this war with the little yellow men. We will be the first to skip bomb their ships and the first to use para fragmentation bombs and the first to devastate an enemy with machine guns and cannon fire on a mass basis.

Early the next morning after chow we are jeeped to our airplanes. We scramble to our positions, warm up the engines, and the Grim Reaper Squadron is at its grim business. As we get ready to go, all gas tanks are topped off and we jockey into position for takeoff. The airfield is alive with thundering engines, and the wind whirls out from under each spinning prop and fills the air with choking dust. I am flying with Captain Connley which makes me the most

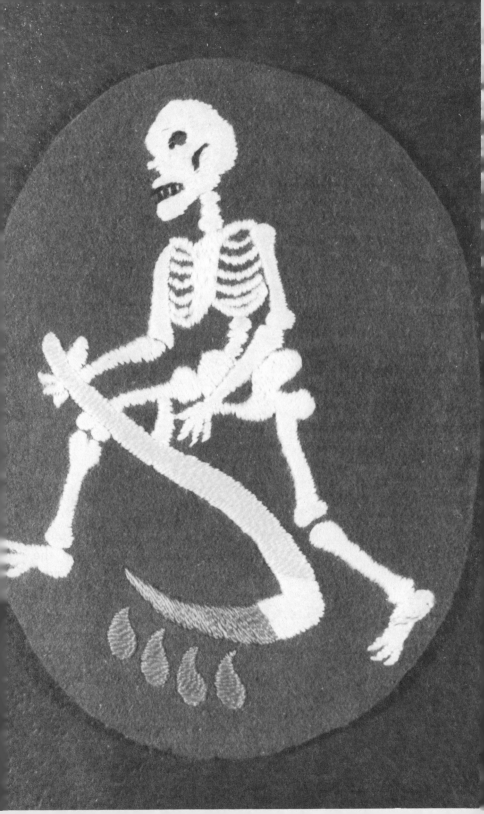

responsible radio operator in the squadron. We roar to the end of the strip, and swing around 180 degrees, then slam both throttles forward to their stops. In seconds our sturdy B-25 is zooming over the trees and we are heading for the Coral Sea. At 5,000 feet we level off and cruise at 250 mph waiting in impatience for the others to catch up to make formation. One by one the other planes appear alongside and take their places. We then gain speed to 280 mph and slowly climb to the comfortable altitude of 9,000 feet.

Townsville is to our right and the coastline is below us. The Great Barrier Reef can now be seen dead ahead. After about an hour I call the Captain and tell him that for practice, and for the first time in the air, I'm going to shoot bearings for our location. The first step is to turn on the radio compass receiver, then lay out a chart of the area on my table with a book of frequencies of local radio stations. I tune to a station in Townsville and run a line on the chart from Townsville the number of degrees the compass dial reads. Then I do the same with another local station in Cooktown. Where the lines cross is our location. The cross is directly in line between Townsville and Port Moresby. Then I call the navigator and ask him to reach back through the tunnel for my chart so he can see my fix and check it with his bearing. He calls me in a few minutes and says "right on." I feel good about this, my first attempt at navigating by radio.

With nothing to do now but wait for our landing, which is about two hours away, I now tune my liaison receiver to a commercial station in Townsville that plays popular music. I call the crew on interphone and ask them why they don't switch to liaison. We all enjoy the bands of Benny Goodman and Glenn Miller while coming into Port Moresby. A real treat.

It began to rain and visibility was only about 3,000 yards. This presented a problem because we were going to land at the new runway at 7 Mile Field. This new airfield was cut out of the jungle and was 7 miles from Port Moresby. From Port Moresby we knew how to find the new strip, so finding Moresby was our only real problem. Then we spied the coast line and saw the old hulk. We banked to the right to find the town and to the left to 305 degrees. I saw a road cut through the jungle that led us to the new field.

As we landed it was still raining cats and dogs so we parked our airplanes and stayed inside. This field was packed earth that was not packed much anymore. It was soft everywhere in the area except on the mesh runway. It was too hot to stay in the plane so I stripped down to my shorts and crawled out to tie down the airplane. In spite of the hot rain the mosquitos were having a feast on my bare skin. So I went back inside, but a few thousand mosquitos dove through the door with me. The airplane was leaking and we had to rig a place to sleep. It was either in the leaky plane or under it. We could not rig our nets inside so it was under the wing.

The downpour went on and on, and the water was hot. Most of us were under the airplane trying to keep out of the rain when a GI weapons carrier pulled up alongside. The driver asked if we wanted a lift to their mess hall. There wasn't a man who didn't want to go. We had the usual spam, powdered potatoes, and powdered everything else. The mess hall was a tent screened, just like the ones the Aussies had.

General Kenney had let out the word before we left, that in New Guinea we would be subject to minimum discipline, and our dress would be just about anything that would suit us. A pair of suntan pants cut off high above the knees

90

seemed to be the most popular attire. The sharp Aussie flying boots went great with shorts if you had them, and most combat crews had traded for them by this time.

Having flown combat missions before, I have an ill feeling about this mission tomorrow. We have a good airplane. It is fast and we have a lot of faith in its ability to take a lot of punishment. But it is poorly armed for defense just like the old A-17. It is vulnerable from everywhere below horizontal. I am afraid that it will prove mediocre and our losses will be too high.

For two days and nights it rained and it was impossible to fly this type of mission in the rain. Our only recreation was to go to Moresby and there was nothing at Moresby to do but swap our cigarettes for what the few merchants had. There were no air raids either during the rain.

On the third day the rain eased off and we spent the day checking our airplanes. I inspected ours from wing tip to wing tip and from nose to cone. We loaded 500 pound bombs, ammo, oil and gasoline. Our target was to be the airstrip at Buna and any planes we could catch on the ground. When I learned we were to fly at 9,000 feet I knew the Zeros would be up to their old tricks and waiting for us. Their radar was their warning and it would pick us up long before we got there.

Before take off on our first B-25 mission we checked our equipment again. After we got our engines started we double checked all the systems on our airplane. I strapped my carbine to the bulkhead near me where I could grab it if we went down and I was still alive. My ammunition containers were filled to the brim and I checked all water containers and survival kits, flares, cartridge belts, steel helmet.

Previously I had tuned my liaison transmitter, because it

takes time to tune and also, it transmits while tuning. It is illegal to clutter up the air waves for more time than needed while tuning.

We top off the gas tanks, roar down the taxiway, whip each airplane around to face the wind, and we are on the steel mat accelerating for our take off. For a change there is no dust. The earth is soggy from all the rain, and soft, except for the steel mat. The propellers in high pitch slap the air with a deafening and throbbing sound and the trees are coming up so fast they appear to crash into us. The tremendous power of our 2,000 horsepower engines do a great job and we are on our way.

"Connley to flight, follow me."

"Roger." "Roger."

We circle once over the strip while all the others get airborne, then point toward the alpine peaks. As usual the Owen Stanleys are covered with clouds, but that is no problem now. Our new B-25's have a ceiling of 30,000 feet. While the planes behind us are catching up and making formation we are steadily climbing to get over the rain clouds.

"Pilot to crew, check your guns."

"Roger." "Roger."

I kneel over the stupid sight and swing my turret around in search of a target. We are too far away from the trees to use them for a target so I swing my guns down and forward and hit the gun button. My tracers arc out of sight. The upper gunner fired his at the same time and the vibration shook the whole waist section of the airplane. We keep gaining altitude and level at 14,000. We can now use only our interphone. We are in enemy territory and the radios are taboo.

Our orders are to bomb any ships that could be anchored out from Buna, and any buildings we see will be targets also. But we are to stay in formation if at all possible for protection. If we break formation for any reason we are to re-make formation as fast as possible. The Japs will have something to say about that. When we are attacked some planes will be forced out of formation, and if there are ships we must bomb them individually.

Now we are down to 9,000 and the Buna airstrip is in sight. I know exactly what is happening at Buna. Their radar has picked us up and their Zeros are taking off to intercept us. And their ack-ack gunners have their fingers a hair from their triggers.

"Bombardier to crew, I see fighters below."

"Roger, get ready."

"Bombardier to crew, they're climbing."

I pointed my turret at 12 o'clock low then zipped aft. Then I swung it to 6 o'clock low. I see them now, they are gaining altitude.

"Bombardier to crew, more fighters below."

"They are going to clobber us," came over the interphone.

By this time we are almost over the runway.

"Pilot to bombardier, you've got the plane."

Then the airplane jumped like it had hit a stone wall. An ack-ack burst had nearly got us. We could hear the shrapnel splatter on our airplane. I am all eyes now watching for those Zeros to attack us.

"Radio to crew, those Zeros are coming up on us from behind."

"Roger."

We see no ships or barges so we are still a perfect formation.

"Pilot to gunners, keep those Zeros away."

"We'll do our best."

I am still watching out my window and all I can see is flak bursts below us. I see them on our port side. I swing my turret toward them as they begin to flash which means they are firing at us. I fire a long burst and rake across their formation. They are still too far away. I watch them gain on us and fire again and again. Other tracers are arcing at them too, and then they break away to gain altitude to dive on us. I'm so scared I can't think about what I'm doing.

"Upper gunners, they are diving on us from above."

The upper gunners open up on them and two begin to smoke but the rest continue their attack. They splatter us with lead and steel and dive right past us and now I swing my guns in their direction but, by the time I'm in a position to fire at them they are out of range. If all the lower gunners could sight them we could murder them. They come up from below again and this time I get one in my next to worthless sight and bring smoke. He turns away and I look out the window to see an acre of black puffs so thick we could walk on it.

"Upper gunner to crew, I see more Zekes at 6 o'clock low. Give 'em hell."

Our plane jumps again from concussion, and more shrapnel smashes us and we keep on flying. There are five more Zeros behind us and we all open up on them and two explode and the rest high tail it away. Now this is more like it. It is unbelievable how fast they gained on us. We were going 300 miles per hour and they came up on us at a fantastic rate.

"Upper gunner to crew, five more at seven o'clock high."

"Roger."

If they are coming in at a high altitude I can't fire on them yet so I scan the skies and see a B-25 smoking with Zeros on its tail. We are being slaughtered.

"Zeros diving on us from above."

There's a deafening explosion and I tell myself we are going down. There is a gaping hole in the side of our plane. But the props are not stopped and we are still flying. When we land we learn a Zero bullet had hit an oxygen container and it exploded.

I switch to command and hear: "They're on us, upper gunners, upper gunners."

I switch back to interphone. We are now out of range of their flak guns and moving fast toward the mountains, but the Zeros are still up here swarming around us. They are above us and I can't fire at them but the upper gunners are now keeping them away. I'm almost buried in the empty shell casings that pour down in the airplane from the upper turret.

"Radio to upper gunner, do you see any more Zeros?"

"Yes, but they are staying out of range now."

"Pilot to radio, what was that explosion we heard back there?"

"I think it was an oxygen bottle that exploded. We'll be o.k."

I scan the skies again and see another of our airplanes smoking.

"Radio to pilot, there is a smoking B-25 on our starboard side lagging behind. Can we ease closer to it to protect it?"

"Roger."

The Captain throttles back and we eased near the

smoking B-25. I switch to command.

"This is Connley, can you make it?"

"We can make it if the fire doesn't get any worse. Besides the fire, we have wounded aboard."

I switch to interphone.

"Upper gunner, do you see any more Zeros?"

"No, they have left us."

By this time we are near the tops of the jagged peaks and getting closer to our base. Our worry now is whether or not that smoking B-25 could make it.

"Pilot to radio, call Moresby and report two aircraft lost, one smoking, and many more damaged."

"Roger."

I tap out my first message in the air. The message is far from perfect:

(Call sign Moresby)

"Heading home. Two aircraft lost. One airplane smoking. Several damaged. Several crew members wounded."

Call sign/time-date

# CHAPTER 8

## BUNA, LAE, SALAMAUA

Our first fight with the Japs with our new B-25's let us know just how vulnerable we were. Our losses were too high. They hurt us badly. We left 12 crewmen in the jungle probably all dead. Many were wounded and we lost two brand new B-25's. It was a nightmare getting enough altitude for the smoking airplane to fly over the mountains. We watched the crew throw just about everything overboard to lighten the airplane so it could make it. But once over the top it was downhill all the way to 7 mile, and it went straight in while the rest of us made a wide circle to give the pilot room and time.

After all airplanes were parked we gathered under our airplane for a briefing. I had been so busy with the Zeros I had not noticed if we had dropped our bombs. But I learned we had dropped them all in the area of the Buna strip. We had done plenty of damage to their installation there besides shooting down six of their fighters. Only three were counted as official however, because all kills must be either photographed or witnessed.

Taking photographs of the damage is part of the business of our attacks. When the pictures were developed they showed that most of our bombs had exploded in the Buna area.

Now we could assay our damage and prepare to lick our wounds. To mend the damage meant we would have to go back to Charters Towers. In the meantime, the damaged planes were fixed up enough to get them there. The Aussies came to help and Kilroy was there to do all possible.

"What are you doing this for?" he asked.

"Oh, I don't know. I suppose because it's the only way to get back to the States." All combat crews can go back when they have flown 50 missions." I told him.

"Fifty missions?" "You won't fly twenty five missions from the looks of these planes." Kilroy said. "Why don't you bomb them in the night like they do us", he asked.

"We are in a different league. We want to take pictures and see what we are doing," I told him.

Kilroy patched up all the holes and I did the best I could without parts to make mechanical repairs. In two days Captain Connley led us off 7 Mile Field and we headed toward Australia and Charters Towers. We were never so relaxed and we listened to our beautiful music all the way back to our base. We came back conquering heroes. After turning our airplanes over to the ground crews for repairs we had some hot chow and hit the sack.

We had no duties until the planes were put back in shape. Now it was time to get our airplane named. Our crew got together to get each others ideas, and we decided to name it "The Widowmaker". Our squadron painter went to work with his brush and soon we were christened. He also painted the first bomb on the fuselage for our first mission in B-25's.

With a little time on our hands, while waiting for our next mission, my friend Kerstetter and I decide to brave the rough ride to Townsville to get a taste of city life. We were thinking about those pretty girls plus a steak dinner. Our money was short, but we had a barracks bag full of cigarettes for barter.

Kerstetter was good company. He was very handsome and came from the Pennsylvania area of the Pennsylvania Dutch. He was a decided asset in meeting the young sheilas from any town. We both flew 50 missions and saw Japan weaken in the Pacific. Kerstetter, my friend, was the best of the best, and his death was a sad casualty of the great war. We both survived 50 hazardous and dangerous combat missions in smashing the Japanese war machine. He was through with war and on his way back home to a well deserved reprieve, and was on the same C-47 with Hartman when it crashed, killing all aboard.

It was my sad duty to write to his parents. They would not accept the truth. Could justice be in this kind of fate? Kerstetter's parents invited me to their home and offered to pay my way there. My good intentions never got me to their home, but my sympathy was sent in letter after letter. What can you say?

We stayed overnight in Townsville and had a nice dinner which was worth the trip after the GI food we were used to. We found some girls I used to know and strolled along the beach just in time to catch the lone Jap bomber air raid. It comes every night to harass the people and the display of the ack-ack shells bursting in the sky was still impressive. The Aussie anti-aircraft gunners were still shooting at it and their ack-ack shells were still exploding all over the sky, everywhere except where the bomber was.

Back at the base the ground crews had just about finished their work of repairing our aircraft. I had a job to do on my plane which was not the work of the ground crews. I needed something to stop the Jap bullets and shrapnel we got from the rear. I conceived the idea of another armor plate like the ones we installed on the A-17's. I knew of a wrecked Aussie airplane in the boonies with armor plate. I cannibalized some of this plate and had a welder cut it to size and burn four holes in it for mounting. That plate saved my life more than once and I made it portable so I could mount it in other planes because I flew combat in many other airplanes.

More B-25's have arrived and we now have 12 airplanes. We are now about ready for our second B-25 mission with some new crews and new planes. This will be their first mission and there is much excitement in the air. Our base is a long way from the target, but one advantage we have is most of the time we are in Australia, far away from the Jap bombers. As for now, we must fly the long route over the Coral Sea to reach our takeoff point at 7 Mile Field where it is only a hop over the Owen Stanley Mountains to the Jap bases.

The weather forcast is in our favor. Light variable clouds and sunny skies. We have our briefing which is pretty much routine, load our gear, and warm up the engines. We have a new upper gunner named Nelson and he is a scared kid. His questions reveal his lack of experience. They seem stupid to me, but they are the kind that come from nervousness and fear. He has been through gunners school in the States and that should help. He at least ought to know how to fire his big 50 caliber machine guns.

I'm still flying with Captain Connley so I am still the responsible squadron radio operator. The other operators will probably not even have to turn their sets on. How lucky can one get?

It is the crack of dawn, and all our engines are started and we shake up Charters Towers and the roos with the deafening roar. One by one Grim Reaper Squadron rolls to the end of the strip and swings around into position for takeoff. The whole field is covered with a blanket of red fog stirred up by spinning props. "The Widowmaker" is the first to roll down the strip and I wonder how the Captain is able to see the runway through the dust cloud. We rocket into the air and suddenly the air is clear. He pulls back on the stick and we clear the eucalyptus trees by inches. This new B-25 could almost fly itself. The vibration in the waist section of the plane eases off as we bank to port 360 degrees and circle once over the town to give the others a chance to get airborne. We head east out over the Great Barrier Reef, and one by one the others fall into formation, wing tip to wing tip. As we climb, it is getting cool and we don our jackets.

I tune my liaison receiver to frequency "one" and listen for my call sign, then tune my transmitter to the same frequency and tap out:

"Grim Reaper to Charters Towers. In formation. Everything o.k."

Call sign/time-date

At 10,000 feet everything is relaxed. There is nothing to do but wait for the miles to pass, so again we listen to the peacetime music of a favorite radio station.

"Radio to crew, our music is on liaison."

We all switch to liaison and dream of our carefree days back home, of friends and family, and our memories of the past. The deep blue sky above and the aqua sea below make it hard to believe in the reality of our mission.

Nelson, our new upper gunner, crawled out of his turret and tapped me on the shoulder. He yelled in my ear: "That music is really something", he said. I could tell it gave him comfort. "Nothing but the best for the troops," I yelled back. He said he did not expect such a treat in music way out here. He crawled back to his position. I switched to "call" which blocks out all other interphone positions.

"Radio to Nelson, switch to interphone."

I asked him if he knew how to operate this interphone system. He said he was not acquainted with it. I told him I would check him out.

"You will be concerned with the "interphone" position mostly. If you want everybody to be concerned switch to "call". If you want to hear the ship to ship or ship to shore radio switch over to "command". When you talk be sure you remember to press the mike button."

"Roger."

"Radio to pilot, over."

"Pilot to radio, over."

"Captain, our new gunner has never fired a turret like this one. Is it o.k. if he fires it now?"

"Pilot to upper gunner, make sure you don't hit our airplanes."

Nelson does not fire.

"Radio to Nelson, why don't you fire?"

"They won't fire," he replies.

I looked at his guns and they had not been charged. There was no round in the chamber. So I told him to charge them, then they fired. The 50 caliber machine gun is a very potent weapon. The slug is one half inch in diameter and the gun will fire 1,100 rounds per minute. The top gunner can fire in almost any direction except below the horizon.

The Grim Reaper Squadron gradually lowers altitude as the coast of New Guinea appears as a flat line on the horizon. We are coming into 7 Mile Strip as the high Owen

Stanleys loom in the background. Our tires touch the metal runway and hum on the matting. We are back in the steaming jungle.

It seems miraculous how the climate, in a few minutes, can change via the speed of the airplane. We are greeted by swarms of starved mosquitos. Since we were here last they surely have doubled their population. It seems our "stay away" ointment is useless. You might as well let them have their fill rather than to smear the blood all over your skin.

Our B-17 reconnaissance plane has reported enemy ships steaming south through the Vidiaz Straits. If they do not change their direction by tomorrow they will be within our range. Perhaps we will fly our first combat mission against enemy shipping.

After we service our planes, and load our bombs for tomorrow's raid, we build our mosquito nets and have supper with the engineers who built 7 Mile Field. Then it is to our sacks, as we will be up before daybreak. The latest report is that the Jap ships are still on course heading south. They will get the surprise of their war on the morrow. We have 500 pound bombs in our racks and they'll sink any ship afloat if hit in a vulnerable place.

Just as we were dozing, the Jap Air Force paid us their nightly visit. There were nine this time and they were headed for the town of Moresby. Too bad they didn't know what we had for them at 7 Mile. They could have done us in had they dropped their bombs on us. But there was no sweat for us this night.

As I lay waiting for sleep my thoughts are on the morrow. Again we are to face the Jap Zeros at high altitude. They'll dive on us like cat birds on a chicken hawk. If we only had a pursuit escort to drive them off, then our bombing mission

103

could be much more effective, and our lives would be much safer. General Kenney has told us that we must have superiority in the air first. This means we must have fighter escort on these missions. Rumors are that there are a few P-39's down in Australia now. What we are looking for is P-38's, but so far there are no fighters at all in New Guinea. I have seen P-38's in the States. They are probably the most advanced fighter in the world. It would really be great if we had some of those with us tomorrow. They would be a match for the Jap Zero. But this night, this is only a dream. General Kenney said we would have to go it alone and take our losses until we can get more planes from Stateside.

At 0530 hours the Grim Reaper Squadron is ready to go. Captain Connley leads the thundering herd to the end of the strip for take off. Until we get a control tower it is follow the leader. The steel matting sings under our tires as "The Widowmaker" accelerates to fantastic speed. We zoom over the trees and climb out of the vermin infested jungle in seconds.

We circle 7 Mile one time watching the rest of the squadron take off, then point toward the lofty mountains slowly, while the others come up from behind and make formation.

"Gunners and bombardiers, check your guns."

We all fire into the jungle which is just a few feet down as we climb the steep wooded foothills of the mountains. Like arcing cobwebs the jungle is alive with white tracers. The upper turret guns fired o.k. this time, and Nelson poked me to let me know, as if I didn't. When his turret fires it shakes the whole airplane, and his empty casings rain down in the fuselage.

We clear the mountains with a thousand or more feet to

spare, and it feels good to have so much power. Our course this time is north and a little east to avoid Buna and their radar there. We are interested in nothing but that convoy. By this time it should be way south of the Vidiaz Straits and within our range. If we have extra bombs after attacking the ships we will strike Lae and Salamaua on the way back.

All eyes are on the sea ahead. We are also looking for other ships that our reconnaissance, in their flights, might have missed, but all we see is the coast of New Guinea and the open sea. Our pilots are watching the fuel guages. To be safe we will have to turn back before they are half empty. Our bombardier has field glasses and the gunners are using their telescopic sights in a search of the horizon for the ships.

"Bombardier to crew, I think I see them. I see smoke on the horizon at 1 o'clock."

The gunners point their turrets forward and sure enough, there is smoke on the horizon.

"Pilot to crew, it appears the convoy is in sight. Everybody get ready. We expect flak and a Zero escort."

The Grim Reaper Squadron with twelve beautiful airplanes holding their "V" formation in the sky like a proud clutch of wild geese, wing tip to wing tip, on their first encounter in WW II with enemy shipping. Our flight represents a lot of years of mechanical evolution that made it possible to put American fighting men up in the firmament of the heavens. From the days of hand to hand combat with clubs and cutlasses, we now can rain death from the skies and let mechanical power and explosives do the majority of the work. There is only one problem. We are confronting an enemy who has the same power.

"Connley to flight, break formation for the bomb run and

regroup after the run."

The "Widowmaker" continues straight on her course. The Jap ships are getting closer, but I still can't make out what type ships they are. If they are transports or freighters we do not have much to worry about. Then it is clear one is a warship—a destroyer.

"Bombardier to crew, fighters at 1 o'clock."

"Pilot to bombardier, take the airplane."

"Radio to Nelson, do you see them?"

"Roger, they're above us."

I can't see them so I watch out both windows and listen over the interphone.

"Pilot to upper gunner, they are diving on us. Fire at them."

Nelson finally fires on them, a short and long burst, and then another. I think he was a scared kid, and maybe too scared to fire. Then I spin my turret in hopes that I could catch a glimpse of them as they dive by. I looked out the window again and could see them climbing a vertical for altitude. There were four of them glittering in the sun.

"Pilot to crew, four more Zekes are diving at us at 12 o'clock high."

"Bombardier to pilot, bombs away, take the airplane."

We bank to port and I can see the Zekes out my right window. The bombardier and upper gunner are both firing as I jump for my turret to try to get them in my sight. Finally they are in my sight and I hold down my gun button for a long burst. My tracers smash into two of the leaders and it's like spraying them with a big fire hose.

"Pilot to crew, the first four are at 12 o'clock again."

I see the others again but a B-25 is in the way. Then I try to catch them as they pass and swing to 9 o'clock. I see a smoking Zero spinning toward the water. The sky now is full of tracers and ack-ack puffs. The ships are firing at us, but the flak is not as thick as at Buna. Down below we can see our bombs exploding around the ships and all are hits or near misses. Those 500 pounders carry an awful wallop. Smoke is billowing from one ship, then I see another ship begin to smoke.

"Connley to flight, make formation."

Now three more Zeros are coming from below. When they are about 1,000 yards I fire one, two, three bursts, and the air is filled with tracers again and one of the Zekes is smoking. This is just like shooting ducks. Who got it? Who knows who got it?

We are on our way to Lae in formation. All airplanes are still flying. The little monkeys have been hurt but they are tough. They go all out and regard life as something to give. A lone Zero is still chasing us. He comes at us in a reckless way that shows he intends to sell his life. He fantails his airplane to try a flock shot at us, and our gunners annihilate him. He explodes to small pieces of junk.

"Connley to everybody. Stay in formation. We will bomb Lae and Salamaua, but now they know we are coming. Good luck."

Lae appears at the waters edge at the same time as does five Zeros above us and that's the worst place they can be. Now they can dive on us which they immediately do as all our upper gunners blast them. One Zero smokes and spins toward the water. They zip past us and the lower gunners try to follow them in their sights. Some tracers follow them as they go out of range.

We are now over the target and bombs away. We bank to port and here come the Zekes again. Ten dive on us in formation in what looks like it's a suicidal attack and they spray us with their guns. Our upper gunners retaliate and one more Zero begins to smoke.

Our remaining bombs are dropped on the Salamaua runway and our nose is now pointed toward the mountains. But we are not yet free of Zeros. They come at us from behind again and one is my target. I hit my gun button for so long my gun barrels get hot and the Zeke begins to smoke. But there are hundreds of other tracers zipping in the same direction. At the same time a ripping sound shakes our airplane. The Zeke hit the tail of our airplane and my armor plate. We are now half way to the peaks and the enemy fades out of sight. We all made it back to our base to lick our wounds.

After landing, parking, and tie down, the Captain called a briefing under the wing of an airplane. It seemed miraculous that we all got back. There was only one casualty—one gunner had been killed. He was shot through the head by a Jap machine gun bullet. Our planes again, had taken a beating but the Captain told us we had done "one helluva job". He said it was 100% effective except for the loss of one man. We did much damage to those ships and they are now going to be finished off by the 89th Squadron with their A-20's and the 90th with their B-25's. But the 13th did the initial damage, also the most hazardous. We shot down four Zeros, three probables, and damaged many others. But no gunner will get credit for the kills, as it is impossible to prove who did it when everybody is shooting.

"The Widowmaker" was perforated with small and large holes. The big ones prove the Zeros really do have cannons. My armor plate had indentations on the aft side made by Jap bullets and shrapnel. Our photos showed that all our bombs fell in the area of the targets. Many of them were direct hits on the ships and runways.

Our Aussie friends, Kilroy and his helpers, came and patched up the worst of the holes so we could fly back to Charters Towers. Most of us pitched in to help repair what damage that could be repaired with what we had to do with.

The second day after our second mission we all took off for our base back in Australia. When we got airborne and in formation I tapped out this message:

"Grim Reaper to Charters Towers. Mission accomplished. One gunner killed. Several aircraft damaged. Coming home.
Call sign/time-date

"Radio to crew. Enjoy some good music now on liaison."
We rode the skies back to our base on a dream, thinking of times past and times ahead. Time proved that for most of us our dreaming of home was nothing more than a dream. Most of us would never get home. But for now we could rest and relax.

The combat flyer of the 13th Attack Squadron was like a modern day Roman Gladiator. We were given the best that was available. Outside of a combat mission to fly we had few duties. When we had flown about one fourth of our 50 missions I was told we would get leave in Australia. Also, we were the only personnel in the Pacific that could look forward to going home before the war was over, if we could survive 50 missions. Those who did not fly combat, and about 90% did not, would not get home for six months after the war because there were so many men overseas it was slow to get them all home. We were kept fat for the slaughter. It was all voluntary and it took the young, naive, foolish and stupid to do it.

Needless to say, we are not very popular in ground crew

circles. They resent the deference given to us. They are envious and some of them hate our guts, but it is those guys who do not have the guts to fly combat. When we fly on a mission and stick our necks out, they are safe on the ground. Few of them mourn our losses in combat, but they turn green with envy when we are given leave to go to Australia. Most of us think it is worth it, but then, we are very green behind the ears. I overheard my crew chief say one time that he didn't care what happened to the airplane after it took off. That is bad.

# CHAPTER 9

## TENS OF THOUSANDS OF DEATHS

After our second B-25 raid on Lae and Salamaua, Captain Connley called me into his tent for a special briefing. And it turned out real special. Without hedging he came to the point: "Would you help test the new B-25?"

"The new B-25?" I asked. "Aren't we flying and testing the new B-25?"

"Yes, but this is different," the Captain said. He told me that, "the B-25 is a good ship but it is just another medium altitude bomber. We all know your lower turret is no good, also we have found out what the Zeros can do to us. So we are going to modify them to an airplane not dreamed possible before this time. We are going to remove the lower turret and install a huge gas tank in its place. Then we are going to remove all the navigators and bombardiers equipment and do away with them. Then we are going to install guns, guns, guns. We are going to install so many guns you will think it is a battleship. And then we are going to change our whole format of attack. We are changing it from a high altitude bomber to a treetop altitude bomber or mast height bomber. We will fly so low the enemy can't pick us up on their radar, and we'll be so near the water or trees that the Jap Zeros can't dive on us or maneuver around us. With all these guns we are going to strafe them, and with parachute frag bombs we will saturate their bases, and with larger bombs we will learn to skip them on the water into the hulls of their ships."

"You've got to be kidding Captain, is it not dangerous enough as it is?"

"We are going to learn to skip those bombs on top of the water just like we used to skip rocks on the water when we were kids," said the Captain. "We are going to drop the bombs at 50 feet altitude as we fly straight into the big ships. We will be going so fast our bombs are not going to sink, but will skip on the water into the hull, then sink below the water line before they explode to cause the most damage. And we've got to learn to avoid hitting their ships with our airplanes as we do it," the Captain said.

"Sounds like we are going to commit a sure suicide," I said.

"We are going to transform the B-25 to the most destructive air weapon the world has yet to see," the Captain countered.

The Captain went on to say that there was a Major Paul Gunn who had conceived the idea of converting the B-25. This Major Gunn was a civilian pilot in the Philippines and was a friend of MacArthur. He had been experimenting with armor on airplanes to try to improve them to meet the formidable types of planes the Japs had developed. He had to leave his family in the Philippines and was anxious to do anything he could to defeat the Nips. It's because of his aircraft experience and his ingenuity, that MacArthur made him a major in the field. He believed the Japs had confiscated his wife and he was hell bent to destroy them.

The Captain told me that Major Gunn was the test pilot I would be flying with. "Will you do it?" the Captain asked.

I asked the Captain why I should risk my neck testing the B-25 when I could be flying missions and getting closer to going home. He told me that if I would do it he would give me priority in flying missions and therefore I would be able to stack up missions faster and go home sooner. Then I told him I would do it.

Connley tells me we are moving to a new base in New Guinea called 14 Mile Field which is 14 miles from Port Moresby. This new field is now being dug out of the jungle and we are going to move there immediately. We are through with flying back and forth to Charters Towers. 14 Mile Field will be our new base and we'll be vulnerable to Jap air attacks. This looks risky to me.

Our planes were repaired and ready for combat again and we were taking all our equipment from Charters Towers. We built a wooden rack in all the bomb bays of all the airplanes and filled the bomb bays with equipment. We also loaded supplies in all other available space. Our planes looked more like freighters than bombers. But we could not take it all and the C-47's hauled the rest of our heavy equipment.

Our flight to our new base was routine and we had no trouble finding the strip. The slash in the green jungle was easily discernable. The new steel mat reverberated through the jungle when our tires touched it. Revetments had been cut out of the jungle for parking for each airplane and they were all dispersed. The initial job was to build a fox hole near each airplane. Then we dug another fox hole near where our new tent location would be. After that we covered our airplanes with green foliage cut from near each airplane. Later we had camouflage nets for covers but they proved to be useless. The Nips always seemed to know where they were. How they found out was always a mystery to us especially because they always bombed at night.

Our next mission is to bomb Lae and on the way back

home, to dump the remaining bombs on Salamaua. This is to be a conventional mission at 8,000 feet and without escort as usual. The Japs will be waiting for us because their radar will tell them we are coming. This means we can plan on a hot time.

This will be my last high altitude mission. My future bombing and strafing missions will be so close to the enemy that I can see the blacks of their eyes.

The Grim Reaper Squadron is ready to go. My position will be with Captain Connley again. Our racks are filled with 500 pounders again and we will do our best to drop them where they do the most damage. Those little yellow monkeys are to know we have been there. At first light we take off and the air of the jungle is choking with the dust of our new runway, and the roar of our thundering engines reverberates through the mat of foliage. It is always a challenge to clear the trees at the end of the runway. Everything has to be just right to make it. With the heavy bomb, fuel, and ammo loads, most of the time it is a sweat, but only once in a while will we hit the top of a tree.

This time our course will be around Buna. We veer to the left after making formation to stay our of Buna's radar zone, and steadily gain altitude to be high enough over the target. They come to meet us however, before we get there. I believe they have spotters in the hills. There is no other way they could know we are coming.

The Zekes are above us again which puts us at a disadvantage. They dive on us from straight above as if they know we can't fire straight up. They must be the same pilots who attacked us on our last mission. They seem to know where and when to attack. They can come at us in ways to make it extremely difficult to line them up in our sights.

Down they come like greased lightning. It is impossible for our upper gunners to fire on any of them until after they fire on us. Their bullets rip through our wings and fuselages. I am watching out the windows and see the tracers falling like hailstones. Our upper gunners finally start shooting after they are down below the horizon. Almost all the action comes from above. I finally get one in my line of vision but when I am ready to fire it is out of range.

They bank off and come at us from starboard. This time the upper gunners have a second to train their guns on them. As they come in our tracers converge on them like a huge funnel. Two Zekes explode while another one begins to smoke. They are below the horizon now but I can not find them at all. It is good for us they don't know how weak we are from below. Tracers are rocketing now in all directions and I see a B-25 smoking.

"Bombardier to pilot, bombs away, take the airplane."

"Co-pilot to flight, more Zekes above us."

"Fire on them, fire, fire."

I can not see what is going on. Lae is behind us now and Salamaua is ahead.

"Pilot to bombardier, take the airplane."

We drop the rest of our bombs on Salamaua, bank to starboard, and head for the mountains.

"Connley to flight, stay together, close up formation. Gunners help each other."

The ack-ack lessens as we move away from Salamaua. Five Zeros make more passes at us but this time they brake their dives quicker and do not come in so close.

"Norton to Connley, we can't make it, we are bailing out."

I look out the window and see a smoking B-25 far below.

One parachute appears, then another, then two more. In about 15 seconds I see one more parachute, but there are no more. This means that one man did not get out. The doomed plane crashes into the jungle in a ball of fire. We never saw any of the crew again.

We had taken a mauling from the Japs, and our planes had been badly shot up again. However the rest of us made it back to our base. I saw gasoline streaming from the plane next to us as we flew back over the mountains. Also, one more plane was losing gas. Their tanks had been punctured by Zero bullets. But now we were at the summit of the Owen Stanleys and could almost coast in to 14 Mile. The two leaking airplanes landed first and the people on the runway did not know of our plight because as yet we did not have a radio shack at 14 Mile.

Luck and skillful handling of the shot up airplanes was with us. They made their landing safely while we circled the field slowly. Then we came in nose to tail. We all taxied to our revetments and then gathered under "Widowmaker" for our report and briefing.

Captain Connley told us we had done a good job. We dropped all our bombs in the target area. It was too bad about Norton and his crew, Connley told us, but we would just have to take losses like this until we could get fighter escort. The Captain questioned all of us about how many Zeros we saw go down. He decided we would get an official credit for five shot down and six probables. The photos showed the extent of the damage our bombs did.

We thought we were through for a while so could take a well earned rest, but the little yellow men had another thought. They were out for revenge. That night as most of us were in our sacks and the ground crews were busy repairing our airplanes, the air raid siren went on and startled us into action. Our spotlights cut through the black night and spotted 24 Jap bombers approaching. They were coming directly over us. Our anti-aircraft guns opened up on them from every direction. Our ack-ack filled the sky around the approaching bombers and the air was full of smoke. Then one of the bombers began to smoke and it turned tail and ran for Rabaul. The others kept coming. It was a breathtaking and fascinating sight. The sky was full of search light beams, ack-ack explosions, and enemy bombers. They dropped their bombs above us, and when the bombs got closer we could see them in the light beams coming straight toward us. We were all in fox holes—three deep in some. When the bombs exploded the earth heaved with concussion. They all exploded in the dispersal area where our airplanes were. In a few seconds it was all over. The Japs had let most of us live. Three men were killed. We all jumped in jeeps and tore down the dusty, bumpy road to see what had happened to our airplanes. Our beautiful planes had been hit and were all burning. They were all damaged beyond repair. When the fires burned out there was nothing in the dispersal area but junk. We loaded all the wounded into trucks and drove them all to a hospital in Moresby.

We had waited almost a year for those airplanes, and now we would have to start waiting all over again.

Some of us stayed in Moresby that night to help the guys who had been wounded. The facilities were short, but the Aussies did all they could. Arrangements were made to fly some of the worst cases to Australia.

This was the biggest bomb raid we had had in New Guinea. In one night the little yellow monkeys had com-

117

pletely wiped us out. But this was not the end. This was only temporary. We'll come back and with something so destructive the little monkeys won't have a chance.

I went to see my friend Kilroy while in Moresby. He was not surprised at our bad luck. We were wide open for such an attack at 14 Mile. It was inevitable, he said.

Moresby now is the dirtiest mess I have, in all my life, ever seen. There must be 10,000 vehicles in the area—all military. There is so much dust it's next to impossible to breathe. And the bomb craters are everywhere. The buildings are the same color as the dust. The heat, humidity, mosquitos, and flies have taken over completely. It is a stinking mess so I high tail it back to 14 Mile to brood over the loss of our planes. How long will it take now to fly my 50 missions and get out of this stinking jungle?

The next night the Jap bombers came again. Because they had wiped us out at night they did not know what they had done. This night was the same as before. They dropped their bombs in the exact same places. But of course, they did not destroy anything because it had previously been destroyed.

Some of the bombs did not explode and they had to be removed by Army bomb specialists. All the next day we had to stay out of the area. And the specialists learned that some of the bombs were duds. The little monkeys were playing some dirty tricks. They shoot us in the water and in parachutes, and now they are dropping dud bombs on us to cause confusion and waste our time.

When the duds were removed we went to check the burned out junk. I found my carbine and it was just a charred barrel. All my 50 caliber ammo had exploded leaving the empty links scattered about. The aluminum skins of the planes had been burned leaving just the skeletons. All my gear had disappeared. The gas tanks in all the wings and the oil tanks had exploded. The tires and insulation had burned. Everything that was not solid metal had burned. There was nothing salvageable.

How do they do it? How can they bomb so accurately in the dark? It is unbelievable. We can not do it. There is something about it that is uncanny. As soon as we hear them, on go our searchlights. Do they use these for a bearing? If they do they must use some kind of a filter to kill the glare. Or perhaps they have spotters in the jungle with lights for guiding their pilots.

We all went to work clearing our dispersal area. The engineers dug a big trench with bulldozers. They crushed the airframes and pushed all the junk into the trench and buried it. Our long months of waiting for airplanes was now under the ground. The little yellow monkeys had us where they wanted us. They would really have gloated had they seen that.

Now that it is over I am the only one in the Grim Reaper Squadron with a project. Major Gunn has been working on the modification part of the B-25 for some time, and he is about to start testing them. My orders are to catch one of the C-47's at 7 Mile for the flight across the Coral Sea again to Charters Towers. This is my first flight in a C-47. They are called the workhorse of the Pacific. Just about all equipment and supplies is moved with them. They are probably the most indespensible airplane west of the States. In November of 1942 alone they moved 15,000 troops to the Buna area. When the Pacific island hopping started, they moved just about everything the military used.

We are ready for take off and the rain is coming down in

torrents, but that does not stop this bird. The plane is almost empty because very little freight is going south and just about everything is going north. The C-47 features a wide open cargo compartment with a row of metal bucket seats on either side. Cargo tie down fasteners are all over the floor and are built flush with the floor so crates and boxes will slide. These planes seem slow compared to other aircraft I'm used to. But they are built to carry troops and cargo. To have to sit in those backless metal seats is about as tiresome as any experience I've had in this man's war. I thought we would never get there. But Townsville finally appears and I am looking forward to a fine steak dinner.

Townsville has certainly taken on a different look since I was here. There are thousands of Yanks. So many it looks like an Army base. I'm sure they have taken over the town including the girls. I've learned one thing about women so far. If they can't get what they want, they will take what they can get.

The steak is good for a change, however the price now is out of sight. The Aussie merchants are getting rich while they can.

We finally get back to Charters Towers. It is here that I will meet the famous Paul Gunn, the genius who is transforming the B-25 to be the most destructive air weapon in history. The Major is tall, slender, and his tales match his appearance. He is known as "Pappy Gunn" to the troops because he is about forty and not as young as the combat troops. But he is not too old to be the most exciting and daring flyer in the Southwest Pacific.

Pappy was really involved in the modification of the B-25. This was his life, and it took just such a character to do the job that must be done. His idea was to make the B-25 bristle with 50 caliber machine guns and to make it a skip bomber, that had never been done before. At first he put too many guns in the nose of the plane which made her nose heavy and almost ended the project because it was so hard to pull her out of a dive. So he took some of them out and shifted some farther aft. Then we had problems with the skin plates next to the muzzles. The concussion would crack them, so we installed felt pads to take the shock. But when the felt got wet and dried, it turned hard. So that problem was solved by using rubber instead of the felt. Materials were hard to get in Australia at that time, but Pappy was a scrounger as well as a "gadgeteer". We had a problem of engineering the locations of all the ammo containers, racks, and chutes. There isn't a lot of space in the nose and aft of the nose in a B-25, and when you attempt to install ten big 50 caliber machine guns with all their chutes, racks, and ammo cans, you have an engineering problem.

The first big job was to remove all plexiglass that was originally built into the nose. Then all the bombardiers equipment was removed, and all the navigators equipment had to go. The next big job was to junk that worthless lower turret, which left a gaping hole in the bottom of the fuselage.

A huge gasoline tank was installed aft of the bomb bay to give us a very long range. This tank filled the whole fuselage from where the lower turret used to be to the bomb bay. Shackles were installed for the tank so we could drop it before going into combat. It was too dangerous to fly over the target with one of our gas tanks empty. Four rails were laid to guide the tank out of the plane. It was the radio operator's responsibility to get rid of that tank when it was empty. An empty fuel tank in combat is a menace. If an enemy bullet should hit it, it would explode like a bomb. The full tank gave us much more range and too, it helped to balance the airplane because of all the weight in the nose. This tank gave us the range to fly to the northernmost enemy bases in New Guinea. It also gave us much trouble. Because of the suction at high speed, it did not release every time. The radio operator had to pry it loose when it did not drop. This was very dangerous because when it went there was so much suction it pulled the man prying it out the hole with it. One had to be tied inside the airplane to stay there. The tank always dropped when on the ground, but when flying it was another story.

Also there was the problem of the installation of the 40 millimeter cannon. It was positioned in the bottom and center of the nose, and it had four 50 caliber machine guns around it. Later we replaced it with a 75 mm cannon. Shock mounts had to be installed to take part of the stress off the airframe. In the beginning each B-25 was equipped with 15 machine guns and the 20 millimeter cannon. Ten of these were fixed and pointed forward. The top turret had two, there were two in the waist, and one in the tail. Also the bomb bay carried a full load of bombs. This gave the B-25 about twice the guns as the heavy B-17 or B-24, and it was only half the size.

Our first strike was with eight forward firing 50's and the cannon, the upper had two, and there was one in the tail. All these guns plus a bomb bay full of 500 pounders made it the most formidable air weapon in history against ships, because we could and did put the bombs under the water line next to the hull, and the explosive power there was enough to sink any ship afloat.

# CHAPTER 10

## MOST DESTRUCTIVE AIRPLANE IN HISTORY

All the fixed forward firing 50's and the 40 mm cannon had been zeroed in on the ground to be certain they would spread their deadly rounds along a straight line at 500 yards. Each gun was adjusted so the total spread was equal to the span of the average enemy airplanes wings.

It wasn't long after I arrived until Major Gunn told me that he was ready to start actual testing in flight. Our targets were to be the protruding reefs along the Great Barrier Reef about ten miles off the coast. There, early in the morning, when the water was flat, we could see exactly where each round hit the water. It was my job to man the upper turret and operate the radio equipment if necessary. I was to operate the tail stinger and tail camera also.

The Major gunned this overloaded B-25 over the tree tops at first light. If the people in town did not guess that something big was soon to happen they must have been indifferent. The thunder of our powerful engines was enough to wake the dead.

As soon as we were airborne I knew we had had it. It would be the roughest flight of my life. This Major Gunn was the roughest, wildest, toughest airplane driver in the Pacific. It was clear he had never learned to fly in any U.S. Army Air Corps cadet school. He played and toyed with death like a friend, and I swore we'd never get back alive. He made that B-25 fly as a pursuit plane in an acrobatic show. We were upside down half the time. We did vertical and horizontal loops, spins, dives, and many near stalls. I couldn't believe what he was doing with that airplane. My thoughts were on a big number of things, but mostly the carburetors. I knew that this type of Holley carburetor wasn't designed for upside down flying, and I would have bet my shirt the Major did not know this. So while sick to my stomach, I called him on interphone to tell him those carburetors would not function in an upside down position. He told me they would be o.k. But, for some magic that seemed to ride with us, they continued to function.

For the first time in my life I got airsick. I had prided myself in my ability to take it in the air or on the sea. On that long sea voyage to the land down under, in the hot and crowded ship "Republic", when everyone was retching and vomiting, I did not get sick. This guy Gunn was giving both of us sensations I had never felt before. He must be some kind of a nut.

"Radio to pilot, are you trying to kill us?"

"Don't worry, we'll be o.k."

You are some kind of a nut, I thought again to myself. You would get washed out of cadet school the first day, and here you are a Major in the Air Corps thanks to your friend General MacArthur. My only consolation was that General Kenney had more know how as to what this guy could do than I do.

We skimmed the trees all the way to the ocean, except when we were doing acrobatics. Among other things, I worried about all that weight up there in the nose. This guy will probably dive on the target and not be able to pull out.

The Major pulled the plane up to about 1,000 feet then pointed the nose at the reef. He slammed the throttles forward to the stops. In six seconds we were doing 330 miles an hour. Our sturdy plane quivered with the strain. Four thousand horses in our two engines plus gravity were pulling us down like a rocket. The reef zoomed to meet us as the Major hit the gun button on the wheel and pandemonium let loose. The recoil of our awesome firepower braked the airplane as if full flaps had just been applied. Water engulfed the reef and it disappeared. When the water subsided there was nothing left of the work of millions of little creatures who had worked so many centuries to build it. The boom, boom, boom of the cannon plus all the machine guns vibrated the airplane to the point of falling apart. But the steady hand of this flying fool saved us. He hauled back on the stick one second soon enough and we skimmed the water by inches. I had been firing at the reefs broad side with my turret guns. My tracers arced a huge "C" out over the placid water.

We pulled up to a near stall and dove on another reef wide open. This time I swung my turret forward and attempted to aim my firepower to the same area as the fixed guns. In advance I fired a burst over the cockpit plexiglass to let the Major know what I intended. At maximum gravity speed he let go the fixed guns and the cannon, and I cut loose with the turret guns at the same reef. Now we had ten forward firing 50's plus the cannon all concentrated on the same spot.

"Pilot to radio, that's great. We'll try it again."

We banked off to a vertical position and immediately we were zooming at full throttle. We pulled out of the roll and the reef rushed to meet us as we both opened up with an extra long burst that ripped the reef right out of the water. As we skimmed the water some water and debris splattered on the nose and leading edges of the wings.

We leveled off over the aqua water, then banked to port and pointed toward the Australian coast. On the way, in level flight, while hugging the water, we polished off one or two more reefs then watched the dark line of the coast enlarge into trees and rocks. We stuck to the tree tops until we got about a mile from Townsville then lifted to 1,000 feet to get gravity speed. At full throttle our nose pointed to the airstrip. At 330 mph we buzzed the air field then pulled up, up, up until it seemed like we were just hanging in the blue. Then we did a slow roll all the way to mother earth before pulling out and lining up to the strip for a perfect nose heavy touch down.

I sat in the airplane too dazed to get out. Why did I ever join the Air Corps? The solid immoveable terra firma never felt so good. It took me a few minutes to learn to walk again. What I had come through was just too much. If this is what it takes to combat the Japanese in the air, fate would have to be kind to us.

I did not know it then, but I soon became aware of the fact that this job had to be performed by someone. To beat the Japs down here we've got to have a superior weapon. And, I guess it took just such a daring man behind the controls to do it.

When I got to know the Major better, then I could understand why he was like that. He hated Japs with all his might and could imagine only the worst as to what happened to his family. Perhaps that was why he drives an airplane like a mad man. He evidently did not value his life much, but maybe he should have thought about the people flying with him and their lives. He was totally dedicated to killing Japs.

126

After our first test I could have refused to fly with him again, but I didn't. I guess I believed in what we were doing. I caught on to his spirit and wanted, more than anything else, to get this grim business over with and get back home. There was no other route.

I took a cool shower and jumped on a bus for Townsville. That the Americans were in the land down under and meant business was evident. The town was jammed with GI's, and it did not take long to see that they had taken over all the girls. I had to wait two hours to get into my favorite restaurant. And, thanks to the big spending Yanks, the prices had gone sky high.

The next morning I was anxious to give our airplane a good inspection. While the armament department was cleaning the guns, I took a magnifying glass and flashlight and checked the airplane for cracks around the gun mounts, the airframe, and exterior plates near the guns to satisfy myself that we were not falling apart. I was sure that after all the stress and vibration there would be cracks. But, to my amazement, there were none. This was good news. Maybe the B-25 could take all that punishment.

After the guns were cleaned and ready, again we fired them on the ground at a fixed target at the end of the runway. They were in good shape. We loaded up our ammo containers, 500 rounds in each can, and took off again for another go at the reefs.

This time we had another man with us. He was an upper gunner and his name was Dickerson. Within two minutes after take off he was sick. As he scrambled out of the turret I threw him a bucket. I told him it would help if he got back in the turret so he could see the horizon. However, when the airplane was upside down mostly it was a problem to tell where the horizon was. He asked a lot of questions including: "Does the Major fly like this always?" I told him this was only my second trip with him and it may be my last. "Why don't you switch to liaison for some music, that may help?"

We are going to try to drop our tank today. When, and if it drops it will leave a huge hole in the bottom of the fuselage. This is a trick that has never been done before and we do not know what will happen.

"Pilot to radio, drop the tank."

"Just as soon as I get myself tied in."

I had brought along a rope because we didn't have anything else. I tied one end around my waist. Then I poked Dickerson so he could watch. I pulled the drop lever and down went the tank, but the suction was terrific. We watched the tank spin to the water through the gaping hole. We had trouble at least half of the time with that tank.

"Radio to pilot, the tank dropped o.k."

"Yes, I felt it."

The Major swung our ship around to gain a little altitude for our full power glide. Then he slammed the throttles forward and we gained speed to 330 mph when the ship shook violently. I was firing at protruding coral when all fixed forward guns exploded into action and the brake action felt like we had flown into a net.

"Wow", came over the interphone.

The coral reef the Major had in his sights disappeared into a wall of white foam. Then all at once my body seemed to weigh a ton. Then I turned on the tail stinger as we pulled up and away from the target.

"Radio to upper gunner, how do you like it?"

"Wow."

"Pilot to upper gunner, on our next pass I want you to fire exactly where I fire."

"Roger."

We zoom for altitude, do a half roll, then dive again at the reef. Dickerson fires a very short burst and the empty casings rain down in the fuselage next to me. Our ship is groaning and rattling under the stress and strain. The fixed guns simultanously explode as Dickerson fires, and more lead and steel is concentrated in one spot than ever before in past history. I really expect our airplane to fall to the water, but we are still flying. We skim the water and climb away from the target that had been disintegrated.

It is enough of this and we point again to the shoreline, firing at protruding reefs until there are no more targets. The trees in the distance grow in size until we have to rise to miss them. We bank to port and head for a looked-forward-to touch down. Our airplane, and two shaking gunners, clear the buildings by inches, buzz the field, bank off, line up with the runway, and touch down nose-heavy.

This was our last strafing practice at the Great Reef site. There were many modifications to improve our model B-25 to make it a deadly strafer, but they could be made in New Guinea. Some had to do with weight and balance.

Dickerson and I went to town to celebrate our survival and see the girls again for the last time before flying back to New Guinea. We would have to survive at least 12 strafing and skip bombing missions before we could come to Australia again.

I called a girl I knew and she said please come pick us up. She had a friend for Dick. He fell for her and there was nothing I could say that would change his mind. I told him that it would cost him all the money he made in three years just to buy tickets for her back to the States, then back to Australia, then back again. And it would never end. But he was in love and would not listen. The next morning we took off for Moresby and that was the end of the love affair.

Our B-25 was loaded with troops. There was no place for them to sit so they were all over the floor. I tuned to our Townsville music and we passed our headsets around to help kill the monotony. It was a long ride, but Dick enjoyed it. ·He was saturated in music and in love.

As we descended to 14 Mile I could see the hulk of the old ship lying near the shore. This old ship would be our target for our skip bombing practice.

The runway was deserted as we buzzed it at full throttle and gravity speed. The Major had to show off a little, so he pulled us up, up, up, then fell off the wing to near the dirt before pulling out. Our hitchhikers couldn't believe it. We banked off, just like a pursuit plane, and came in for a perfect landing.

Major Gunn was here with the airplane and the armament that would blast the Japs out of the Southwest Pacific, and he wanted everybody to know it. Captain Connley and most everyone came to see the renovated B-25. The combat men were expecially interested in all the guns, the cannon, and the drop tank that would give all our airplanes a range that was unheard of. The word spread and the troops from other organizations came also. Pappy was vociferous. He told them that this was their future airplane, and we were going to have a whole new mode of attacking the Japs. No more high altitude bombing. "We are going to hit them from so close we will see the black of their eyes. We are going to fly right down the barrels of their big guns while skip bombing. The 500 pounders will skip into the hulls, sink below the water line, and blast a hole as big as a house. As the bombs skip we will saturate them with all these guns. We already know what these guns will do. They will obliterate anything. We know this because we have tested them." The Major told them that he was already working on a bigger cannon. And with this gas tank we could fly to their northernmost bases in New Guinea and New Britain.

Flying at tree top and mast height altitude we can surprise them. They won't be able to see us on their radar. We will strafe and drop parachute fragmentation bombs on their ground installations from tree top altitude. These para frag bombs will have delayed action fuses to give us time to get away before they explode.

With 500 pounders we will fly broadside into the sides of their ships while strafing them and plant our bombs under the water line next to their hulls. They will sink any ship afloat. You are looking at the weapon that will drive those little monkeys back to Japan.

The Major made a big impression on the Grim Reaper Squadron, but as for me, I'm going to get away from him as soon as possible. He is slated to kill himself and everyone with him. After a few days of skip bombing practice I am going to refuse to fly with him. He has had no formal Air Corps training and has no regard for regulations. He smokes his stinking cigars around the ship as if it means nothing, which is against all safety rules. He gets away with it because there are no officers around with more rank than he has.

Now that we have this new remodeled B-25, we don't want to be designated a bombardment squadron anymore. The 13th Squadron has always been a proud organization as a dive bomber squadron. Now we are going to be called an Attack Squadron, not a Bomb Squadron. Word comes from Brisbane which makes it official.

√   The Nip bombers are still flying their usual nightly raids in the Moresby area. Now they have many targets because the Yanks have cut several more airstrips in the area. We learn that one more field has been cut at Lakoti, and P-38's or P-39's will be stationed there. We are hoping, at last we will have fighter escort. The P-38's are going to have wing tip drop tanks also. This will give them a very long range. The Aussies are now at work building the tanks.

We are about ready to try our first skip bombing practice mission. This has never been tried before and everybody is waiting for the trial. Our bombs will be duds and we'll make our first runs on the old shipwreck along the coast. My job, in addition to radio operator and waist gunner, will be to operate a camera. To learn faster we must have pictures. I am to lay on the fuselage floor over the opening for the gas tank and photograph the bomb. We know the bomb will skip. What we do not know is the speed it should be dropped and at what altitude. I dread this because the Major will fly the airplane upside down half the time. I will have a problem in keeping myself on the floor and to keep from falling out.

The bomb bay is loaded with 500 pounders. They are duds but for practice they are just as good as the real thing. In fact they will be better because we won't blow ourselves up. Our ammo cans are filled with 500 rounds for each gun, as we roll down the singing mesh runway vibrating the jungle. The major pulls it up over the treetops while I tie myself to a nearby bulkhead. Dickerson is with us and he will fire with the Major into the hulk. We'll make our first run on the ship at full speed in a dive at 100 feet altitude. We climb fast to 1000 feet and point the nose at the sunken ship accelerating rapidly. Our speed is well over 300 mph and the ship zooms to meet us. I position my camera as the bomb drops and all the fixed guns explode along with Dickerson's turret. The hulk momentarily explodes into a cloud of dust and smoke as the bomb in a spin bounces high off the water once, twice, three times, then completely over the target. We gain altitude to 800 feet, bank off, and come at the hulk again at full throttle and in a dive. This time the hulk disappears under a cloud of smoke when struck by the awesome fire power of all those guns and the explosive projectiles of the cannon. The bomb drops at a little less than 150 feet and bounces high in the air. It bounces twice more then smashes in the hulk. It seems we were too low the first time.

The Major hauled back on the stick again to pull the heavy nosed airplane up to an attack altitude and aimed it at the helpless old hulk. He slammed the throttles forward to give it all it had. The structure of the airplane began to groan in agony as he pumped the rudders and wheeled the ailerons for evasive attack. Then he walked the rudders while all guns were firing to hose down the full length. The boom, boom, boom of the cannon was drowning out the noise of all the other machine guns. Simultaneously the bomb left its rack to skip off the water three times, then smash into the mid section of the stricken old hulk. It seemed to be working at 150 feet in an accelerated dive.

"Pilot to crew, we'll make another attack."

I cinched up the rope holding me inside the airplane and made ready for this other run which I knew would be the big show. I did not want to tumble inside the plane while he was showing off to the crowd on the beach. On this run he came at the hulk at about 100 feet once more and dropped the bomb sooner, while fantailing the airplane to spray the full length once more, while Dickerson concentrated in the same area. The bomb bounced about five times before it smashed into the old ship. We are now free of a lot of weight and it is time for the good Major to top off his show to the audience gathered on the beach. We gain altitude just like a fighter, to about 1500 feet and dive straight down to the beach before pulling out. We must have been flying faster than any medium bomber ever flew before. We skimmed the water at only about one foot all the way to the trees before pulling up. Then he climbed vertically to the end of our prop bite before falling off a wing. We fell nearly to the water again before leveling off to gain altitude again for a swing out over the jungle and one turn to line up for a perfect landing.

Some of the troops were waiting for us at the operations tent to find out if it had worked. We told them we hit the target three times out of four and next time we could hit it four out of four. It's a lot more accurate than any other way of bombing, and a lot more destructive to explode the bomb under the water beside the hull. "Yeah," someone said, "and a helluva lot more dangerous too."

Through the grapevine we learn that our tests tomorrow will be watched by Generals Whitehead and Kenney. General Kenney has command of all the 5th Air Force and Whitehead has command in New Guinea. We are told that General MacArthur is in the area and he will probably watch too. This skip bombing is Kenney's baby, so the Major will really put on a show, you can depend on that.

It takes a lot of blood and guts to draw a moment of interest in this outfit. The ground troops are indifferent to just about anything that happens, including plane crashes. But this modified B-25 with all its armament has the attention of most everyone, even the guys who push pencils. This represents a great advancement in our chances to win the war, so when we are ready to go, there is a big crowd gathered on the beach and the flight line. This is the big day for the Major. This is the day he is going to prove himself. He will put on a good show because he is the show off type.

A photographer is going along on this one so I won't have much to do but fire the waist guns. But the way the Major drives I'll probably be on the ceiling most of the time. The upper turret is operated by Dickerson. He will not have to worry about tumbling around when we are doing our acrobatics because it is impossible to fall out of his turret.

At the end of the taxiway the Major swung the airplane around to align with the runway. As he hit the brakes the nose strut collapsed and bounced back as the engines snarled like two wildcats. With the brakes released, our flying battleship thundered down the singing mesh runway accelerating like a rocket. Before our wheels cleared the mat, the trees were on top of us.

"Pull it up." "Pull it up."

That crazy pilot is going to hit the tops of the trees, and he did. The right wing hit a tree and the Major didn't even notice.

We gained altitude to 1,000 feet, then it was straight at the people on the beach. From three feet above the water and ten feet from the crowd we pulled straight up again hanging in the sky.

"Pilot to gunners, fire with me."

Now I can't fire straight forward, but I will fire for the tracer effect because Major Gunn wants to impress the Generals. The nose of the airplane is pointing at the hulk while the throttles are wide open, and Dick is shaking with fear. He is not alone. The guy up in the cockpit is showing off and we are paying for it. We pass the 300 mark and the ship is dead ahead as the guns explode into a huge ball of fire. In evasive action the hulk is engulfed in white water and our bomb leaves its rack to ricochet off the water and come back to meet us. Our guns continue to saturate the ship. As usual, our bomb bounces and lags behind. The area is a huge ball of tracers and white water as we bank away and the bomb now smashes into the side. The ship is boiling in foam and smoke and we are in a vertical climb for altitude. At 1500 feet we fall on the right wing and dive again for water. We pull out at 100 feet and the airplane sounds like it's falling apart, when once again we are pointed at the target. Then the Major walks the rudders to fantail the plane as all guns again spray the ship and there goes another bomb. The bomb bounces one, two, five times and crashes in the hull of the ship. We bank away again and do not fly over because we'll have to do this to avoid crashing into a high superstructure. It is dangerous to do this because it exposes the bottom of the airplane to the ships gunners, but it is better than crashing into the ship.

On our last attack we are going to drop the bomb from a lower altitude so it will have to be dropped sooner or it will bounce over. With all possible speed and all guns blasting again, the bomb switch is initiated, but the bomb does not drop.

"Radio to pilot, the bomb didn't drop."

"Pilot to radio, I dropped it."

"The bomb did not fall, I'll take a look."

I look in the bomb bay and the bomb is in a vertical position hanging by only one end. I call the Major and tell him I will crawl in there and try to pry it loose. We have no tools so I find the landing gear downlock pin, inch my way to the bomb and manage to pry it loose. Then we come in for a beautiful landing.

## CHAPTER 11

## FIRST MAST HEIGHT ATTACKS

Mast height skip bombing is now a fact. It, strafing, and the use of para frag bombs will be our answer to the hellbent invasion of the Pacific by the Japs. We now knew we had a mode of attack and a superior weapon that, in time could beat them. Our impetus now is dependent on more planes.

Pappy Gunn scurried back to Australia to do the supervision of converting more B-25's.

"We will convert them as fast as possible," Pappy told us, "and you will be the first to get 'em." "The new airplanes will be equipped with a 75MM cannon instead of the 40MM. This cannon shell is about three inches in diameter, and with a steel point armor piercing explosive shell, you can bet your life we can penetrate the hull of a battleship," the Major told us.

I was happy to see the Major go. Now I am not obligated to fly with him anymore, and it gives me a new lease on life.

The model B-25 we have tested was now the training plane for the Grim Reaper Squadron. A different crew was assigned to fly it each day to give all the combat crews some experience. All the crews would go through the training I had gone through, but with more conservative pilots who had been trained in the Air Corps. They will all be checked out on the new techniques of skip bombing, strafing, and yet new parachute fragmentation bombing. I'd had my "go at it", as the Aussies say, so I spent a lot of my time observing. There's not a lot to do anyway as we are still waiting for airplanes. I have been waiting for airplanes for about 99% of the time since leaving Stateside.

Those "kids" as General Kenney called us, learned fast. They had a new hope now and the motivation was "kill Japs". Their job was to learn the mechanics of the operation. When to drop the bomb, how high they should be and a proper speed. All this had to be synchronized with the strafing. Some would never fail to smash the target, and others would be too low or too high and the bomb would either bounce over the target, or sink before it reached the target. But they would try again and most of them would come up with a pretty good score.

I was flying with Lieutenant Norwood some now, and what a relief it was. The crews in a lot of cases were all mixed up and without any organization. It wasn't like the movies would have it. The crews didn't stay together longer than a few days. You made friends in a hurry just to lose them. Most of us were destined to be killed or be missing in action, which was most of the time, the same thing. And there was a constant shifting of personnel, and new replacements coming in all the time when we got started in the business of killing Japs. There was not one crew that I know of in the 13th Attack Squadron who stayed together for their full 50 missions. At any rate, I flew most of the time with Major Connley who was the Commanding Officer of the Grim Reaper Squadron, a majority of the time.

Finally we received two more fully equipped B-25's. Now our training crews could train three times as fast as before. Our big worry again was losing them. The Jap bombers were up there every night, and we knew their uncanny accuracy in hitting their targets. We had one thing in our favor now, there were several runways in the Moresby area, so they had quite a few targets to choose from. To save our precious planes we camouflaged them well and put them in a different area nearly every night. One night the Japs turned all hell loose on us at 14 Mile. We huddled in our foxholes watching the bombs fall on us. We were sure they would wipe our planes out again. Our dispersal area and the runway were heaved into mountains of dirt and bomb craters. But our three precious planes took only a few shrapnel holes. Those Japs were too audacious. They needed a lesson, and we were just the guys to teach them.

All the crews are ready now to fly combat the new way. That old wreck off the beach has served a good purpose. We are now able to hit it with our bombs 95% of the time, and always 100% with our guns. We have been told that we will fly our first skip bombing or para frag mission when we receive two more airplanes. We will have only five planes, and it is not as many as we need, but it will let us know just what we can do with them.

Since we lost our other airplanes the two other squadrons of the 3rd Attack Group have been flying conventional missions on Buna, Lae, Dobadura, Salamaua, and other Jap bases across the Owen Stanley Mountains. There are also a few B-24's, and B-17's now that have been hitting Rabaul, Wewak, and Madang. These planes have been bombing Jap shipping also, but what can a high altitude bomber do to a ship? By the time the bomb has dropped all the way to the ship, it has zigged or zagged out of the way. There is only one effective way and that is to fly right down to the ship and drop the bomb from so close it's impossible to miss.

November 1942, and the Grim Reaper Squadron has five

new converted B-25's, and we are going back to war and revolutionize it. Our reconnaissance has informed us that there is a Jap convoy of five ships churning south of Finschaven and headed this way. The Yanks and Aussies are closing in on Buna and this convoy is loaded with little yellow men on their way to reinforce Buna. This is our opportunity to prove skip bombing. I am going to fly with Lt. Norwood at daybreak. We will fly over a little village called Kokoda, to the left of Buna to avoid any warning and hope to surprise them. We will fly at tree top level, even over the mountains, and then ten feet off the water way up to the convoy. This will be a long flight so we will use our drop tanks for the first time in combat. It has been calculated that we can pounce on them almost before they have time to jump into their gun seats. Their radar will be no good, and even if they happen to see us in the distance they will only have a few seconds before we will be on top of them. So, we feel we can hit them so quickly they won't know what hit them.

At 0330 hours the guards wake us up. We have some quick powdered eggs and head toward the flight line. The 500 pound bombs had been loaded the night before, the ammo cans filled, and all fuel and oil tanks topped off. In the half light we thunder down the mesh strip and rocket into the half lit sky. We nose north to climb fast over the high peaks. At 15,000 feet the peaks are far below us and we don our oxygen masks only to take them off again as we hang to the trees and come right down again. As we zip along the trees become a blur. I see a native village and am tempted to check my guns on it because this is enemy territory and we know the natives are helping the Japs. We fly over a huge coconut plantation with a mansion in the

141

center and we hope the Japs do not have spotters there to give us away. Suddenly we're out over the water and we quit bouncing. It is always smoother over the water. The water is as glass—completely flat in the early morning when there is no wind.

"Radio to pilot, what about checking guns?"

"Pilot to gunners, check your guns."

It's great to fire onto the water. You can see exactly where every round crashes into the water which makes for good practice. The cannon drowns out all the other guns.

I fire broadside into the water, which to my surprise, creates huge arcs that are formed by my tracers, and the rounds strike the water forward of where I aim. So, when firing broadside, to hit a target, I have to aim behind it.

Nelson is our upper gunner and his guns, to say the least, shake the whole ship and shower me with empty casings. The other four aircraft see us firing and they too open up to saturate the water with hot lead and steel.

"Pilot to crew, everything o.k.?"

"Roger."

We are way out over the Solomon Sea and I am worried about that tank. It is my responsibility to get rid of it, and if it won't slide out we can't attack. If the Nips hit that tank and it's empty, it will explode like a bomb.

"Radio to pilot, how much gas left in the tank?"

"About one fourth full."

We are working with the B-24's. They will bomb the convoy from high altitude a few seconds before we attack, to put the Japs in confusion while we are sneaking in. If we can put our bombs under the water next to the hulls we should be able to cut their ships in half. Any 500 pounder should do ten times the damage in that location than on top of the deck.

This is another first for the 13th Attack Squadron. None of us know what will happen to us when we attack those ships. As far as we know, it has never been done before. There is one thing we do know, if any of us go down it is certain death. Even if we survive the crash the Japs will shoot us in the water, or first they may haul us out of the water to torture us before they kill us. In a crash we cannot plan on using a parachute. We would hit with terrific impact and instantaneously. Our plane would shatter and break in two, and our odds in favor of surviving such a crash are about 40%. Our odds of surviving after such a crash would be about zero. I have thought about the chance of survival in the water and what I'd do. We know the little Asian monkeys will try to kill us in the water. I consider myself a strong swimmer, and I know I could swim many hours. Perhaps I could stay afloat a day or two if the sharks would leave me alone. We have no means of rescue yet, so I would try to swim to the shore of New Guinea. If the shore is not visible I have a small compass strapped to my wrist.

My plan, if we get shot down is to dive when they shoot at me. I can hold my breath well over a minute so I'd come up for air and dive again before they would have time to get a bead on me. Then I would make for the shore, even if it was 20 miles away. Once I get to the beach I can live off the land and start working my way back to our lines. I would not go ashore until dark and not be seen in the open in the daylight. It would probably take years or months to get back, because sometimes there were 600 miles of jungle between our base and our target. The Mae West I'm wearing would be in the way, because it is bright orange, which would make a good target, and I couldn't dive with it on anyway. I would take it off and get rid of it.

"Radio to Nelson, everything o.k.?"

"Roger."

"Pilot to radio, tank's empty, drop it."

"Soon as I get tied in."

I cinched a boline around my waist and tied to a bulkhead. I hope that damned tank will go. I pulled the tank lever with a prayer. It did not go, so I grabbed my pry bar and with some leverage it went and almost took me with it. Thank God for that rope. It spun all the way to the water and bounced back at us in the same way as the bombs. It bounced a few times and settled on the water like a box.

"Co-pilot to crew, I see smoke."

"Pilot to crew, I see the ships."

We change course slightly and head toward them about six feet above the water. We have five airplanes and they have five ships. We'll now see who is superior. The ships are growing fast in size and now appear to be two warships and three troopships. There are water geysers, which means our heavies have already dropped their bombs and we hope the Japs are in shock. The heavies missed as usual and we hope again that they think the raid is over.

Our slip stream screams a crescendo as we accelerate faster and faster toward the troop ship directly in front of us, and our airplane is rattling from the strain of flying too fast.

"Pilot to upper gunner, fire with me."

All our fixed guns and the upper turret together, rake the ship from bow to stern as the Lieutenant fantails our airplane. Dust, smoke, and explosions engulf the deck of the ship and a 500 pounder leaves our bomb bay to fall on the

144

water. All our guns and cannon now concentrate on the deck because that is where their gunners are, but we see confusion on the deck. The deck is alive with naked Japs falling over each other trying to find shelter from all our guns. Our bomb skips along behind, as we spray the deck without opposition. We bank to miss a mast and I have a view of their troops as if I was on the stage of a packed theatre. My guns mow them down like I was spraying them with a fire hose. I flip the tail gun and the camera switches while our bomb crashes against their ship and we zip away to see an explosion that knocks the ship over on its side. The naked Japs pour off the deck into the water while the ship rights itself and begins to sink. Then we pull away from the ship and come in contact with a Zero escort.

"Zeros above." "Zeros above."

I cannot see them, but Nelson begins firing at them as they zoom past us and I can hear a burst of lead splatter into our airplane. As I try to get a bead on them they are already out of range. Then they circle and come up from a different angle.

"From behind." "From behind."

Nelson swings his turret all the way around and opens up on them with a long burst and I thing about what a fool I am to be without my armor plate. Zero tracers whiz past us and Nelson keeps on firing when I look for them to see a B-25 chasing a Zero. I can't believe I'm seeing a bomber chasing a fighter.

The Lieutenant is making a run on another ship. Our's will sink and this destroyer still is under way, so we bear down on it. It has been hit on one side so we will plant another bomb on the other side. The destroyer is smoking a lot from the first bomb and it has turned, but that won't

145

slow us up. This bomb run will not be as safe for us because their gunners won't be asleep on the job this time, and now it is plain they will know what to expect.

The destroyer tries to turn her bow to us but we make a wide circle and come at her from the side. She is firing at us now. I can sight white flashes on the deck. But some of her gunners have been hit, which should reduce some of her fire power. At full throttle in a dive, we open up on her deck with all our guns and rake it the full length of the ship while our bomb skips along behind us to smash into the ship. I am spraying the deck when a blast jolts our airplane and I think we've had it. The concussion from an ack-ack shell nearly got us. We bank away as the bomb skips to the hull, sinks, and explodes to throw water and debris to the sky and a hole in the ship as big as a house.

"Zeros behind us."

Nelson's turret spins aft and fires at two Zeros full in the face. We are on top of them, only a few feet away from the confusion on the deck. It is covered with debris and bodies. Our guns and bombs have hurt them plenty. I sweep the deck now with my guns and Nelson is firing at the Zeros. Our bomb almost cut that warship in two, and it has another house sized hole in the other side. It will sink immediately. Our airplane now hugs the water and heads toward a lone B-25 for its protection. We make a bee line for home in formation close to the water. The Zeros make one more pass at us and our gunners knock one to the water, then they stay at a distance and leave us alone.

Two ships are listing and all are burning. But it will take time for them to go down. Our reconnaissance airplanes check the area soon after we leave and report all ships sunk. The water is littered with debris and bodies, while many

Japs are swimming and hanging to junk in the water. There were about 4,000 Japs on each of the troopships and about 1,500 on each destroyer which would total about 15,000 Japs and all their supplies. But the warmongers back in Washington have given us a free license to do this. In fact we will be heroes if we kill many Japs. The more we kill the more noteworthy we become. If we kill enough we will be famous. A high ranking general will give us medals and a heroes welcome. We will go home to be welcomed by a grateful people. And when it is all over and the little piece of paper is signed, if we did the same thing, we would be murderers.

Our first skip bombing strafing mission is a smashing success. We can do it. We can pulverize them. We sank those ships with thousands of men and all their equipment and didn't lose one man. Two gunners are wounded and four airplanes are shot up, but we didn't lose a man.

"Radio to pilot, should I send a message?"

"Roger."

"Grim Reaper Squadron to Hq. Mission a success. All ships burning. Some sinking. Most A/C damaged. Two gunners wounded."

Call sign/time-date

One airplane is leaking gasoline badly. I can see the gas streaming from the wing. If they can make it to the top of the peaks they could almost dive all the way to 14 Mile. Then I switch to "command" and listen.

"How much gas do you have now?"

"About 200 gallons."

"We'll stay with you."

"Remember this, if you bail out here, we will probably never see you again."

147

The leaking plane is still with us so it looks like they are going to make it. We begin to climb for altitude as we pass over Gona on the beach. The Kumusi river is below us and I can see the mountains grow bigger. If we only had some way of transferring gas. All the other planes have plenty of gas. We could give them 200 gallons easily. Or if we had a long towing rope one of us could tow the stricken airplane back. The crew of the leaky plane have one consolation. They know the U.S. Infantry and the Aussie Diggers are moving toward Buna through the Jungle. If they have to crash in the rain forest there is a chance to make contact with our forces. Then comes:

"We are almost out of gas. We can't get up over the peaks. We'll have to crash land."

"Let her stall. Don't power into the trees. Maintain flying speed until she stalls, but hug the trees. Try to walk to the coast. Good luck."

We all watched the doomed B-25 as it descended. It lagged behind, then disappeared. None of us ever saw any of the crew again. There was nothing we could do to help and as yet, we do not have air sea rescue. We were all counting our lucky stars that we were not with them. The power we had to carry us over the jagged peaks was never more appreciated.

We gave 14 Mile a victory buzz, then swung one circle and came in one by one. After we got parked the ground crews came running.

"Where's the other plane?"

"Did you sink 'em?"

"Is anybody dead?"

We all went to our briefing tent and everyone was so excited that we all wanted to talk at once.

"We sank that transport with naked Japs."

"Did you see the Zero I shot down?"

"That ack-ack was something else."

"I thought you were in the crashed plane."

Our operations officer asked us how many Zeros we shot down as if it mattered with all those thousands of Japs in the water and five ships sinking. A Zero more or less makes little difference. They are just the tip of the iceberg. But a ship loaded with men and equipment means something in winning a war.

Our photos showed we sank three ships immediately and the heavies finished the rest, however, the heavies probably couldn't have bombed or hit them if they had not been stopped. The credit for breaking the back of the convoy went to the Grim Reaper Squadron.

The next morning we had another briefing and the whole squadron attended. Supreme Hq. in Brisbane has ordered an invasion of Buna. The Yanks and the Aussies have Buna surrounded and are in waiting for us to annihilate them from the air before they start the slaughter by land. We are to sink all shipping coming south and to pulverize their base with parachute frag bombs.

We have two more converted B-25's now which make a total of six. This is only one third the number we are alloted, but we are rarin' to go. We have confidence in our planes now. We know what they will do. And the most important thing is that we are not afraid of the Japs anymore. I believe the B-25 as a skip bomber and a strafer is now a proven success. Our next assignment is to prove it is a success as a para frag bomber. Our mission next Sunday will prove that we can wipe Buna and all their other bases off the map.

# CHAPTER 12

## PARACHUTE FRAGMENTATION BOMBING

After our first fight with the Japs with our new skip bombers we had to admit our losses. We had been hurt some. One of our beautiful planes with its crew was somewhere in the enemy rain forest. Two of our gunners had been wounded and our planes carried many gaping holes inflicted by the agile Nip Zeros and ack-ack. I made up my mind I wouldn't go on another mission unless I had my armor plate. I just knew it was a good idea, especially since those Zeros usually came at us from behind.

Our ground crews went to work on our planes around the clock repairing the damage. Until we had fighter protection and more planes, those on the flight line had plenty to do.

In the meantime we used the two new planes for practice in dropping parachute frag bombs. Our bomb shackles had already been modified to hold the clusters of frag bombs. Each bomb had a little parachute attached to it. When the bomb was released from the shackle the chute opened and would slow the fall to give us time to get far enough away not to be blown up. This made it so we could bomb at tree top level and not get damaged by our own bombs—we hoped. The bombs were designed to explode, throwing small jagged metal fragments horizontally for anti-personnel and anti-anything on the ground. They wiped the ground clean of anything.

We made several runs on 14 Mile Field using duds for practice. The equipment had been pretested by Pappy

150

Gunn in Australia. Everything was o.k. It seemed to be much easier than learning to skip bomb. It was just a matter of flying at tree top altitude at top speed, and to separate the airplanes to cover all the area on the base. The pilot would just flip a switch and the bombs would fall one at a time to space them at about 100 feet apart on the ground. It was during this practice that I had the opportunity to rig armor aft of my gun position. This saved my life many times. Some of the troops thought I was out of my mind to haul that piece of metal from one plane to another. But a lot of those guys would be alive today if they had done the same thing.

It was just a square piece of armor plate in which I had burned a hole in each corner for the mounting. I attached a piece of short cable with a turnbuckle to each corner and secured it to a bulkhead aft of my machine guns. It stopped many bullets and junks of shrapnel that would have, on many missions, struck me.

That night the Japs bombed 14 Mile again. We were in our tents when they came over, and they seemed to have our exact location again. All the bombs fell in our dispersal area and we jumped in our jeeps and lit out for our revetment area. We were glad to find out that they had not been as accurate as we thought. Only two planes had been hit and the damage was minor. The raid only delayed our para frag mission one day.

We had our pre-attack briefing the day before our attack. This gave us all night to sleep on it. We would take off one hour before dawn to be over Buna when the Japs were waking up. We felt that even Japs have to sleep. We would fly over the target abreast and spread out to cover most of their base, and make only one pass. We could drop

151

all our bombs in one pass. We can't damage their runway with small bombs, but we can level everything above ground. We will fly three airplanes on each side of their runway spaced about 100 feet apart. This will cover most of the area of their installation. Our bombs will cut everything above ground and leave it bare.

In case they are alerted and are making any attempt to get airplanes off the ground we will change tactics and one B-25 will fly down their runway to destroy the take-off planes.

At 0200 hours the guards awaken us and we go to the mess hall for powdered eggs, powdered potatoes, and spam. The bomb bays are all loaded with our new bombs with the little parachutes. Our ammo containers are filled with 500 rounds for each machine gun and 100 rounds for the cannon. All our equipment is loaded including our parachutes and survival kits. Why we take parachutes I do not know. We will never have enough altitude to use them. Maybe there is a stupid regulation that states we have to have them.

In the darkness each of the six crews crawl into their airplanes, start the engines, check equipment, and begin to switch on and off many systems. While the engines warm up, the bomb bay doors are still open for the armament people to remove the fuse pins from all the bombs. After the pins are removed, the bombs will explode on contact. The ground crews remove the chocks and landing gear lock pins, and each plane moves toward the end of the strip.

I am flying again with Captain Connley, our squadron commander, who is one hellava guy. His promotion to Major is in the paper mill and if anyone deserves it, he does. He spins our plane around as he slams the throttles forward and we rocket down the strip by the light of the moon. The nearby jungle is vibrating from the blasts of the engines as we clear the trees. He eases off the prop pitch and the throttles. All five other planes are close behind and getting near us as we must stay close together in the dark.

As we climb the south slopes of the mountains our planes are burning their little running lights, but when we get over the top, every light will go off. We are in formation now and at maximum rate of climb, as the mountains in the moonlight grow in size. I can see the always present rain clouds now, but it isn't a problem now. In a few moments they will look just like a cloud below us.

"Connley to flight, check all guns."

Outside the window fireworks light the sky. The trees below us are blazed in a glow of white light from the seventy two machine guns and six cannons. Our airplane shakes and brakes from the recoil of this awesome power.

We are over the peaks now and all lights go out without radio command. We will not use radio now until we get over the target. In the moonlight the other five planes are easy to see flying on either side of us. The glow of their exhausts is the only light emitted from them.

We are descending with the terrain at 300 miles per hour, and at ten miles before target we'll throttle up to 330. The wind coming through the gaping hole in the bottom of the fuselage where the auxiliary gas tank should be, is spinning through the airplane. We are not using it for this short run. But the wind feels good in this unbearable heat.

"Radio to Nelson, I don't think the Zeros will be up. What do you think?"

"Hope not."

We plan to catch them on the ground. We'll be under

their radar and they don't know we are coming unless they have spotters in the jungle. We'll soon find out, and we'll learn also what our new para frag bombs will do.

There are no lights anywhere down there. This is Jap territory and everything is blacked out. Inside our planes it is dark except a few blackout lights are showing on some dials and switches. The moon dodging in and out of the clouds gives a beautiful light.

"Pilot to crew, we are coming in on Buna."

The trees are a blur from the speed we have picked up. We can feel our momentum gain, and our plane begins to shake as we approach its maximum speed. The dawn is breaking and Buna is dead ahead, and we hope dead asleep. Now we spread out into groups of three, and then separate farther. We have attained all the speed possible now and "wham", there go our guns. All planes fire at once and saturate the area with hot lead and steel which lights everything forward with arcing tracers. I point my guns down point blank, rake the ground, not being able to see what I'm firing at. Then I see our little bombs start leaving the bomb bay as I flip the camera and tail gun switches. Our airplane is groaning and shaking from the recoil of many guns and cannon, and Nelson is showering down the interior with empty casings as I look out the window to see planes and buildings on fire from our incendiary shells. They are like huge flame throwers that explode everything to fire far ahead.

Then I see tracers going the other direction which means they are firing on us. We are still dropping bombs and our guns are turning red from heat while the airplane continues to shake with the strain. My gun barrels turn red and I look aft to see their whole base ablaze with our bombs and fires and explosions which are shooting for the sky. All our guns now are hot which fills the airplane with the smell of hot steel and burned gun powder.

Their airfield is behind us now and off go our guns except for the tail gun and the upper turret. They will stay on to try to keep the Jap gunners down while we get away. We turn to the right to come part way back to take a look at what we had done.

I turn my camera and tail gun off and turn to take a look. The airfield is ablaze with fires and exploding ammo. Airplanes, buildings, and equipment, are exploding like the fourth of July, shooting projectiles skyward, and the airbase looks like an inferno.

We hug the water and make formation. The Jap gunners are still shooting at us but we're out of range and all still flying. I switch to "command".

"Is everybody o.k.?"

"Roger." "Roger."

We must have really clobbered them. No Zeros got off the ground. We sneaked in under their radar and they were totally surprised. Our new frag bombs are murderous to everything but the runway. This will revolutionize aerial warfare, but our cameras will tell the true story.

We turn right again and pass over the coast, then look back for a last view of their burning base. The smoke is billowing high over the jungle. We can see it while climbing the lofty mountains for a distance of twenty miles.

"Pilot to radio, contact our base."

"Roger."

"Grim Reaper to (call sign) 14 Mile. Mission success. Buna afire. No airplanes lost."

Call sign/time-date

.

We climb to 14,000, cross the peaks, then drop down to 14 Mile. After a three foot buzz down the strip, we peel off and come in still nose heavy. A quick check of our airplanes told us only two had been hit and their damage was minor.

The photo people grabbed the film and we all went to the briefing tent.

"We caught them sleeping."

"They didn't know what hit them."

"We must have clobbered all their Zeros."

"We know now we can annihilate them."

Our pictures revealed a sight we had hoped for, and more. Many buildings, airplanes, fuel dumps, ammo dumps, and tents were on fire. It appeared everything on the base was on fire. We are however, going right back again and do it all over again. This time the heavies will hit them from high altitude a few seconds before we pounce on them again from the tree tops.

After fighting the mosquitos and flies at the flight line for two hours, we get the word to go. We are to start firing our guns at 0210 hours. The high conventional bombers will release theirs at 0205 hours which will give us a two minute margin of safety. If we miss the time by one minute we could be blown up by our own bombs.

It is usual procedure to synchronize every watch at briefing time, but this time we check and double check. One minute error could mean our lives. If we make a mistake it won't be a first time Americans have been killed by their own bombs. In the near future we will drop our bombs by mistake on our own kids in the Markam Valley and kill hundreds of them. But that part of the war is hush-hush.

We took off at 0100 hours which allowed us one hour

and ten minutes to reach our target. This time over the mountains there was a haze that covered the peaks as well as the eternal rain clouds. As usual we descended on top of the trees, and when the haze disappeared, the smoke was visible again from Buna. The smoggy haze was caused from the burning we created at Buna this morning.

We have no mercy for the little yellow Asian monkeys. I wouldn't want to be one of them at Buna. They are doomed. In one month we will be using their skulls for landscaping around our tents. They will be used for rock gardens and their skulls will be grinning from the tops of our fence posts. When Buna was taken over there were thousands of skeltons all over the area mostly from the result of our bombings.

We came into Buna over the same route as we traveled that morning because we knew they had no warning. We were anxious to see what it looked like now and to hit them again when they least expected it.

"Pilot to crew, are you ready?"

"Roger." "Roger."

The smoke is getting closer as we throttle up to full speed and break formation to three airplanes on each side. Now we are spread out to about 200 feet apart and all 72 guns plus the cannons break loose in concentrated power that smashes nearly 80,000 rounds per minute of 50 caliber plus the cannons into what used to be Buna Air Base. All pilots are fantailing to spread the bullets over a wider area. In a flash the bomb bay doors pop open and immediately our bombs begin to trail each other out to snap into their little chutes. My guns are firing forward strafing the area when I see Japs running and airplanes burning, so I swing both guns on the running Japs. Some fall in a cloud of dust as we flash by and in a split we are behind them and more Japs are running.

Tracers are flashing by our line of fire which means they still have some gunners alive and capable of firing back at us. And there are flak bursts around, so we didn't kill all the Japs here in our raid this morning. The ground is covered with skeletons of airplanes and the runway is full of bomb craters. The whole area is a mass of piles of ashes and burned things hard to make out.

As we cut across their airdrome like a big scythe we almost run out of something to destroy. It seems everything is already destroyed. We zoom to the end of the base and turn toward the mountains this time in case they expect us to take to the sea as we did before.

It was plain that our strike this morning broke their back. They could not get any airplanes off the ground. The tremendous force of our attacks leaves their field a total shambles. We have no need to worry about the enemy mounting any further attack on us from Buna. All they have left is their ack-ack guns which are dispersed in the area. Our photos will show where the guns are and unless they move them we will get them tomorrow. There is no chance for them to recoup their losses. If they try from the sea we will sink their ships as fast as their Navy can send them. Our infantry and the Australian Diggers have them surrounded on all the jungle sides and they are cut off from any supplies, but they will not give up. They will let themselves be slaughtered to the last man.

Three of our planes have minor damage but they will be ready to fly in a few hours. We've learned already, that it takes more than some holes to knock down our airplanes. With plenty of airplanes we would not be afraid of the biggest bases or their most powerful ships.

We take to the tree tops back to our base. We don't have to worry about Zeros on our tail this time unless they come from another enemy base. From the foothills we rise up, up to the higher mountains, then over the peaks and down, down, still on the tree tops, to a victory buzz across our base and then touch down.

They will be crying the blues tonight in Tokyo. The Japs have lost Milne Bay and just about lost Buna. In their conquest of the Pacific they have been stopped. They will never again take land that does not belong to them. We will smash all their bases just like Buna, and when we have driven them out of this area it will be down hill all the way to Japan.

Our rapport with the ground crews is picking up. Even the pencil pushers are treating us with respect now. The combat crews flying these dangerous missions were regarded as expendable and stupid. Now we are being sent to Australia on leave and given promotions. Also we will have earned the right to go home—if we live. The non-combatants will not go home for the duration and six months.

Pappy Gunn has sent us three more new B-25's all ready to go with 75 mm cannons. Now we have nine which is something, considering a total absence of airplanes for nearly a year. It is time for a couple days rest after bombing Buna. The squadron painter has a chance to install the names on our airplanes. Captain Connley, Nelson, and myself decide to name our airplane "The Widowmaker". It seemed appropriate, and in time everyone thought it was the best name in the squadron. In fact, it was not long until she proved to be a widowmaker. All aboard were killed, but our crew was in another airplane at the time.

Other new planes were named "Virgin Mary". "Hellzapoppin'", "Ruptured Duck". and "Jim's Folly", etc. The squadron painter had a job for a few days. He not only painted names, he also painted shark's teeth on the nose and a bomb for each mission flown. We would be on a mission almost every day and losing planes on most of our missions, so the painter had his work cut out for him.

The Japs now know about our flying battleships. But they have a lot to learn yet. What they do not know is that we can fly all the way to their big base at Wewak. And when our new base at Buna is ready we can attack them all the way to Hollandia which is their last big base in the north of New Guinea.

This night the Japs hit us with everything they have. They bombed Port Moresby, 14 Mile, 7 Mile, and all other bases where we could be in a position to strike at them.

Our ack-ack gunners are improving now. Our shells are exploding near the Jap bombers, and one is knocked down. Our searchlights beam all the bombers and follow this one all the way to the ground. The next day we go into the jungle to see the downed plane. We think we could learn something about their bombers, but it is so smashed up we could learn nothing. Later, when the Aussie Diggers and the Yanks take Lae and Salamaua I am in a position to inspect many of their fighters and bombers.

Their big retaliatory raid hurt us. Some P-38's were hit at Laloki, some B-25's got it at 7 mile, and we had one gunship knocked out of the war for a couple days. Because we were short of planes as usual, we waited until the damaged plane was repaired before we made our next strike.

After devastating Buna we turned back to the sea.

Always, our orders were to sink all shipping. Not one ship escaped us. There was some mopping up to do at Buna, but it was for those bombers with bomb sights. We were without bomb sights, so we could not destroy anti-aircraft gun emplacements.

The Japs continue to try to reinforce the lost cause at Buna. We sunk all the big ships they sent, so now they are using motor driven barges. They move the barges down the coast at night and hide them in the coves in the daylight. They cover them with green foliage cut from the trees to camouflage them. So we fly the coastline during the day to sink barges. Mostly we use 500 pounders, but they are designed to sink ships and are too powerful for barges. When they explode under their barges, the power is so great that the barge is blown 200 feet skyward. Sometimes there is nothing left but small bits of junk and blood.

The barge runs were ducksoup. We called a barge mission a "milk run". We called an easy mission a milk run. The barges were armed too, but their guns were smaller than ship's guns.

Reconnaissance informs us that there are two troop ships heading toward Buna again. It is evident they are trying to sneak in while it is raining. The Japs seem to be utterly in a stupor. Even if they make it and unload, we will sink their ships on the way back.

Our para frag shackles are removed and we install the big ones for 500 pounders. We are going after big game again. Armament has all our guns ready, and loads the bombs. Maintenance has pre-flighted all the planes. Every plane is topped off with 100 octane gas, and we are ready to go. The combat crews are in the briefing tent getting the latest dope and time check from the operations officer. I get the

161

code book for the day and head to Hellzapoppin'.

The two ships are south of Gasmata, about ten miles from the center of New Britain. They were last seen heading directly southwest toward devastated Buna. We have nine planes, not enough, but more than we're used to. We will go out there, find them, and sink them.

# CHAPTER 13

## SLAUGHTER IN THE WATER

We are chafing because of the weather. It's been raining for two days and those Jap ships are taking advantage of the rain to try to get to Buna with their re-inforcements. Our planes are fueled and waiting, but we can't go until the weather clears. We must have good weather to find those ships.

The forecast is for better weather in the morning, so we are looking forward to it. The Japs haven't bothered us either since it has been raining, so all we have to do is wait. To wait is sometimes worse than going. But we are going to chance it tomorrow.

It was raining when we took off and we had to fly entirely by instruments. After crossing the mountains in the rain, we flew an hour more at 46 degrees magnetic and it was still coming down. It was no use, we would never find those ships without visibility. So we turned 180 degrees and started home. Now we've got to find a little place called 14 Mile in the rain. We'll now see if I can be a radio navigator.

"Pilot to radio, can you give me a bearing for 14 Mile?"

"What was your compass heading from home?"

"46 degrees."

"46 plus 180 is 226. Fly 226 degrees until I can tune the radio compass."

I tuned the compass to an Aussie radio station at Moresby and called the Captain.

"Radio to pilot, follow your radio compass pointer to Moresby."

Nobody knew exactly how many minutes we'd been flying, but we estimated, and flew back. Then the pointer flipped all the way around to 47 degrees which meant we had passed over Moresby. We descended, turned, and followed it all the way in to Moresby. Then it was easy to find our base. Well, we didn't sink any ships today but we found our way home with almost no visibility.

The next morning the rain had stopped so we took off and flew the same course looking again for the ships. We dropped down to the water and found them coming in to Buna.

We made our deadly skip bombing attack in a quick, catlike way, so fast that their gunners did not have time to man their guns. We each skipped a bomb into a ship and shattered the deck 10,000 times with our guns and cannons. Each ship took four bombs and sank immediately. They sank while we were circling and only a few troops could be seen as survivors. Most of them went down with the suction of the big ship. We didn't even see any life boats which led us to believe they may not carry life boats, so they can haul more men.

They had a Zero escort too but they did not attack us until it was all over, and we stayed in formation after our attack for protection, so the Zeros made only one pass at us. Our gunners knocked one Zero down and they didn't come at us again.

We can chalk up two troop ships, about 9,000 Japs aboard, and all their supplies as our work for the day. Not a slow way to kill Japs. Some of course survived, but not many.

The Grim Reaper Squadron with the Widowmaker in the center and four on each side, heads south, low over the water. Soon the beach at Gona is a blur on the horizon. Then we hug the trees all the way to Kakoda, climb the foothills, then up over the peaks, and down down to a victory pass three feet above our runway. One by one we all come in, in perfect order.

On the way back I contacted 14 Mile:

"Two troop ships sunk. About 9,000 Japs in the water. We are all o.k. Grim Reaper.

Call sign/time-date.

We came back from this mission almost without damage. After a quick inspection we found only one airplane had been hit, and that was minor. Captain Connley said it was duck soup. Those Japs were helpless. I wish there had been more ships.

"How about that Captain? You chasing a Zero with a B-25. That's one for Ripley."

The ground crews hung around the area to get in on the chatter. Even they were getting worked up. All bombs skipped into the targets. No bombs missed the ships. The 13th Attack Squadron took credit for two big transports sunk with all the supplies and equipment and possibly 9,000 Japs killed.

Pappy Gunn has sent us two more brand new B-25's with 75 mm cannons. Pappy had improved the balance by moving the side guns farther aft which was a big improvement. We tested the new airplanes on the old hulk at full throttle and ten feet off the water. When the guns opened up and the shock reverberated through the airplane it was a little greater, but the plane seemed to take it as usual.

No army is made up of old men. Old men are too smart to be stupid, and they are not in good enough shape to take it. Our crews were a combination of high school and college kids in their prime who liked games. And this was the most exciting game they had ever played. With our super destructive B-25's the game was even more exciting. We now had the power to destroy the enemy on land, sea, and in the air.

Everybody was eager to strike the Japs way out there where we had not been before. But we seemed to hold back. Perhaps it was because we did not want the enemy to know yet that we had the range to fly all the way to their huge installations at Rabaul and Wewak.

From 14 Mile we can fly round trip to all their bases on New Britain Island. But because of the distance they feel safe from our deadly attacks. Soon enough we are going to pay them a visit up there. Right now we don't want them to know we can fly that far. Now we are going to attack Finschaven which is about 250 miles one way from 14 Mile.

Our planes are loaded with everything we need to give them a dose of what they deserve. The bomb bays are filled with parafrags. All the ammo containers are loaded to their brims with 50 caliber belts, and our big drop tank is topped off with all the rest of the tanks. We will hit them from the jungle side so we can sneak on them without warning. We plan to drop all our bombs and empty most of our ammo in one quick pass over their base, then swoop out to sea and back along the coast to try to sink some barges on the way back.

The night before we went on this mission we got very little sleep. It was very hot, and the mosquitos buzzing around our nets kept us awake. And the Japs didn't make it any easier with their nightly bombing. The worry about a possible crash way up there did not help any either. But

166

dawn finally came and we hit the chow line for the usual powdered eggs. We grabbed our weapons, and equipment, and jeeped to our planes.

Our plans were to hug the trees as far as Salamaua, then cross the neck of the Solomon Sea at ten feet off the water, then cross the coast again south of Finschaven. We will then swing inland at tree top level to attack them from the jungle side. We expect to hit their base so quickly they won't have time to get to their foxholes. We are also hoping they won't have time to jump to their guns.

These dawn raids are becoming routine now. We thunder off the runway at 0615 hours and plan to be over the target at 0730. I am flying with Captain Connley again and Nelson is our upper gunner. When we are on our way and in formation a voice blasts over the command set to check our guns. Immediately 143 fifty caliber machine guns plus all the cannons, in unison fill the rain forest with 157,300 hot rounds of lead and steel per minute. The foliage and trees before us is chopped down like it was cut with a huge scythe.

We will drop a bomb every 100 feet from a point at the near side of their base to their beach on the other side of the base. Our airplanes will be spaced 150 feet apart to cover the complete area of the base. If we see airplanes lined up on the field two B-25's will fly straight down their line of planes to be certain to destroy all of them. We will zoom over their base at maximum speed and will be over the target only 13 seconds. But if their gunners get to their guns they will be able to shoot at us while we are leaving the area and out over the sea. Their gunners will have to be very close to their guns or they won't have time to get to their guns.

167

During our climb to 14,000 feet to clear the mountains, I take the opportunity to tune my liaison transmitter before we get in Jap territory. If I tune it on their side of the mountain they could pick me up.

We hurdle the peaks and nose down the far side, staying as close to the trees as possible so the Japs can't detect us on radar. The foliage also muffles our noise.

Kokoda is an inland base directly in line between Moresby and Finschaven. We will avoid it by detouring around it to the west. A blur is all I see when I gaze out the window. Then there is the beach and we're out over the sea at ten feet off the water. The second we pass over the beach and leave the jungle our airplane stops bouncing. The constant air temperature over the water makes for smooth flying. We see no signs of life over the land or along the beach. That is good because we do not want to see anyone who may give us away.

"Pilot to upper gunner, when we get there fire your guns with me over the cockpit if no Zeros are in the air."

"Pilot to crew, I see the beach ahead. We will be over the target in about 15 minutes."

"Roger." "Roger."

We watch for people on this beach too, and then check our watches. We have leather watch bands with leather covers to protect them. It is now six minutes to go. We are now at full throttle in a power glide at 330 mph and ten feet above the trees. Their runway looms in a scene like most bases in the jungle. From a distance it looks just like a patch of grass mowed out of a big grass field.

Our bomb bay doors pop open, while every gun explodes simultaneously and our airplane jolts from the recoil. Their airdrome is now under us and airplanes are on the ground.

The planes are scattered about the area, and Japs are standing around in groups. I flip my aft gun and camera switches then hit my gun buttons to pour out a steady stream of lead at the airplanes and Japs around them. They are in a stupor and don't know what's going on. I spray them like with a fire hose, and only a few feet under our wing are mechanics working on their airplanes. Their beautiful airplanes begin to explode and burn even before we get close to them. Our incendiaries are like huge flame throwers. Now our bombs are streaming a steady flow out the bomb bay and popping into their chutes. I see a group of Japs just standing and open up on them. They don't even know what's going on yet. The ground, in all directions is alive with tracers arcing in a maze. I am holding down my gun buttons and raking the area being careful not to hit any of our airplanes.

The smell of hot steel and gun powder fills the airplane to a choking degree, as Nelson is shaking and vibrating in his turret and about ten thousand empty casings rain down on me. Now all the Japs are running and our gunners keep hosing them down as they stumble and fall. The Japs are so close I could knock them over with a stick. So far there is no ack-ack—no resistance at all.

We are at the end of their base. Nelson in a frenzy, swings his turret aft and continues to rake them and our fixed guns go off. I turn my guns aft also and see our bombs exploding all over their base. Pandemonium obliterates their airdrome behind us. Fuel dumps and ammo dumps are shooting thousands of feet into the sky. The smoke is rolling and billowing.

We stay in the same formation and lower even farther to skim the water and zip out to sea. It is only then that the

Japs start firing at us. But in a flash we are out of their range. Some of their shells hit the water in front of us and around us, but no one is hit. We continue hugging the water until we are at least a mile out of their range, then slowly turn toward the coast.

We caught them completely by surprise. The Japs did not have the slightest notion of our coming. Before they realized what was in the air it was all over. Their gunners were too slow. We were almost out of their range when they got to their guns. We caught their airplanes on the ground and slaughtered them. You can bet your life those still alive can hardly believe what happened. They have learned something this day about aerial warfare. How will they combat it? We don't think they will.

You little Asian monkeys. You haven't seen anything yet. Before this is over you'll wish you'd never had any ancestors.

"Connley to flight, anybody hit?"

"No, Captain."

"Unbelieveable."

"Pilot to radio, give'em the good news."

I pulled myself out from under what seemed like a ton of empty shell casings and coded a message:

"Mission accomplished. Complete success. Destroyed all aircraft and many people. No damage to us. Barge hunting now."

Grim Reaper/time-date

As we come to the water's edge we swing toward home watching along the coast for square groves of trees. A barge covered with foliage looks like a rectangular shaped cluster. After a few minutes we see one. We all bank to sea and the "Widowmaker" dives on the barge firing all guns and can-

170

non, and the foliage rips off leaving the barge exposed and smoking. We give it another blast and it explodes throwing tons of debris and naked men into the air, and we fly right through the debris catching a piece of junk in the right wing.

Then we fly down the coast about ten more minutes and see two more. Sure enough, two more rectangles right next to the shore. We attack each barge one at a time until they are like two big sieves. They sink immediately and the Japs still alive scramble ashore. We circle to watch them and their junk floating in the water, then continue south.

It is like shooting fish in a barrel. Those Japs don't even shoot back. They have guns on those barges, but they are not the big guns the ships carry. The suddenness of our attack seemed to leave them helpless.

Buna is dead ahead and we have plenty ammunition left, so we make a pass over Buna. We fly over the beach to the jungle side and come over the trees to muffle our sound. We come in like a rocket, so fast they don't have time to get us in their sights. We shatter their base on one pass with all our guns and cannons, then hug the tree tops up the foothills to the peaks and down to 14 Mile for a victory buzz. At two feet off the runway we lift to scrape the trees and brake up for one at a time landings.

It had taken us just two and a half hours to raze Finschaven, destroy their airplanes, destroy their fuel and ammo dumps, kill hundreds on the base, sink three barges with all supplies, kill more Japs on the barges, and strafe Buna again.

On the 2nd day of January, 1943, the 32nd Infantry Division with help from the Aussies, captured Buna mission. Immediately the 13th Squadron prepared to move there.

Everything we had at 14 Mile was moved to Buna.

During the Buna Campaign we led most of the attacks that sank 300,000 tons of their shipping, the destruction of 2,000 airplanes, the killing of thousands of their military, and the destruction of untold millions of dollars worth of equipment. And we were just getting started.

# CHAPTER 14

## TENS OF THOUSANDS OF DEATHS

What is the Japanese mentality?  What makes them do the crazy things they do?

In the war in the Southwest Pacific we did not understand them.  They seemed to want to go to their ancestors.  At Guadalcanal they sacrificed the lives of thousands of their troops in what we thought was insanity. They sent their troops, wave after wave, charging into the Marines shouting "Banzai", only to be cut down by our machine guns.  Then they would charge again over the bodies of their dead until the bodies piled so high they could not get over them.

It must be a great honor to die for their "Son of Heaven."  It must be for some fanatical religious reason.  It would not make sense any other way.  Or like the lemmings of Norway, they became obsessed with their own psyche, and did follow each other to certain death.  They seemed to want to commit mass suicide.

They never give up or admit defeat.  Since we have taken Buna, Milne Bay, and Guadalcanal, they are trying to reinforce Lae and the other bases in southern New Guinea, with ships.  They are using barges too.  When they send ships and barges south to reinforce we fly out over the Solomon Sea and sink them.  We always sink them but they keep sending them.  With our new B-25 skip bombers we can sink them as fast as they send them.

Once again reconnaissance reports a five ship convoy, with two destroyers and three transports heading south through the Bismarck Sea toward the Vidiaz Straits. This means, as usual, that they are going to try to reinforce their southern bases.

Our B-25's have the range to fly all the way there, but we don't want them to know that yet. Our strategy is to wait and let them get closer.

The next day the convoy is spotted once more still steaming south. It is time for us to strike. The weather forecast is good, and we are ready. We will need our big drop tanks so we'll have additional problems in getting rid of them. This will be a late afternoon attack which will add to our hazard. The winds will whip up and the water will get rough which is also a hazard to skip bombing. Also, we will not get back until after dark.

While they are loading our planes I have a chance to install my rear armor plate. And while all the gas tanks are filled I check my equipment and gear. When the plane is fueled and ready, I am ready.

Once again Captain Connley is our pilot and Nelson is our upper gunner. We have a new co-pilot who has never flown a mission. "Widowmaker" is the first in the air and we head slowly for the mountains while the others get off and catch up. Then it is over the clouds and down with the terrain to the sea. The sea is already covered with white caps from the afternoon wind.

"Pilot to crew, check your guns."

Our bullets send up small geysers out on the water. Nelson and myself are shooting out to the side and our plane shakes and rattles. The other planes see us shooting and do the same. Everything is going smoothly as we ride over the peaceful expanse of the Solomon Sea. It is hard to believe we are carrying so much death and destruction to hundreds, and maybe thousands of men trapped in overloaded troop ships somewhere out there ahead of us.

The music that comes through our radio as we pass swiftly along, carries nothing but a good memory. The Japs on those ships may be listening to the same music. Our scenery at ten feet off the water is nothing but water.

Our command radio, which has a range of about 30 miles, gives us no indication of an attack yet. The heavies are supposed to hit the ships just before we do, to cause turmoil. Some of us are thinking about a promised combat leave to Sydney. We are promised this as a reward for completing about 15 missions. We will board the plane for Sydney, the most desired place in the whole Southwest. All our ground crews and pencil pushers, who cannot have such blessings, will turn green.

We must be getting close to that convoy. Now we are due east of Finschaven and it was last seen off Cape Gloucester.

"Radio to pilot, how much gas left in the drop tank?"

"Just about empty."

A few minutes later the Captain said, "I want you to get rid of that tank."

"Well Captain, I want to get rid of it as badly as you."

I strapped myself to a bulkhead and gave the lever a hard yank. As usual, the tank is not willing. I pull it again and it is what we call "no soap". Then I use my pry bar to try to get leverage. It still hangs on. Now I poke Nelson and ask for help. "Nelson, we have got to get rid of that damn tank. If we don't we'll have to abort."

"Hang on to that lever and push with the other hand," I tell him.

Together, we push and pull and in a minute, it goes out

like a bullet. It left a huge gaping hole in the bottom.

"Radio to pilot, tank's gone."

"Yes, I felt it."

We watch the other planes to see if they get rid of their tanks. We see two fall to the water and bounce high into the air. And we see more fall and bounce high off the water. Then one plane banks away from the formation, makes a 180 degree turn and high-tails it for home. We can't use radio, but we all know they could not get rid of their tank. Lucky guys.

"Pilot to crew, the convoy has been hit by the heavies, we can see the smoke."

"Pilot to Nelson, I want you to fire with me on the ship unless Zeros are attacking."

"Roger."

One ship is smoking and we are going after it because it is a destroyer, and the ships are close now. The destroyer zooms to meet us as I brace myself and shake with fear. Down we go gaining speed every second and the airplane is rattling from the strain as the fixed guns explode to shake the plane even worse. Nelson and the Captain hold down their gun buttons while raking the deck as our bomb leaves the bay to smash the water and bounce back, then lag aft while we all pour everything we have into the ship and bank to miss the superstructure. This gives me what I've been waiting for—a clear open close-up shot at the deck. I hold my triggers down and rake the deck back and forth as we bank away. The men on board are mowed down like grass in a hay field while our bomb crashes to the side of the ship and sinks. I am only feet from the deck alive with little yellow men terrorized by our savage attack. Some are prone and some are running and some are operating the guns. I see hundreds of them which proves our bet that they carry troops on warships.

After sinking three seconds our bomb explodes and rolls the ship on its side. A water spout rises twice the height of the masts and the ship rolls back to its normal position as we zip away still blasting it with the top guns, the tail gun and the waist guns. Now another of our B-25's is skipping a second bomb into it as we position ourselves for a second run. The sky is now alive with black flak puffs and several hundred thousand white tracers arcing in every direction like a giant cobweb. Our plane jumps from the concussion of a near miss and shrapnel pocks our skin with jagged holes. The other airplane banks away from the ship as its bomb and guns tear out the other side of the ship. Now we circle to gain altitude for a run on the other destroyer. Already our airplanes have exploded two bombs in each ship and saturated each ship with hundreds of thousands of rounds of machine gun bullets and explosive cannon shells.

Now their Zero escort wings down on us like a swarm of angry bees.

"Zeros diving on us."

The Captain throws the stick forward and we dive for the safety of the water and broadside at the other destroyer. Nelson and I fire head on at the Zeros as our bomb drops to the water to skip into the ship. The Captain sprays every foot of the deck and we concentrate on the diving Zeros. Three Zekes are right on top of us in a dive and one fails to pull out in time. It crashes into the water while we pull away from the ship and our bomb cuts it right in two. The bow and stern immediately point skyward and the sea becomes alive with swimming Japs.

"Nelson, forget the ships, fire on the diving Zeros."

Two more fighters dive on us and we pulverize them with our guns, and one explodes almost like a bomb.

My view from a window shows a sky full of a million tracers, ack-ack bursts, Zeros, B-25's, and smoke. And I see a B-25 smoking and heading for home. Now we are circling to decide if it is necessary to attack again. One of the destroyers is cut in two and sunk, one troopship is half sunk, and the other three ships are a mass of flames and heavy in the water.

We are going to attack one more troopship. Two 500 pounders have already exploded in her belly and we are going to plant another bomb there. She will sink as she is, but the Captain wants to hurry the process. We point our nose at the ship and slam the throttles forward. That ship is hurt badly, but some of her gunners are still alive and firing at us as we fantail broadside into her with all fixed guns raking her decks. Nelson is firing at a Zero behind us and I can't see it, so I focus my attention on the ship ahead.

Away goes our third bomb and here comes a transport loaded with troops and supplies. I have a clear shot now and the deck is just a few feet away so I open up with a long burst right into hundreds of naked and half naked Japs cluttering the decks. I continue firing until the ship is out of my scope, then along zooms another Zero at us and I swing my hot guns toward it and it is out of sight.

"Pilot to crew, everything o.k.?"

"Roger." "Roger."

Our bomb rolled the ship over to expose a room size hole in her side, and we leave them to their fate.

"Connley to flight, get together, get back in formation, we're going home."

"Connley to flight, everybody o.k.?"

"This is Frank, we've been hit, but still flying."

"This is Jacobs, our radio gunner's hit."

"Anybody know what happened to Aberly?"

His plane had gone south smoking.

We circle and watch the ships sink. In a few minutes we head south in formation and let the thousands of Japs who are still alive swim for their lives. If there were 4,000 Japs on each troopship and 2,000 on each destroyer we left about 16,000 Japs back there dead and trying to survive. This will help compensate for the cowardly attack on Oahu.

Aberly, the pilot of the plane that was in smoke had to ditch, and all were lost. We lost the radio gunner who was hit also. He died on the way home. The rest of us all got back home safely.

"Connley to flight, we are going to hunt barges on the way home."

"Roger."

We head west to the New Guinea coast just south of Saidor, then follow the coast south a few miles looking for barges. We found two out in the open without camouflage.

Those poor dumb Japs. They'll die on the spot.

"Connley to flight, I'll hit them first, you guys follow. Don't waste bombs. We'll sink 'em with our guns."

We swung wide to get them both in line. In a power glide at over 300 we ripped into them. The first barge exploded and bodies and debris flew into the sky. We crashed into a piece of metal as we passed over. It must have been an ammo barge. We hit the second barge with every gun and cannon and made a sieve out of it.

"O.K. you guys, polish it off."

We circled out of range of their guns and watched the others make their attacks. The helpless vessel began to sink

179

after the second airplane hit it. The others continued until it was awash with water and the Japs who were not hit began to swim toward the coast.

Like rats they struggled in the water. We were tempted to kill them in the water, but did not do it. It would have been much easier to kill them there than for the ground troops to have to rout them out of the jungle. They have been shooting our men in the water and in parachutes. If they continue to do it, we are going to do the same thing.

We bank off and head for Lae. We have some bombs left and the Captain has a plan. They are fused for three seconds delay and we have no intention of landing with them.

Radio silence breaks.

"I'm going ahead 1,000 yards. Do what I do."

No one answered. The Japs would not have an opportunity to fix our position.

We crossed the neck of land that protrudes southeast of Lae at tree top level. The trees now muffled our noise and they wouldn't see us on their radar screen. As we approached the airfield we rose to 400 feet and our bomb bay doors popped open as we zoomed over their airfield at full speed. At 400 feet and three seconds delay we escaped the savage destruction of our bombs. Our bombs hit right down the center of the runway as the Zeros were taking off and one crashed into a crater and wrecked itself. I turned on the camera and caught the picture just as it hit. None of the planes at Lae could take off because of the craters. At Salamaua our last bomb did not fall and I gave the Captain a call. I have a good view through the tank hole and the bomb did not go. Connley said the bomb was dropped, so I looked in the bomb bay and there it was, hanging by one end again.

"Captain, the bomb is hanging by one end. I will try to pry it loose."

"Pilot to crew, we've got a bomb hung up in the bomb bay."

I secure my safety strap around my waist, grab my pry bar, and crawl in the open bomb bay. Through the open doors the trees are only about ten feet away and flashing by so fast they are a green blur. Our new co-pilot is at the front end watching me. Nelson is still scanning above for Zeros. There is nothing to hang on to but a bunch of tubing secured by small clamps. These clamps are built only strong enough to hold the tubing. The bulkheads are corrugated and I can get my hands in the holes, but the metal is as sharp as a knife. If I have to hang from any of them they would cut my fingers off. I can get a toe hold at the top of the doors but there is little space there. The slip stream is hitting my feet making it hard to hold my footing. One slip and I've had it.

Then I get an idea. I yell at the co-pilot and tell him to throw me his shirt. He rips off his shirt and hands it to me. I have only one hand as I have to hold my pry bar. Then I fold the shirt and put it through one of the holes. I secure my strap through the hole and hope it will hold if I fall. But now I'm not in a leverage position and have to do it all over again.

By this time we are over the rain clouds on top of the mountains. Now I've got to get enough leverage to bend the heavy shackle. Shackles on these airplanes are made out of case hard steel. With a yank it gives a little. Then I position my bar better and pull harder and the bomb falls.

We are passed the rain clouds now so I stay in the bomb bay to watch it explode. It hits the jungle and in three seconds it explodes like a huge ball of fire and sends shock waves over the trees like a rock thrown in a pool. Back in the fuselage I stretch out on the floor over the edge of the hole for the gas tank to cool off. I am hot in spite of the cold over the mountains. It is the hottest trip I have ever made.

Our victory buzz over 14 Mile Field was a victory of victories. Never before had we hurt the enemy like this. But it was only the beginning. We will hurt them much more in the future. We had our losses, but the Japs lost a thousand times more. We lost five lives and a B-25. But the enemy lost five ships, a possible 16,000 men, all their equipment and supplies, two of their barges and all supplies, three Zeros and three probables, and we planted 18 huge holes at Lae and Salamaua.

Our photos revealed the damage we did. Men were running on the decks of the ships in disbelief, bewildered, terrified. They showed the awful destruction of our machine guns, cannons and bombs. Hundreds of Japs were lying on the decks in their blood. They showed the Jap gunners in close ups, aiming and firing at us. We used a magnifying glass to see the fear on the faces of their troops. They still don't understand or believe we soft Americans are brave enough to fly down the barrels of the guns on their warships. A photo of one of their barges showed hundreds of boxes of supplies with Japanese letters on them, and all their supplies floating in the water after the barges sank.

At our briefing we have some good news. Soon we will have fighter escort on some missions. Well, it's about time you guys got over here. There are several pursuit squadrons in the New Guinea area now. They have P-40's, P-39's, and P-47's and P-38's. The Aussies have been working to build auxiliary wing tip fuel tanks for the P-

38's. It's another example of the blunders of the people at the factories who send us airplanes that can't be used until modified. We have been told the P-38 is the fastest pursuit plane in the world. There was a little kid by the name of Richard Bong who flew P-38's with us. He eventually shot down 40 Zeros to become one of the heroes of the Pacific war.

# CHAPTER 15

## MOVE TO BUNA

These American kids are in the Pacific for just one reason—to kill Japs and destroy all their property possible. General Kenney made a point to make it clear. For combat personnel in a B-25 skip bomber outfit it is a risky way to go. To motivate it he offered us anything that was available in the area. If we would kill the little yellow men we could have medals, all the booze we could drink when available, dress like we want, no duties except fly combat, and leave to the best places in Australia. And don't forget, when you have flown 50 combat missions you can go back to the States to stay. In the Army Air Corps, no person will go home until the war is over plus six months, except combat crews and the disabled.

One of our B-25's is going to Sydney with a load of combat crews and I'm one of them. We'll leave in the morning for one whole week, and we will have two days travel time. When we return, the bomb bay will be full of booze for all the thirsty troops in the outfit. We will be first to go to Sydney on combat leave. We, so far, do not believe it, even though we have been told a hundred times. We'll stay in Sydney's very best hotels paid for by the taxpayer. We can do anything we want as long as we stay within the law and show good conduct. Sydney—the most coveted place in the whole Southwest Pacific. It looks like the General is a man of his word.

Our squadron commander, now Major, not Captain Connley, will pilot the plane and I'll be the radio operator. There'll be little to do on this peaceful mission except see that we enjoy our music.

This leave has additional kicks when we all know how envied we are. You can feel the resentment among the troops in the squadron who are not in a position to go, especially those who push pencils and complain about how rough it is in the jungle. They are not talking to us. Not one has said, well, you deserve to go. One pencil pusher was nice to me for a reason. He asked me if I would bring a case of booze for him? This for the liquor, and here's a fifty for you for your trouble. He said he was sick and tired of drinking "jungle juice."

Jungle juice is brewed in the jungle and made from a concoction of any fruit, grain, or whatever can be found in the jungle or mess hall kitchen. The stills "work" well, because of the heat and nobody cares what the troops do in their spare time back behind the camp area. Mostly the guys who know how to make it are from the south. But there are plenty guys in every outfit who have made it, and some of them have been ridge runners and moonshiners.

One kid in radio school was hopped up on it all the time. He was a mathematical genius and said it helped him. Here in New Guinea he has a still out in the boonies that is working continuously. But they get tired of their jungle juice and will pay anything for good store bought liquor.

On our trip to Sydney, our B-25 was packed with troops with no seats. But there were plenty of parachutes that came in handy. It's better than sitting on the hard floor. Also, they could be used for a pillow. To ease the boredom we had music via radio, but we didn't have enough headsets, so we had to pass them around. The music of Artie Shaw, Glenn Miller, and other big name bands brought back so many memories.

We viewed the Coral Sea and the Great Reef at a comfortable 10,000 feet. It was so good to wear our A-2 jackets and our garrison hats with a 50 mission crush. Our anticipation was intense. We felt like we were getting some kind of reprieve from doom's day. We were on a leave from the humid heat, the mosquitos, the flies, K-rations, and killing for a whole week in a world that some of us had almost come to believe didn't exist. We were going to indulge in fresh milk and ice cream, fresh eggs, steak, and all we want for a whole week. Also, there will be the sights of the big city, and we'll have our pick of some of the most glamourous girls in the world.

We circle into Townsville for gas. What a change. Townsville is bustling with G.I.'s and American war materiel. Why all these troops so far away from the war? It is said it takes as many as seven men behind the lines to keep one man in combat. From what I see here it must be more like 100 men behind the lines. How can a wasteful fouled-up military like ours win any war? I say it is possible only because we are less fouled-up than the enemy.

With our tanks full of petrol and our stomachs full of Aussie mutton, we thunder off the runway and point south for Sydney. Our flight speed is 300 mph, but this land is endless. It has been said that Australia is an island, but it is as big as our 48 states. Australia holds out for us farther and farther. We are anxious to get there, and the miles and long hours add to our anxiety. There is nothing to see but blue sky and nothing to do but listen to the steady drone of our big Wright Cyclone engines. High altitude flying loses the interest of watching the scenery flash by.

Again we nose down for fuel. This time at my old base at Amberly Field, and again plenty of American hustle and bustle. It seems there are more than half the Air Corps here. It takes us a half hour to find parking so we can gas up. There are so many people we have to sweat a half block chow line. Now we will not make it to Sydney until after dark. But we finally get our gas and chow and again head toward the great metropolis.

At last we see the lights of Sydney. Two command cars are waiting to take us to where we want to go—down town. The city is loaded with troops and we thought we would have it to ourselves. Again, what are all these guys doing 2,000 miles from the war? I'll bet these guys will never get any closer to the war, and when they go home they'll tell how they were able to win the battle of Sydney.

Dulce Faye Ann Shirley. There she was in full bloom just waiting for me. She was the cutest girl I had ever seen. Every day was a day with Faye Ann. We went to breakfast, lunch, and dinner, then out on the town. A full week of the beach, picnicing, and the sights of a big city. Let this be heaven.

While Beecher and his friends were trying to drink the town dry, I was with Faye Ann. She caught the eye of everyone and I wanted not a thing more. Sydney was like any city in America, but for me I wouldn't have traded it for Shangri la.

Seven days can go by like a whirlwind. It was over before we got started, and soon it was time to go back. She stood there with wet eyes and AWOL was strong on my mind. What did young tender feelings mean when there was a war to be fought. I was over here to kill the little yellow men. It was goodbye forever.

Our take off was held up. Newcomb did not show. We tried to find him but he dropped out of sight. He was one of the heavy drinkers, so anything could have happened to him. When he was saturated in alcohol he was nothing but a lot of trouble. Anything could have happened to that guy. We had to leave him.

Three months later he showed up back at the Grim Reaper Squadron. Why had he deserted? Well, he told us he was fed up with life in New Guinea. His money gave out and he decided to come back to face his court martial . He could have been before the firing squad, but all he got was denial of his next combat leave. He was the fightingest kid in the squadron. Every time he got drunk he came back with his face like hamburger. Poor Newcomb, like so many others got his in a flaming crash in the jungle.

On the way back we had engine trouble. It was not serious. It held us up just right for an additional leave in Brisbane. One cylinder on number two engine showed excessive heat on the cylinder head. This was great for anybody who did not have a hangover. Some of us jumped on the train at Ipswich and went to Brisbane.

When we got there I could not find a girl I used to know, so we had a good meal and bummed a little around the town until train time. Then it was back to Ipswich on the little train with the screeching whistle. It was early in the morning and there were no rides to Amberly. There was no other way, so we hired a car with a charcoal burner and chugged up the hill.

In the half light of dawn we were on our way to Townsville. There we gassed up for the flight over the Coral Sea. We were a bunch of tired old men when we got back, but it was worth it. After a night of fighting the mosquitos and heat there was good news. Lock, stock, and barrel we were packing to move to Buna.

188

Buna was now our base on the Japanese side of the Owen Stanleys. Things were moving for us. We were much nearer all enemy bases, but also, it made us more vulnerable to their attacks. This was our second move toward Japan since we left Charters Towers. This was our signal to the Japs that they have been stopped, and they were stopped at the Owen Stanley Mountains.

Our precious airplanes were converted. Each plane had a plank floor in the bomb bay to haul a load of freight. With a full load of our gear we rolled down the runway at 14 Mile and lifted over the mountains just like a bombing mission. Down we powered over the trees to our first and exciting landing at Buna. The U.S. Infantry and Aussie Diggers had just taken the base and the Army Engineers and Seabees had laid down a new corrigated steel runway for us. The Diggers and Infantry moved on through the jungle, but the Seabees came running to greet us. They had been without enough rations, so we gave all we had in our airplanes.

There were still some Jap stragglers in the jungle who had made life miserable for them by sniping at them while they were working. It was hard to rout them out. Japs can live on anything so they didn't starve.

Now we could see first hand the results of our bombing and strafing. There were thousands of smashed and burned pieces of equipment lying around, mostly moved under the trees so we were not able to see it from the air. And worse, there were skeletons everywhere. Our ground troops, at that time had received orders to move on to Lae and had no time for burial. All these Japs had been killed by our bombing and strafing attacks and by hand to hand combat.

Our photos and observation had not shown us half the real destruction. It was an ugly sight at first hand, but it made us feel great to see the extent of the damage, and this would hasten the day when we would not have to engage in so gastly a business.

We unloaded our cargo under the trees to be sure the Japs would not see it from the air. It was then back to 14 Mile for another load. We made three trips hauling freight, then the C-47's hauled the heavier equipment. Our trucks, command cars, weapons carriers, and other big vehicles were driven to the dock at Port Moresby and loaded on a ship for the trip around the southeast tip of New Guinea to Buna.

Our first job was to camouflage our airplanes and tie them down. Our precious planes came first, because you can bet your sox the Japs were going to do everything in their power to destroy them again. Our second work order was to dig fox holes near our airplanes and near our tents. Our tents were pitched in an area away from our planes. We rigged our nets, had some K-rations, and hit the sack. We didn't even have showers or a mess hall yet.

The first night the Japs let us alone, and it was a good nights sleep. They probably did not know we had moved so soon. But they will know and they will bomb us worse than on the other side of the mountain. They'll strike us with low altitude fighters like we do, up to 100 at a time. We are in for a hot time, that we know, but from now on, they will get the worst of it.

We are getting stronger all the time. Now we have two more B-25's equipped with all the guns and 75 mm cannons. New, green crews are coming in from the States to man the new airplanes and replace those who get killed and those missing. With all this equipment, these guys can't imagine how it was when we had nothing to fight with.

The ground crews are busy getting ready for our next strike, and we are trying to get our new quarters livable. We live four people in each tent and have to cope with each other. Some of the guys are landscaping their yards using Jap skulls for rocks to make their "rock gardens". They line their walk ways on either side with skulls, and some are making crosses with old clothes for scarecrows.

It is evening and the heat has eased somewhat. I have wet my shirt to help cool off. Our drinkers in the squadron have made a slipshod bar out of a tent and have cooled some Aussie beer with $CO_2$ bottles. The mosquitos are up to their blood letting, but in spite of it I am fascinated by the giant bats that are winging their way south. They appear to be about twice as big as a gull, but no one has ever been up close to one, so we don't know their size. The sky is filled with them and every evening they fly south. Where they go we do not know. They must come back sometime and probably do this during the night. We don't know where they fly from or where they go.

There are still some diehard Japs out in the boondocks. They keep sniping at us and one of our men has been killed. We stay out of the jungle and off the beach. It is tempting to go swimming, but they could see us for miles anywhere on the beach. We've got to get them out of that jungle. We hope they will starve and come out for food, but Japs can live on almost nothing. There are plenty of birds for them to eat—and snakes. If they would come out for a bite to eat we would give them all they could eat and probably better food than their own. We would make prisoners of them and they would be much better off, but Japs don't surrender.

We are now in a position to attack them at all their bases in New Guinea and New Britain. We have the range to fly all the way to Hollandia, and we will, in time. Our strategy now is to attack them farther and farther until we reach our limit. They know now what we can do with our flying battleships. What they do not know is how far we can fly. Most every time we attack them we will surprise them, and in many missions we'll catch them with their airplanes lined up for us which means total destruction for all of them.

On August 17th, 1943, the Grim Reaper destroyed 36 Jap airplanes in 12 seconds at Wewak. That did not include fuel dumps, storage areas, ammo dumps, warehouses, or the many people who were working and parading at the airfield. We will sink every ship and barge that comes south to bring relief to their harassed troops. And we will destroy all of their bases completely. Some bases will be leveled so flat that our infantry won't even bother to stop there. It is clear now what General Kenney said in the beginning: "We must destroy them by air first."

The Japs hit us the night of the third day at Buna. They used their fighters and came at us at tree top level. They zipped down our runway and fanned out on either side. They came in groups of eight planes, each group taking turns in bombing and strafing attacks. But the destruction they did to us wasn't one tenth of the destruction we do to them. They wounded three men who could not get to their fox holes quick enough, and they damaged four of our planes. We were ready to go again in two days as good as new.

Now we are ready to fly our first mission out of Buna. Our first target is Nadzab, and on the way home we'll try to sneak up on Lae. The base at Nadzab is inland and not far from Lae. We will hit Nadzab from the northeast, then fly round about to Lae to try to catch them asleep. We will pounce on both bases so quickly their gunners won't know what happened until after.

Lae has been re-inforced recently and it is a mystery to us how they did it, because we sank all the ships and barges that have come south. They must have snuk in during the night with airplanes or barges. The base is stronger now, but not for long.

Proudly and full of confidence we take to the air and stay close to the trees. To try to sneak up on them we go the long way by way of the jungle. After making formation we drop even lower to make certain we avoid their radar. Then a jolt shakes our airplane. We hit the top of a tree. This is not very unusual, as many times we hit the tops of trees. The B-25 is a sturdy unit and it takes quite a jolt to bring it down. After each flight the ground crews inspect the airplanes for damage from trees. The wood pulp and leaves sometimes mats between the cylinder baffles and must be removed. And the cowling and leading edges has to be repaired or replaced. Our engines are an asset because they are air cooled and are not dependent on water like the Allison and Rolls Royce engines. We don't have radiators to get fouled up.

"Pilot to crew, check your guns."

Radio is out here but the other pilots see the Widowmaker's tracers and follow suit. Every machine gun and cannon explodes into action to fill the jungle with hot lead and steel. Every branch of foliage is cut down before us.

In a few minutes the Grim Reaper Squadron is on the other side of Nadzab so we gradually turn to the right and approach it from the far side. We are loaded with para frags and enough ammo to cut down everything on their base.

Without any signal all airplanes spread to a distance of 200 feet and all abreast. Some pilots hit their gun buttons for effect, then all turrets and forward firing guns and cannons simultaneously open fire on the near side of their base and saturate it with steel jackets, incendiaries, soft nose, tracers, and explosive cannon projectiles. As the frag bombs begin leaving their shackles every gun we have is wide open and cutting down everything above ground. These frag bombs are mean. They obliterate everything above ground to nothing. They pop in their chutes to slow their fall so we can get far enough ahead to be fairly safe. As I turn on the tail gun and camera I see Japs running in a clearing and I swing the muzzles of my guns on them and hose them down. For the time it takes to zip over their base, about 12 seconds, all our guns are wide open which causes tremendous heat in the barrels and they turn red and fill the airplane with the stench of hot steel. Also, the smoke from gun powder is stiffling. Our bullets and shells resemble a hailstorm as we rocket across the area trailing a bomb every 150 feet to cover all areas. I look behind to see bombs exploding and the whole airbase on fire.

It is finished so fast their gunners do not have time to get a bead on us. Then we do a bank and head for Lae which is only a short distance away. We hope to be over Lae before their gunners get the word. We are flying in formation about 200 feet abreast and our ship is in the center and will take the runway. It is straight ahead and a Zero is on the runway trying to take off. The Major hits his button and the Zero explodes throwing junk into the air. It is too late to avoid the flying junk so we fly right through it and come out splattered. One Zero gets off the ground and one of our B-25's takes after it and pulverizes it.

There were no visible Japs on the ground at Lae. They had been warned by Nadzab. We got a few holes in our skin at Lae, but none from Nadzab. It was five feet off the water in formation back to Buna and our new home.

# CHAPTER 16

## DEATH IN THE VIDIAZ STRAITS

The Jap base of Buna was our new home and there was much to do to make it habitable. It was a morbid place. The bones of the dead had been strewn all over the area. Hundreds more were rotting in the humid heat. They were the victims of our scorch earth attacks. The U.S. Infantry had left them, and they were mostly skeletons when we got there. Our people were disrespectful to them because they had sneaked up on us and stabbed us in the back in Hawaii, so they used the skeletons for landscaping. We used the skulls to make walkways to our tents and the mess hall.

The greatest respect was shown to our people missing and killed in action. Missing in action was not much different from getting killed. I never heard of anyone coming out of "missing in action". And we could not expect any mercy from the Japs if we fell victim to them.

A monument was built in the jungle in respect of our men who were killed and missing. Their names were inscribed on a bronze plaque. As the names increased, we added more plaques. The Grim Reaper Squadron averaged about 100% killed or missing every three months. This is to say that if 60 people flew combat for this time, about 60 would be killed or missing. A few of the original 60 would still be around because green replacements were coming in all the time from the States.

Our mess hall was surrounded by a screen to keep out the flies, and there was a crude bar in an old tent that sold booze when there was booze to be had. We dug a large hole for our latrine and elevated 50 gallon barrels in the trees for showers. Holes were punched in the barrels and they made a pretty good shower. Some guys bathed in a nearby stream that was a growing mass of algae. For our drinking water we hung lister bags in the trees. A little evaporation would help to cool it. We paid the local natives a few shillings to do the dirty work in the squadron and they never had so much wealth. Most of the natives could speak pidgin English, but it was not easy to understand them.

Reconnaissance has reported an enemy convoy of warships and freighters moving west near the north coast of New Britain. They are heading to the coast of New Guinea and probably came from the big base of Rabaul. This is a long way from Buna but with our drop tanks we can make it. Our job is to fly up there and sink them and we'll do just that. The 90th and 89th Squadrons will help us. The weather has held us up, but it is reported to be good tomorrow. We are ready for the mission with our bomb bays full of the big bombs and our ammo cans up to the brim with 50 caliber belts. The convoy consists of three destroyers and three troop carriers. We like those troop carriers, because they haul thousands of Japs and we can kill them all or put them swimming. They'll be armed to the teeth and we know they'll have a fighter escort, so our work now is cut out for us.

This would be our longest mission so far, and we were eager and ready. The ground crews were on the flight line doing last minute chores during the night when the red alert siren screamed. All our beautiful planes were out there making good targets for the Japs. They swarmed in on us at tree top level and zoomed over the dispersal to cover our runway and supply areas. Their guns blazed across our base while they dropped small bombs that split the air and our eardrums. Our ack-ack gunners could not throw much flak their way because they were so agile and quick. Their attack was after dark and our searchlight men could not get them in their beams so our ack-ack gunners were firing everywhere but where the Zeros were. They splattered us with their machine guns, cannons, and bombs, but failed to do much damage. They don't have a fraction of the destructive power in their Zeros as we have in our flying battleships. They killed two mechanics, wounded four, burned one airplane, and damaged three. I rushed out to my airplane to check it for damage and found not one hole.

After the raid we did not find it hard to sleep and morning came all too soon. At 0445 hours we had the usual chow of powdered eggs and powdered milk, then hightailed it out to the flight line. Our mechanics had been working all night on the damaged aircraft and had two of them repaired, so we were only shy two planes which didn't slow us up. The destroyed airplane will be cannibalized for parts. This will help to keep all the other planes flying.

The rain is still coming down in a light sprinkle, but it isn't going to stop us. The earth is muddy and slippery on the taxiway as we all maneuver to the end of the runway and one by one all pull onto the steel mat. Then the Widowmaker blasts down the runway making enough noise to wake the dead Japs. There are no mountains to climb now and this will help us greatly in reaching our target. Our formation is made out over the Solomon Sea as each plane comes alongside the Widowmaker. Magnetic north is our course which will put us several miles east of Finschaven so they can't locate us by radar. Visibility is not good, but near the water we can see better.

"Connley to crew, check your guns."

Water spouts erupt as we smash our deadly fire power into the sea. All goes well so I tune my liaison receiver to Townsville and call the crew on interphone to let them know we have Bing Crosby on liaison.

As the crow flies it is about 250 miles from Buna to where the convoy should be, and it will take us the most part of an hour to get there. We may not find them so easy, as the sea is big and we have poor visibility. But we have plenty of gas and can afford to spend a little time in search.

After about 45 minutes we sight three enemy barges, and the Major decides to swing back and give each one a bomb. Evidently they are trying to sneak through under the cover of the rain to bring much needed supplies to their troops. The convoy is trying to do the same thing.

We break formation and rise to dive on them. At full throttle the Widowmaker attacks one of the barges. The driver of the barge tries a zig-zag, but they can't get away from us. They are doomed. All our guns concentrate on it as our bomb bay doors open and out goes a 500 pounder to skip and smash into the barge. Our firepower turns the barge into a smoke cloud and the 500 pounder penetrates the side of the vessel to explode inside. The barge blows into ten thousand pieces. There was nothing left but debris, foam, and parts of bodies.

Four other planes make runs on the rest of the vessels and they all go down like rocks.

We make formation again. The rain now eases off and visibility gets better and I am worried about the tank.

"Radio to pilot, how much gas in the tank?"

"Pilot to radio, just about empty."

I strap myself to a bulkhead. Then the Major calls me to let it go. This time I am lucky. I pull the lever and down it goes. It tumbles in the air, hits the water, bounces, and spins again and again far behind us.

This is the first time our tank went without a problem. But now we have other troubles. The one way check valve at the connector line for the drop tank is leaking gasoline into the airplane. I called the Major and told him that when I fire my guns it could cause a spark and blow up the whole airplane. So I grab my faithful little pry bar and tap the valve to try to jar it into its seat. This is risky business, and if I make a spark all of us could be blown as high as the barge we just destroyed.

"Radio to pilot, I can't get the valve leak stopped. But if you open all your windows and vents to let the air rush through the airplane, it will come through the tunnel and out the big tank hole. That should prevent any explosion."

"Pilot to radio. Roger."

With the wind blowing through our plane to carry off the fumes, we decide to chance our luck and continue on our mission. The 90th and 89th squadrons are flying with us. They are up ahead of us about a half mile. When we get to the target area we'll separate to search for the ships. The first to find them will attack once, then call the rest to give the location. I hope we will be the first to find them. We have a good chance to surprise them, and the squadron making the first pass will have the best chance. Surprise is our best weapon.

Now we are in the Vidiaz Straits west of Cape Gloucester. The convoy should be near us. Our plan is for each squadron to separate and spread out about ten miles apart to search. We all switch to command and listen for any word. In about twenty minutes smoke appears on the horizon and voices come over the command radio. The 89th with their A-20 Havocs have found the convoy and are already attacking.

We immediately change course and head toward the smoke like vultures sensing death. Now we can use radio. They know we are here.

"Connley to flight. We'll go straight in."

Now we bear down on 'em with every inch of manifold pressure we have while a battle is in progress with the A-20's and the Zeros. This is great, the A-20's will keep the Zeros away during our attack. Also their flak gunners, must be concentrating on the A-20's because we can see a sky full of black puffs.

Three ships are smoking so three have been hit. The Major picks a destroyer that is not smoking and here we go. In evasive action down we go. Our guns explode and our airplane is in fantail to hose down the deck as the first of our 500 pounders leaves the bomb bay and skips off the water. The momentum bounces it high in the air, then it lags behind to skip into the hull of the destroyer.

We bank to the right which gives me a wide open shot at the deck at point blank range. In one long blast I pour bullets into the men on the deck. As the superstructure flashes by Nelson swings his muzzles onto the ship as I turn on the tail gun and camera to catch all action below.

Some of the Zeros then pounce on us, but we dive to the water to force them to pull out of their dives. Their bullets smash into our tail with terrific impact which can be heard above our machine guns and cannon. They flash by so fast I can't get them in my sights.

We jockey into position for another run. In the meantime

the other B-25's and A-20's continue to make their bombing and strafing runs. The sky is full of A-20's, B-25's, Zeros, flak, and tracers. All the ships are smoking now, and dead in the water. One is cut in two. Two more are very heavy in the water which means their damage is taking on water very fast. The Major points our airplane at a freighter wide open. We are in the midst of black puffs of flak and it blurs our vision. Our plane is shaking from the recoil and stress caused by all our firepower and the boom boom of the cannon. Like a bunch of cornered rats those Japs on that ship are putting up a desperate fight now for the right to breath a little longer. The deck of the ship is strewn with their dead and the dying, and some are running to try to escape our hail of death.

Our bomb smashes into them amidships and a geyser of water covers the ship as it rolls on its side and the men fall into the sea. As we zoom away Nelson and I keep raking the deck as the ship rolls back. Then a mountain of water floods through the room size hole we just put in the hull below the water line.

The Zeros dive on us and two fail to pull out quick enough and crash in the sea. Two of their Zeros are chasing an A-20 and another A-20 is chasing a Zero. One of our B-25's is low and smoking. There will be some Americans down there in the water with the Japs.

I switch to command and everyone is talking at once, as we circle wide like a bunch of panthers eyeing our prey. Now it is up to the Major to decide if they will sink as is, or do they need some more. Each ship has taken three bombs which is plenty. All ships are on fire. A destroyer is cut in two. Three are very heavy in the water. One now has rolled on its side. We can't linger too long and have enough fuel to get home. Sometimes it takes hours to sink a ship, even though it has huge holes in it. The survivors can seal off compartments.

The Major decides to strike once more, but only on the three ships highest in the water.

"Connley to Grim Reaper, we'll make a run on the highest ships and head for home."

This one shouldn't be so bad because most of their gunners are killed or wounded, but we are not free of their Zeros yet.

The fear never leaves us. We know what they will do to us if we get shot down. As yet there is no provision for rescue. None of our people who have been shot down have ever been heard of again which proves how hostile the ocean and the jungle is. We can expect no mercy from the Japanese. We know they will torture and kill us.

Major Connley selects one of the warships that appears to be less damaged and we brace up for another attack. As we make our bomb run the Zeros dive on us again, but that does not slow us up. The other B-25's and A-20's are chasing the Zeros and their pilots know now that if any of them get in our sights they are doomed. Now they try to stay out of our range.

As we accelerate and vibrate toward the destroyer while they are firing at us with some of their guns, we can see big fire balls on their deck as we barrel in on them. We never know how close they come to us because their big cannons do not have timed explosives like their ack-ack guns. Near misses don't count. They've got to hit us, and when they do it will be over before we know what has happened.

We rake their deck as our bomb skips to the hull. There is a B-25 on either side of us this time to help give us protection. We bank to the right to miss the superstructure and Nelson and I keep spraying the deck and the terrified men on the ship.

The fantastic power of our bomb next to the hull and under the water breaks the ship in two. It had been hit twice before, and our bomb cut it in two. The bow and stern point toward the sky. The Japs slide and fall into the water and we make formation and head for home.

As we point for our base we look back to see unbelievable destruction. The ships are all on their way to the bottom and the Japs who are still alive are forced to the water without a lifeboat in sight.

The B-24's came in and finished the job, but when they got there all ships had sunk except one. It was helpless and dead in the water, so it was easy prey.

I coded a message and tapped it out:

"Grim Reaper to (call sign Buna)  All ships sunk or sinking.  Also, we sank three barges and lost an airplane."

Call sign/time-date

While we were high tailing it for home it gave me a chance to check our damage.  So I crawled past my armor plate to the tail section. The cables and pulleys looked o.k. They were the most important.  The auto gyro had been hit, but that operated the auto pilot, and we didn't have to have it.  I called the Major and told him about the damage, then tuned to our music and lay over the gaping hole in the wind to watch and be cool.

Usually on the way back to base we hunt barges or attack one or more enemy bases, but we used up all our bombs and most of our ammo, and we didn't have a lot of gas left, so it was back to Buna as the crow flies. When we got back in formation I counted the planes, and saw our outfit had lost one. We learned later that the other outfits lost a B-25 and an A-20.

On landing we checked our airplanes, then lit out for the briefing tent. The Major congratulated us on a job well done, and we tallied up the Zeros shot down. But we were not much concerned with credit for shooting down Zeros. An enemy airplane was a drop in the sea compared with a ship loaded with troops and supplies. The photos of the ships and barges showed total destruction. Debris and supplies were blown hundreds of feet into the air, and bodies were decapitated by the awesome power of our bombs and guns. The photos of the Jap ships showed huge holes below the water lines with water pouring in and the decks awash and strewn with a maze of equipment and dead and wounded Japs on the decks and in the water. We could see that both the freighters and destroyers were loaded with troops. Our damage was only minor. Four of our planes had enough damage to merit some delay for repairs, and one copilot had taken a bullet through his arm which would keep him out of combat a while.

Great news at our briefing. From now on we will have P-38 fighter escort on some of our missions. Everyone yelled and threw their hats to the top of the tent. This is what we have hoped for since our first combat mission. We can hardly believe the good news. These P-38's are the best pursuit planes in the world. The Jap Zeros will now meet their match. Our fears are lessened and our confidence soars to the sky.

Pappy Gunn is now supervising an assembly line, converting the B-25's in Australia, and they are coming to the 3rd Attack Group three at a time. With them we will destroy all Jap shipping and all their bases. Also, we have received news that North American Aviation is at last building them at their factories like they should have been built in the beginning.

# CHAPTER 17

## THE BISMARCK SEA BATTLE

Hot? Man was it hot! This steaming, green jungleland was not my kind of country. Those Japs could have it, but our orders come from Supreme Headquarters, and they are to drive them out. That is why we are here.

To a man, we hated it like hades. But if we were ever to get back home, that was what we had to do. We were here to fight these little yellow men and give our blood if necessary, to defend this land. General Kenney, who was commander of the 5th Air Force, informed all combat crews that if we could survive 50 missions of this type we could go home. A very few made it home.

After many months of waiting for airplanes we now had something to fight with—new modified B-25's, which we had developed into the best air battle wagon in the war. They were armed with 500 pound bombs with delayed action fuses, fourteen 50 caliber machine guns, and a 75 mm cannon. Our planes were also equipped to carry para frag bombs for killing enemy troops and destroying airdromes and ground installations. To man this equipment we had the best people that could be mustered in the 48 states. All were eager to get the job done and get back home, knowing full well that the odds were in favor of the enemy. And we had the experience. Most of the crews had flown many missions of this type. At this time I had flown 26 strafing, skip bombing, and para frag missions. So we knew what to expect.

This was the big one. This would be the turning point in

the war in the Southwest Pacific. Rumor had it that there was a big naval force of cruisers, destroyers, troop carriers, and freighters loaded with troops and their supplies, on its way to re-inforce the southern bases in New Guinea, in the name of the invincible one—Horohito. Our reconnaissance in recent flights proved this rumor to be true.

We faced this stark reality in Buna, New Guinea, where we were stationed at the time. In a frenzy of action, fear, and rising hate, we psyched ourselves into readiness.

This combat would be between air power and sea power. No United States warships would be involved because there were none in the area. The sole contenders would be the B-17's, the B-25 skip bombers, some B-26's, P-38's, P-47's, and a few Aussie Beaufighters. Much debate is about regarding which is superior by the military. Apparently the Japs put their faith in their sea power because only about 100 of the Zeros were involved. We were at last prepared, and we all had the long range droppable fuel tanks. They do not know yet that the B-25 can fly so far.

We had literally remade the B-25. We have adapted them to low level flying which made it possible to get so close to the target it was nearly impossible to miss. And at treetop and mast height their radar could not detect us. We had developed the new technique of using para frag bombs and skip bombing, and were daring enough to fly straight broadside "down the barrels of their big guns." We had a 75mm cannon that fired an explosive shell and this gun would penetrate the armor of a warship. We had 14 fifty caliber machine guns for defense and strafing. This literally made them a flying battleship, and the most formidable flying machine in any man's war.

We have the element of surprise going for us. They will

not know we are coming until we get there, if we are lucky. We hope they will be within firing distance before any of them see us.

Hitler had used the airplane to terrorize the world when he invaded Poland and Belgium. He called it lightning war. He used dive bombers and tanks. The dive bombers were equipped with screamers. This gave the illusion of invincible power. His psychology was to create the feeling of utter useless of resistance. We do not need this illusion. We are now prepared to totally destroy the enemy.

When the Japs struck Oahu they tried the same tactics. They would terrorize the stupid pleasure loving Americans into submission. But they made a mistake in not following up. They did not realize the extent of the damage they had done.

These American kids facing this stark challenge in the Southwest Pacific had never been blighted through generations of puppet soldier playing. They had a fifth column going on their side. When the chips were down they had something in reserve on which to draw. This was the American spirit still alive from the days of '76. It was this spirit that they had when they needed it most. They were not for glory or to intimidate. With this tough job on their hands they could use their ingenuity, imagination, skill, and spirit to get the job done.

Waiting in the shade of the wing of our aircraft with the rest of the crew was not a time for panic. Nervous as we were, this was a time to think and plan. What to do in case we went down and were still alive. What would you do if you were swimming in the water with the enemy all around you, and you knew they would shoot you in the water?

We decided first to play dead. Eventually the Japs would

be wiped out in New Guinea, and the best thing to do would be to try to swim ashore and live off the land until we slowly could work our way back to our lines. However, those I knew who went down, I never saw again.

The sweat that oozed from our bare backs in this unbearable heat did not all come from the heat. Hearts were beating fast and we were shaking with fear. But this fear became an asset. We were tremendously conscious of each other. Every man depended on each other. If each man did his job and the airplane did not fail we would come through. We all knew we were afraid, but each of us knew the other had the guts to go out and face whatever there was.

At such a time, a man's mind can cover many years in minutes. My humble home and family was a first thought. My father who had passed away and my mother praying for the safe return of a "little boy". My carefree days down by old Bear River, and the long string of bass I caught and cleaned. My brothers and sisters complimenting me on my skill and luck, and the smell of them frying on mother's old wood burning cook stove.

The backache and long hours on the farm and in the sugar beet fields where my only tool was a beet thinning hoe. How I chopped my way to a realization of dreams to earn enough money for a big Harley Davidson bike so we, my cousin and I, could tour the country, the same country we are now fighting for.

We saw the Congress in action where the law was made that put me here. Washington, the city way back there that is the nerve center of this land of America, the object of so much of our griping. But now we are all ready to give our all for the land we all knew we loved.

"Report for another briefing."

We jumped at those words and ran to where we held our briefing. This is it. We are ready and finished with waiting. My reveries vanished and I was back to the stern realities of this life and death struggle.

We knew what to expect. We had done it many times before but never so big. But we needed a briefing to bolster our confidence. We were, of course, to stay in formation and fly as near as possible to the water, attack the ships in evasive action at maximum speed, level off at mast height, drop our bomb on the water, all the way raking the ship with our machine guns and cannon, bank off while the upper gunner and radio gunner continue to strafe them, turn on the camera and tail gun, and re-position ourselves to do it all over again.

We were told at the last briefing that there are about 25 ships in the convoy and they formed in one group heading south toward the New Guinea coast and the Vidiaz Straits. The word is go, and we scramble to our airplanes. The hot breath of the inside of the airplane is unbearable. It was just like climbing into a bake oven. We wear nothing but a pair of shorts, Aussie flying boots, a shoulder holster filled with a loaded 45 automatic, a knife, and a Mae West in case we have to swim.

Up we go over the tree tops and down next to the waves heading magnetic north. We make formation, check our equipment again, and open a vent for a little air.

The sea is flat which is good. Luck or providence favors us with perfect weather.

Because America had not been prepared for a war with the Japs, they had been successful all over the Pacific to gain new territory. But at last, in this area of the war, we are ready now to hit them hard. Today the little Nips will see if the soft Americans really can fight.

"Pilot to crew, check your guns."

The gunners fire short bursts into the flat water at anything that may be floating. To hit a stationary target we have to fire behind it.

We are two hours out of Buna now and the big auxiliary gas tank is empty. It has got to be dropped or we'll have to turn back. I secure myself, pull the lever, and the tank goes out like a rocket. Now I have some air to breath.

According to plan, the B-17's are to bomb them seconds before we attack them from mast height. We hope the high altitude bombing is a shock to them and they won't see us coming.

After a few more minutes smoke is visible on the horizon and we change course to point at the smoke. In a few more minutes the ships become visible and we see airplanes swarming over them like bees around a hive. We are getting closer now and can see water geysers in the area of the ships which means the heavies have dropped their bombs. The P-38's are here too, and they are beginning to fight with the enemy fighters. Far above I can see the sun reflecting on the wings of Zekes about to try to dive on us. The P-38's chase them away. It is a beautiful sight to see those P-38's way up there.

Ships are everywhere. We have never seen so many ships. There are so many and so despersed it would be nearly impossible to count them all. The Major slams the throttles forward to the stops and we head for a big warship that turns out to be a cruiser. Our airplane rattles and creaks in torture of flying at a speed it was not designed for. A short burst of all forward firing maching guns is a jolt to our airplane, then all guns including the cannon smashes everything we have into an already damaged Jap warship. The ship is now alive with white flashes which are guns firing at us, and black flak bursts begin to arc closer and closer. Then we hear the shrapnel splatter on our airplane. Connley now flips the bomb release switch while all our machine guns and cannon rake the deck of the big warship and we bank to miss the superstructure and gain altitude while Nelson and I continue raking the deck to allow us to get away. I turn on the tail gun and camera which will prove to our generals what we did.

Then two Zekes got on our tail.

"Upper gunner, get those Zeros."

We fire on them but there is no smoke, then the beautiful P-38's chase them away.

Our bomb skips to the hull, sinks below the surface and explodes with devastating power. We gain altitude slightly for our second attack on the same ship. This time we come at the ship on the other side in hopes we can cut it in two. As the sea and the ship rise to meet us, we see the "Widowmaker" next to us giving us support. She is being flown by another crew this trip and every crew member is a friend. We attack the ship in the same way, filling the deck with everything we have as we drop our second bomb. The gunners on the cruiser are firing their big guns in the water in front of us and the "Widowmaker" crashes into one of the water spouts. It was just like crashing into a mountain, and the "Widowmaker", at full speed went down right beside the cruiser. Our pictures showed she broke in two, and those guys, right under the Jap gunners never had a chance. We, of course, never heard from them.

The Japs learned it was easier to knock us down by

throwing up a water spout in our flight path that to hit us directly.

Our bomb, and the "Widowmaker's" bomb found their target and nearly cut the cruiser in half. We went after other ships and the cruiser sank during the battle.

Our next target is a freighter and we attack it without mercy. When we bank away from it, the deck is alive with Japs, and Nelson and myself have a field day hosing down the hundreds of Japs on the deck.

Black flak puffs fill the sky, and I see a B-26 afire and crashing into the sea. Our P-38's are high above chasing Zeros. Thank God for those P-38's. So far they have kept those Jap fighters away from us. It isn't like the old days when we had no fighter escort.

Through my windows I can see Jap ships in every direction. Some are sinking and all are smoking. The sky is filled with ack-ack, airplanes, and tracers. The command radio is a mess of garbled American voices all screaming at the same time and none can be understood. A few words come through:

"Get him off my tail."

"We are on fire and going down."

"We're going home. Our co-pilot is dead."

A destroyer is ahead of us so there's our next target. It has already been hit with one skip bomb so we give it another one amidships on the other side and cut it in two parts. Now we see another troopship and bear down on it. This is easy prey. The troopships have plenty of guns, but they are not the big cannons. When we begin to rake it with our guns, a flak junk cut a big hole in the side of our fuselage. We keep on flying without even easing off. There is one bomb left so we attack another troopship that is

214

already heavy in the water and starting to list. Some of the Japs aboard are leaping into the water as we dive on them in an attack that would have sunk them had they not already been sinking.

Our bomb bay is empty so we attack three more ships with our guns then check our fuel. Our gas is almost half gone and it's time to head for home.

As we leave the area we look back to sight a view hard to believe. All the ships are on fire and sinking. It appears the whole ocean is full of burning and sinking ships.

I get on the liaison transmitter and code a message to 3rd Attack Group Headquarters:

"Mission accomplished. About 24 ships. All burning or sinking. Two planes lost in Grim Reaper. Heading home."

Call sign/time-date.

We are going to make it. We've been hit but we are going to make it. Upon landing at Buna we bail out, pat the ground, grab the film as we make a quick check of our plane, and head for the briefing tent. Some of the crews are already there. Everyone is talking at once:

"Did you see those water spouts?"

"Did I see them? Widowmaker hit one."

"Boy, I never saw so many ships."

Coherency was lost in that briefing tent. Excitement had taken over but in time each of us made a personal report as to what happened, and the film was developed to prove it.

It's going to be hard to sleep after all this, but we are slated to go back and do it all over again at the crack of dawn.

We are up at 0400 hours, have breakfast by 0430, and are out to our planes at 0515. The ground crews worked all night repairing damage, loading bombs, cleaning guns,

215

loading ammo, and refueling. We are on our way back to the Bismarck Sea Battle at 0530 hours.

This time we have a problem. The big gas tank won't drop.

"Radio to pilot, the tank is jammed."

I crawl to the top of the tank and try to get my pry bar between the tank and a rail. It won't budge. I pull the lever again while prying, and it still won't go.

"Pilot to radio, we're getting close to the ships, you've got to get rid of it."

I give one more big heave and it goes. I almost went with it. The suction would have pulled me through had I not been tied in.

Most of the ships are in the same area, but some are sunk. All the rest are burning. Without hesitation we begin to attack the ones that are the highest in the water and listing the least. Resistance is less today because we have really hurt them. Those who were in the water when we left yesterday have crawled aboard the already overloaded ships that are still afloat, and hundreds have been killed. There are fewer Jap airplanes also, but the P-38's are up there to keep them away from us again.

We skip four 500 pounders into four troopships and two into destroyers and they all explode with deadly accuracy. Then we fly across the convoy strafing every ship that comes in our flight path. More are sinking now and two are cut in two. The Japs are jumping into the water and trying to grab on to anything in the water that is floating. As the ships go under thousands upon thousands take to the water, and then voices scream over the command set:

"Kill them, kill them all! Shoot them here like they do us. Don't let them escape to swim ashore."

"Think of Pearl Harbor."

"Shoot them in the water."

We attack another troopship loaded with thousands of troops as they are jumping over the side. Clawing men are clinging to floating debris and each other. It is this debris that offers salvation to the swimming people in the water. A few lifeboats are floating in the water but they are overloaded and thousands are trying to get to or hang on to the few lifeboats.

Then some of our airplanes begin to strafe them in the water and others follow suit.

"It's better to kill them here than have to rout them out of the jungle with the loss of many of our infantry and the Aussies."

They were trying to swim ashore which looked to be about three miles and we made several strafing passes on them in the water. We kept machine gunning them in the water until we were able to see no more movement and the sea turned red. The Bismarck Sea ran red with blood.

We headed for home with a sick feeling. The next day we came back to see six of the battered ships still there but half sunken. We polished them off and went home.

Our total losses were about ten planes and their crews. Their losses were between 22 and 25 ships with all cargo, tens of thousands of men, and about 60 fighters. As a rule they carry about 4,000 men on their transports, and about 1,500 on their warships. Using these figures about 80,000 men were in the water, and very few of them could have escaped.

We could not have done it had they not done it to us first. We were brainwashed by our superiors to believe they were vermin that had to be exterminated.

Our orders were to destroy every vestige of the task force

that had been sent against us. We found it too easy. Our bullets found easy marks. Their blood now mingled with the waters of the sea and the Bismarck Sea ran red. But the American cause had not remained unsullied. If anything, American blood might have made the sea a shade more red.

The Japs were serving a lost couse, and the sadness of it was that it was utter uselessness. The scene of blood and death that will always be with us. Can the world make amends for what happened that day? Has time healed the memories of those who live today to the hopes and fears of those who were buried in the waters of the Bismarck Sea? Lest we forget.

# CHAPTER 18

## MADANG, SAIDOR, THE P-38'S

After the big three day battle of the Bismarck Sea our reward was congratulations from our Commander, General Kenney, on the great victory over the enemy. General MacArthur sent a message of congratulations also and told us we would receive many medals. We thought we would have some rest and respite now, but no, we were to strike Madang the next day when they least expected it.

The Grim Reaper Squadron lost two precious planes in the Bismarck Sea Battle, but we have enough left to pulverize their base at Madang. And we'll hit other bases on the way home. This will be the first time our flying battleships will give Madang a taste of our kind of war.

I am flying with Lt. Norwood on this one so my luck is still holding, and we are in a new plane. The Widowmaker is no more. She went down in the big battle with my armor plate. So while the ground crews are getting the planes ready, I install my new armor aft of my guns.

We will have some green crews, new from the States on this mission. These guys don't know how lucky they are. They are anxious to go, and scared, and they think it was always like this with all these beautiful airplanes. Now we have well equipped airplanes, fighter escort, as well as enough planes to help each other.

At the crack of dawn we thunder down Buna strip one at a time and clip the tree tops. Our course will be jungle all the way to their airdrome at tree top level. We'll avoid Jap bases all the way and stay as low as possible so the little monkeys won't know we are coming. It is a usual plan to try to catch their planes all parked on the ground and easy to destroy. Our course is half way between Wau and Salamaua to avoid any spotters or radar. This will put us west of Nadzab.

"Pilot to crew, check your guns."

Our airplane jolts from the recoil of so many machine guns and the cannon. I arc all my rounds over the trees, but the upper gunner is silent and does not fire. His name is Caspar and he is fresh from the States.

"Radio to upper gunner."

No answer, so I am forced to poke him. Then I notice that his interphone switch is on command, so I turn it to interphone and call again.

"Radio to Caspar. Over."

"Caspar to radio. Over."

"You didn't fire."

"O.K., fire over the trees, but not until you are sure you won't hit our planes."

He finally fires then crawls down out of his turret. I ask him if he has ever had any experience with this type of turret. He says he fired one in school like it. I teach him a few basics and check him out on the intercom system, and tell him how to fire with all the fixed guns.

"Radio to crew. If you want to forget your troubles switch to liaison. There's music from home. It's a long way to Madang."

At briefing we were told to spread our formation just before target to about 200 feet so we can cover every foot of their base. At the same time we will rake the area with 195 machine guns and our cannons. These guns will pour 137,500 rounds a minute on them—not counting our cannons. However, we'll be over their base only about 15 seconds. But those 15 seconds, if our guns are firing all the time, will be time enough to destroy everything above ground.

We have a P-38 escort on this mission. They are so high we can't see them but we know they are there. They will rendezvous with us above the target. They need to be way up there to have an advantage over the enemy fighters. There is a little kid up there named Richard Bong. He is on his way today to become the ace of aces. He will eventually shoot down 40 Zeros with his P-38 and he will have helped us many times by chasing the Zeros away from us and shooting them down. We all would like to shake that kid's hand, and a bunch of other kids who shot down many Zeros. But none of us ever did. He flew his missions then lost his life in an airplane crash in Los Angeles.

We are now deep in the rain forest and about half way between Bena Bena and Nadzab which is in the Markham Valley. This valley has a lot of open spaces and that is good to see in this eternal jungle. This valley is where a lot of the natives live. As it flashes by under our flight it is a temptation to fire on the natives. It is a fact that they are helping the Japs. But they probably know nothing about the war and what the Japs did.

There is a river down there that looks like it would be full of fish. If it were nearer our base we might have fish for a change instead of that dried and powered food.

"Radio to pilot, how about the drop tank?"

"It's ready to drop."

It is me against the tank, and I look personally at it like a contest. I never fail to get rid of it, but sometimes it is a battle. I need a witness to my fight with the tank so I poke Caspar to let him know what I'm doing and to get him acquainted with one of our problems. I strap myself in as usual and pull the lever. Nothing happens. So I get leverage with my pry bar and it still doesn't go.

"Drop the tank," Norwood says.

"It won't go."

Caspar gets a good hold with both hands then kicks with his feet as I pry and pull that stubborn lever. Reluctantly it leaves the plane and tumbles into the trees. There is no bouncing as there always is on the water. When our new B-25's come from the States we hope they will have invented a system that will release the empty tank without risking life and limb to do it, and put a question mark on whether or not we can complete our mission.

We watch for other tanks to drop. Some of them fall, but then, in a few minutes, one airplane turns 180 degrees and heads toward our base. We all know they can not get rid of their tank.

We still have plenty of firepower left to do the job and a lot more than some of us are used to. And a real comfort to us are those wonderful P-38's way up there above us. The P-38 is superior to the Jap Zero and we can't wait to show them. They are manned here by the best trained pilots in the Air Corps. These young kids are eager to do their stuff and prove to the world what they can do. They will make a name for themselves and many will be war heroes. Many P-38 pilots shot down close to 40 Zeros before they went home.

Suddenly we change our course to west and north to avoid a corner of the Bismarck Sea. After a few minutes we change again to northeast on a direct line to Madang.

"Pilot to crew, we'll be there in ten minutes. Everybody ready?"

"Roger."

We hug the trees and pray they don't know we are coming. Surprise leaves them helpless on the ground and gives us a tremendous advantage.

"Pilot to Caspar, fire with me unless we are attacked by Zeros."

The throttles go forward and we feel the airplane surge ahead. There it is straight in front of us. It looks just like all the rest of their bases. Our fixed guns and cannon give a burst for effect. Then all planes open their fixed guns, upper turrets, and cannons. Concussion and recoil shakes and trembles our plane violently as we cut down everything in front of us where our incendiaries act as a far out flame thrower. Our bomb bays drop open and the para frag bombs pop into their chutes. I point my guns down and lay on the triggers. My gun barrels get hot as I rake the field. I see a group of Japs running and know we have snuk up on them. Their airplanes are on the ground. Our bombs begin to explode throwing their metal in every direction and searing the ground. I see more Japs running and swing my guns on them. We are dropping them like tenpins. More Japs are trying to escape our deadly fire on the other side. They don't believe what we are doing to them. They have never been slaughtered in this way before. Their planes and equipment are exploding and burning in front and behind us as we zoom over their once strong air base. Our plane now is full of smoke, the barrels are in a red glow, and I'm buried in empty casings. We continue to rake their field and suddenly it is behind us. Our backward view shows their installation a huge cloud of black smoke.

As we zip away out over the Bismarck their gunners finally begin firing at us, but it is too late. We are out of their range. When the ground fire ceases we look for Zeros. Where are our P-38's? Then I see them way up there ready to pounce on any enemy fighter that has enough guts to attack us.

As we head for home five Zeros dive on us. They must have come from another base. Our gunners all fire on them creating a huge funnel in the sky. One Zero leaves a trail of smoke and turns away. The other four keep coming while a second one explodes. They spray us with several rounds but they are no match for us. Now the P-38's are dogfighting with them and each plane is leaving a vapor trail in the sky. The enemy fighter pilots are running scared of the P-38's, and the P-38's are knocking them out of the sky.

"Pilot to crew, everything o.k.?"

"Roger."

"Radio to pilot, we don't have a scratch in the waist or tail section."

"Pilot to crew, we are going to follow the Major and do what he does."

This means we are going to hunt barges down the coast or strafe other bases. We fly toward home along the beach looking for barges. Most of us know what a camouflaged barge looks like, but many new men in our flight don't know anything about barges. In a few minutes we see a light smoke rising from a clump of trees at the edge of the jungle. It's a barge. Those stupid Japs have a fire going. They are probably making tea.

We spread out and dive on the barge, one at a time with all guns blazing. The first volley sets it afire, and the second shatters it and sends debris flying into the air. Most planes are circling just watching the show. The third plane perforates it with holes and it begins to sink, so we head down the beach and do not use any more ammo on it. Most of the Japs are still alive. They jump into the water and swim ashore. We head for Saidor.

We guess what the Major has in mind and approach Saidor with apprehension. This will be no surprise attack. Madang has let them know we are coming, and they'll be ready for us. Our P-38's are still with us and they should be able to handle the Zeros, but they can do nothing to stop the ack-ack. This seems a mistake, to hit them at this time, as there is no chance to surprise them. They can give us plenty of trouble.

The Grim Reaper Squadron hugs the tops of the trees at full throttle for the attack. In a flash their runway looms ahead and our guns cut a path across their base. But there are no airplanes on the ground and there are no Japs running. All at once we are surrounded in the center of a sea of tracers and flak. I switch on the tail gun and camera, then open up on a source of their tracers. Then their bullets go crashing into our side. I jump in fear because they are giving us more than we bargained for. I hold down the triggers on my guns until they turn red hot as we zip over the far end of their runway. One of our B-25's is on fire. They clobbered us. They had moved all of their equipment off the base and were ready for our attack. This strike is a mistake. We should have let well enough alone.

The B-25 that was afire had to ditch. The crew talked to us on the command set until it hit the water. We could not help the poor guys and we had no air sea rescue yet. There will be some sad letters for the Major to write tonight.

The Major had planned to strafe one more enemy base on

the way back, but after the sad experience at Saidor, he decided against it. We left the coast and crossed the Solomon Sea as close to the water as possible on a straight line to Buna. Our mission was a fantastic and one hundred percent success but for the men on the lost airplane. After a victory buzz across Buna we quickly landed and went to the usual briefing for good news and bad. Our pictures showed the complete destruction of everything above ground at Madang. We destroyed 18 planes, fuel dumps, ammo dumps, much equipment, and at least 94 Japs were prone on the ground, either dead or wounded. One barge was destroyed with about 20 more Japs and a full load of equipment, and we shot down 8 Zeros and lost one plane.

Our target for today is enemy infantry at Lae. They are in the jungle, and of course, we can't see them. To find them we'll have to be on the ball and calculate perfectly. We will bomb and strafe a spot in the Markam Valley. Who ever heard of the Markam Valley? Nobody ever heard of it because somebody made one of the worst blunders of the war there, and it was covered up. We bombed our own troops. No one took the blame. It was the old story of pass the buck and cover up.

Our infantry and the Aussie Diggers were closing in on Lae, one of the strongest enemy bases. The Jap infantry filled the jungle in the Markam Valley northwest of Lae. It was a first attack on enemy infantry for us. At our briefing we were shown a map with shaded drawings indicating where our troops were and the area occupied by the Japs. Our plans were to fly at certain degrees for so many minutes, then change course to fly so many minutes in another direction. Then we were to strafe the jungle and drop our bombs. We were cautioned many times not to make a mistake, and we did not make a mistake. But a

226

terrible error was made by someone and we bombed and strafed our own men.

The sky was hazy which was not good, as we needed good visibility to find the landmarks. After we made formation, one plane hit the top of a tree, but we did not learn this until we returned. We made two passes on the target in perfect order and made no mistakes. There was no resistance and we did not have the P-38's with us. It was a milk run.

The green jungle became alive with our destruction. Those American kids from all places in the States were down there in the hot humid jungle, and we were killing them. There was absolutely no resistance or sign of anyone below. We made our bomb and strafing run over the jungle and turned around and did it again. Our guns became red hot and all our bombs were dropped, so we closed the bomb bay doors still skimming the trees, and went back to our base. It was the easiest mission we had ever flown. On the way back there was nothing to do except listen to our music and think about our leave to Australia.

As usual we gave Buna a victory buzz then broke off and made perfect landings. It was a normal and routine trip to our briefing to get the word that we had bombed and strafed men in our own army. Some radio operator had survived and called his commanding officer and told him of the blunder we had made.

We could not believe it. We have killed an estimated hundreds of our own men, and wounded many more than we killed. Everything about our mission became hush-hush. It is not in the history books. It is not in the novels and other stories about the Papaun Campaign of WW II that stopped the Japanese advance.

# CHAPTER 19

## THE GREAT BARGE HUNT

American kids fighting in the hot jungles of New Guinea needed rest. This task was something new to all of us. We not only had a formidable and wiley foe, but we had to conquer the terrain, which had defied the white population since it had been discovered. The impenetrable green hell of the jungle, the hot and humid climate, the fever it bred, the vermin and swarming insects, and the devaporized and highly processed food we had to eat could sap even the young and strong. But, as an incentive to spur us on, we were given a leave to Australia after about one fourth of our 50 missions. Three cities were selected. They were Sydney, where I had already been on my first leave, Cairns, and Mackay.

Our leave was called in military parlance, R&R for rest and relaxation. This was a misnomer. It might better have been called F & F for fun and frolic. Most of the kids, coming back from combat leave were so exhausted they looked forward to coming back to New Guinea to rest. But the offensive war was now being stepped up and there was little chance for a rest when we got back. This was what we wanted as we had only one goal, and that was to get it over with and get shipped back to the States.

The evening before our departure, while we were busy preparing for the big holiday, the Japs gave us a departing social call. Their greeting came via 100 Zero fighters. They hit us like a swarm of wasps in a big circle zipping

228

over our airfield again and again. They strafed and dropped their little bombs on us and in the nearby area. But they did not hit our tent area where most of us were. Our anti-aircraft gunners were not very effective. The Zeros darted like flies and were hard to hit. Only two of them were hit by our gunners and they got away from the Buna area. They fired a lot of ammo and dropped many bombs, but they did very little damage. They damaged four of our air-planes, but in a few days we had them repaired. Parts were cannibalized from bombed planes in the "boonies."

This raid did not stop us from going on leave. One air-plane was loaded with all the crews it would hold, and we climbed over the mountains heading for Australia. We were packed like sardines and our only comfort was in our parachutes which we used for pillows and seats, but our morale soared with the gradual climb over the mountains into the cool air. We cleared the peaks and pointed straight toward Mackay, which was close enough to make it on the gas we had. It wasn't long before we were dropping down to their little airfield.

Packed in the plane were some of my old buddies. There was Deckelman, Strom, Beecher, Kerstetter, Dickerson, Alford, Whitek, Stretch, and the list could go on. Most of these kids did not get back to the States, but this time out we had no thought but what we might find in Australia.

Deckelman was some kind of guy from Arkansas. We would kid him and ask him why he is not back home taking care of his grandchild. He was too old to be in the war, but he said he had enough left to kill Japs, and he did. He would clean his guns and turret like they were his own guns back in the Ozarks. Guns had been a big part of his life. The guns on our planes were something else and he took great pride in them. He was always reading and all he could get to read were old newspapers. All the learning he had acquired, he said, was a result of reading, and he had a good education. With Beecher it was his still and jungle juice. What he was looking forward to was some store bought liquor in Australia. Beecher is genius and even looks like Einstein. And Strom, my good friend Strom. The big handsome Swede from Minnesota. We had a contest to see which one of us would be first to fly 50 missions to qualify to go home. Whitek was a little eager kid from Wisconsin. He really had a struggle to get his 50 missions but he made it. Stretch. We couldn't understand how he could get in his turret. He was a giant. I never heard whether he made it or not, because he was a late comer and I was back in the States long before that big likeable guy could have made it. If he did it was a miracle because he was so big it was just about impossible for the Japs to miss him.

Mackay lies halfway between Townsville and Rockhampton on the east coast of Australia. It is a beautiful little city quaint as old England. It is nestled on a beautiful beach right next to the Great Barrier Reef, and has enough charm for the whole east coast. They grow cane just like on Oahu, and burn the stalks in the fields the same way. The people have not, so far, been spoiled by the Yanks with their money. The first thing we notice is that they haven't, so far, jacked up their prices.

The word spread that we were combat flyers from New Guinea and that was all the introduction we needed.

Most of the guys headed for the pubs only to find disappointment. They did not open 'til late in the afternoon and then for only three hours because of war stringencies. Kerstetter, Strom, and myself went looking for the best restaurant. We found it and the food was out of this world, or so we thought after all the powdered chow. We spent so much time in that place that the young waitress invited us into her home. She told us about a dance they were having in honor of us New Guinea vets, and you better believe we went for that. What place is better to meet the girls? After the food most of us went to a milk bar for ice cream. Mackay has one of the most beautiful beaches in this part of the world, and part of the Great Reef is visible, but there were many sharks out by the reef so we stayed close to shore. It reminded me of testing the B-25 and Pappy Gunn and the risks we had taken and how lucky I was.

Those Aussies were still wild about American cigarettes. If we had them we didn't need money. I had been saving my allotment and was loaded. They were cheap off brands but it made no difference to the Aussies.

The dance was great and all the girls in town came to meet the Yanks. We took our pick of the sheilas and went to the beach. The moon was full and the night was tropical so the memory still lingers.

It was a full week with beautiful sheilas, good food, swimming, basking in the sun, tennis, horseback riding, and boating. Some of the men were drunk the whole week, but no one got into any serious trouble. Beecher was so saturated the whole thing was like a foggy nightmare. He couldn't remember what had happened.

We have to get back to the war. The tempo is picking up. We are getting more planes and men and we'll hit them harder and harder until we drive them right out of the New Guinea and New Britain areas. Wewak is coming up which is one of their strongest bases. And Rabaul, which is their

Gibraltar of the Pacific. Lae will be taken soon and we will have to pulverize it so the ground troops can go in and slaughter them. Their shipping must be sunk, and we are slated to do that too.

Our trip back to Buna was routine but for the guys with hangovers. They used up all our oxygen, claiming it was good for a hangover. We did not have enough oxygen masks so they were passed around to each sick man.

When we arrived we got the glad news that Pappy Gunn had sent us three more modified airplanes and Major Connley and our crew got one of them so we named it Widowmaker II.

Before hitting the sack we listened to our old friend Tokyo Rose. She broadcasted from the Japanese Empire every night and informed us of the successes of the Japs in the Pacific. She gave us a lot of garbage on how the Imperial war machine was slaughtering the Americans in New Guinea and surrounding islands. We got a bang out of listening to her. We knew the truth and the truth was that we were killing the Japs at a ratio of about 50 to one, and we had the pictures to prove it.

On July 26th, 1943 we attacked Lae again with para frags and strafing. Other units also hit them that day and we dropped a total bomb load of 126 tons. Everything was on fire as we zoomed out to sea again. The P-38's were there with us dogfighting the Zeros. What a sight it was watching them chase the Zeros and knocking them down. They shot down 11 Zeros and did not lose any. We lost no airplanes either, but we got shot up a little by their ground fire.

Then we flew back to Buna and loaded again. As they were trying to clean up the mess from our first attack we hit them again. They were trying to put out the fires when we pounced on them, hosed them down, and shattered them with our vicious little para frags.

The Nips were determined to re-inforce Lae and hold it at any cost. They tried to get the supplies there by using motor driven barges. It was their thinking that they could hide them during the day, then make a run for it during the night.

On July 28, 1943 we went barge hunting up the coast of New Guinea and over to New Britain Island. The 90th Squadron sank two destroyers near Cape Gloucester the day before. We missed out on that, but we'll make up for it on this day. We checked out our guns over the Solomon Sea and kept going to the west end of New Britain Island. After rounding the tip of the big island we turned east and followed the north shoreline. Then we ran into potshot shooting. The sea was filled with barges, motor launches, and torpedo boats. Boy, oh boy, this was for us. Each of us had a full load of 500 pounders, and all the ammo we could hold.

This big Jap flotilla of barges was heading west toward the Vidiaz Straits and we were heading east. In order to attack them broadside we swung north, separated, and dove on them full throttle. Each airplane picked a vessel in the flight path and riddled it with machine guns and cannon, then smashed a 500 pounder into it. We did this over and over until our bombs were gone, then we continued with our guns and cannons. They peppered us with small arms, but we all kept flying. They had to hit us in a very vital spot to bring us down with machine guns and rifles. After a while our guns nearly burned up and we ran out of ammo, so we stayed in the area and watched them sink and explode, and watched all the men jump in the water and try to swim for it. All the vessels we attacked in the area were either sunk, sinking, or on fire. But there were more and we had no more ammo. We heard other barge hunts over the command set, so we headed back to Buna to re-load.

We were now vulnerable to attack with not a round of ammo left. If the Zeros attacked us, it would have been "in the drink." But the P-38's stayed on the ball and kept them busy.

This hunting barges was too good to be for real. We had to get back at them, but when we got back to Buna there were repairs to make and after re-loading there was not enough time left to get back that day. So we prepared to get at them early in the morning. The 89th and most of the 90th Squadrons went with us next time so we had three times the bomb load and fire power. The barge hunting was really good around New Britain because the Japs were getting desperate to re-inforce their southern bases.

All three squadrons arrived at a tank dropping area at 0700 hours. Two airplanes had much trouble with their tank and had to go back. But we still had plenty of airplanes to go hunting barges. Our rendezvous this time was over Arawe on the south coast of New Britain. From there we followed the beach west and around to the north side, then east to the same area where we found so many barges yesterday.

It seems a waste to drop a 500 pound block buster on a barge. The barges are big and heavy, but those bombs sometimes blow them to nothing. If the bomb penetrates inside the barge before exploding, it blows everything into little bits, including bodies.

We spotted two motor torpedo boats and dove on them.

We used two airplanes, each coming in at right angles, but those boats are fast so we dove on them at different directions simultaneously. Both boats exploded with fearsome force. They must have been loaded with torpedos 'cause they went off like bombs and bodies flew a hundred feet in the air.

Then we found six more motor driven barges and six airplanes attacked them. Three of them exploded and the bombs skipped over two, so two more planes skipped two more bombs, then all we could see was debris.

Now garbled American voices came over headsets. It was evident that someone was having a real shootout. The Major cut into the conversations and asked where they were. It took about ten minutes before we could get a clear answer because about ten people were yelling over the radio at the same time. They were sinking more barges about twelve miles east of Cape Gloucester along the north coast of New Britain. Someone said there were so many boats they couldn't count them all. We didn't have to be coaxed. Immediately we headed straight over the west end of the island as the crow flies. When we got there we found a squadron of B-25's sinking Jap barges like there was no tomorrow. The Bismarck Sea was full of barges. There were barges farther than we could see.

"Hello there," the Major called. "We are an eager bunch from the 3rd Attack Group. Can we help you guys sink these barges?"

"Help yourself, there's plenty for all."

In every direction there were barges smoking, sinking, and men in the water. There were Japs hanging on to floating debris, bodies in the water, and blood coloring the water.

We broke formation and each plane picked a victim. The Widowmaker chose a torpedo boat and pointed at it full throttle. When it was a good time to let loose our bomb she had turned, and pointed her bow at us. So we circled the boat a while to confuse the driver. When the stern was toward us we dropped in on her and let our bomb go. It was broadside when the bomb skipped into her. We swept the gunners with our awesome fire power, but they got in some licks too. They hit us with their machine guns hard enough to shake us up, and one of our wing tanks punctured. The devastating power of our bomb turned their torpedo boat into small pieces of junk.

Another of our bombs exploded inside another torpedo boat and threw bodies and chunks of the boat 200 feet into the air. Their motor torpedo boats, like ours, were built out of marine plywood, and when they blew up, they shattered in small pieces.

We continued east to find another barge that looked un-damaged. While strafing it, it blew up like a bomb, so we saved one bomb. It must have been loaded with ammo. The sky was full of airplanes, all out hunting barges and flying about in different directions. Each crew was selecting its target. We had never seen so many barges. The Japanese war lords must have been stupid to expose so many craft to us in the daylight. It was the same with their ships. They kept sending their ships to re-inforce and we kept sinking them. It seemed to us they gloried in unnecessary death for their Godlike Horohito.

After a half hour of constant attack on the barges, we ran out of ammo and bombs, so we had to head for our base. Our bearing was straight over the island, then out over the Solomon Sea for Buna. Our gas leak wasn't bad, but it kept our minds on it. There didn't seem to be danger of fire, but there was danger of running out of gas. However, we were given priority, so we cut straight into Buna and touched down on the much welcomed steel mat.

After the day's work and chow, we had a hot shower from our elevated barrels, then listened to Tokyo Rose. Our sirens screamed the warning and here came the angry Zeros seething with revenge. They came like a flash, burned up a lot of ammo, dropped their little bombs, scared us, but did very little damage. We wondered why they came at night. If they came in the daylight they may have been able to see our camouflaged revetments and airplanes.

The next morning it was barge hunting again. For two weeks we sank barges and we thought we had sunk all the barges they had. Then we added up our kill. We had helped sink 240 motor torpedo boats, motor driven barges, and launches. A report came that the P-38's had shot down about 29 Zeros during that time and lost none. One B-25 was lost and four damaged, and 2 of our P-38's were damaged. The great barge hunt ended so we went back to para frags.

The next morning we hit Lae hard to try to help our infantry. Our infantry and the Aussie Diggers were closing in on Lae and they needed all the help they could get.

There was a new fighter base at Marilinan, in the jungle southwest of Lae. We had P-39's out there, and the word was that they were not very good. But we took them. We took anything in preference to nothing. This new base at Marilinan was close enough to our base that they were able to escort us on some missions. To make this base less vulnerable to attack we were constructing a dummy base not too far away, in hopes the Japs would think it was a real base and waste their bombs on it. However, on August 14, a Jap reconnaissance plane spotted our P-39's there, and the next day about 15 Jap bombers in formation with 35 Zeros came to bomb the base. The P-39's were warned by radar and were up to meet them. In the fighting 3 P-39's were lost, but they shot down nearly all the bombers plus 3 Zeros. They gave a good account of themselves and we felt they were not so inferior after all.

The P-38's will rendezvous with us over Lae. We clear the trees at Buna and head for Lae via the jungle. We hope to sneak up on them as usual and slaughter them. Our big drop tank is not installed and the wind really feels good as it rushes through the airplane. Major Connley is driving our plane and Nelson is in the upper turret so we've got a good crew. We check our guns and cut the jungle like a giant scythe. All throttles are slammed forward, the plane surges, and begins to shake and rattle. But we are used to that now and know she can take it. Now all guns and cannons begin to rain death down on a battered enemy below. Our tracers, armor piercers, incendiaries, and soft nosed bullets cut through everything above ground as our bomb bay doors pop open to let out a continuous stream of the deadly little para frags. They are spaced 200 feet apart and they will scatter their jagged, cutting fragments in every direction. As our bombs begin exploding our guns begin to get hot, and everything behind us is laid flat as fire and smoke cover a burning field.

There are no airplanes on the ground. They are above us fighting our P-38's. If we can't have it that way, that's where we want them. We are their target, but now, they have to go through our P-38's to get to us.

My guns are hot but I continue raking the airfield below

until we sweep out over the water. Now water spouts begin to appear around us. The Jap gunners are hoping some of us will hit the spouts.

The airdrome behind us is a mass of smoke and fire. We escape unscratched except for a few holes in one B-25. Our fighters are making vapor trails high in the sky. One airplane is falling to the water. I can't tell if it is one of our planes.

The Grim Reaper Squadron stays in formation, heads for Buna, and lands. The ground crews work feverishly to reload and re-fuel our planes and we have a hasty snack. Within one hour we are in the air again and heading for Lae. It seems like the trucking business. We're hauling bombs and ammo to the Japs. This time when we pounce onto them they are out in the open putting out fires. They scatter and try to avoid our guns, but we hose them down and chew them up again with our frag bombs. Then we zip out to sea at ten feet off the water and back to our base.

## CHAPTER 20

## 36 ENEMY PLANES DESTROYED
## IN 12 SECONDS

August 17, 1943 was called by the Japanese "The Black Day of August 17". It was on this day we mounted the biggest air attack of the war on the Wewak area. And it was our longest flight so far of 1100 miles round trip. It was a total surprise and we clobbered them plenty. They did not know we could fly so far with the tremendous clout we carried.

The area around Wewak had four big runways with big bases around each one. The squadrons of the 5th Air Force were ordered to hit Borum, Dagua, and But. The Grim Reaper Squadron was a special outfit and had orders to hit Wewak. It was the first time for the B-25's to fly that far north. Our big drop tanks earned their keep on that day.

The whole day of August 16 was spent in preparation for the big attack. Our mission that day, as usual, was to kill Japs and annihilate everything above ground. This again was a sneak attack and the whole operation was based on whether or not they knew we were coming. The Major drove my airplane and Nelson again was our upper gunner. Our takeoff was at dawn and the weather forcast was good. This was another day the Jap war lords would have been better off without ancestors.

We took off with all the para frags and ammunition we could hold, and all our gas tanks were topped off to the brim. Everyone was more than eager to go.

"Connley to Grim Reaper, check your guns a short burst only."

Our course is over the trees all the long way. We don't want to be seen by anyone and it is safer over the trees. I tune to our radio station for music and it helps get our minds off what lies ahead. But this time I can't keep from a thought of going down 550 miles from our base. That would be a long walk through the jungle if one was to survive the crash, and could avoid the enemy and live off the land. So we put faith in our trusty airplane.

We are passing between Salamaua and Wau to avoid their radar so Nadzab will be close to us on our right. Then we come to the Markam Valley and follow the Markam River for a few miles to the Romu river. But it is straight all the way. There is no changing course.

The heavies will hit Borum, But, and Dagua from high altitude at the same time we hit our target. There is another group of B-25's equipped the same way we are that will hit the other bases. As far as we know, we are the only ones who will hit Wewak. It is estimated by reconnaissance that the Japs have over 200 airplanes in the Wewak area.

The Markam Valley is far behind us now, and the Sepic River is coming up ahead. It is about time to drop our tank.

"Radio to pilot, how much fuel in the tank?"

"It's empty, drop it."

I secure myself and pull the lever and the tank goes. The rushing hot air feels good. I watch the other airplanes to see if their gas tanks go. One by one their tanks tumble and spin into the trees. All airplanes get rid of their tanks and I lay over the gaping hole trying to relax.

Tension is beginning to mount, as we are getting closer to the target. We do not know if they are aware of our coming. If they don't know, we can slaughter them. If they do know, they can do the same to us. We are told we have a P-38 protection, but I can't figure out how they could fly so far. They have wing tip drop tanks, but even with those they would not have the range we do.

"Pilot to crew. Get ready. We'll be there in two minutes."

"Pilot to Nelson, fire with me unless we are attacked by Zeros."

I check my equipment again and look ahead to see nothing but jungle.

"Pilot to crew, hold your fire 'til we go over the target."

There's the runway. I see no activity. At full throttle and maxium speed all our fixed guns explode into action and the recoil slows us like flying into a net. 195 machine guns and 15 cannons rip into their base at a rapid rate of 136,500 rounds a minute. Our bottom doors pop open and I flip the tail gun switch and the camera switch. The Jap planes are all lined up for us and I hold down my gun button to rake down the line of airplanes. Their airplanes are in a straight line and the stupid Japs are standing around them. Some of their engines are running and the mechanics are all around the planes working on them. They are looking at us like we were one of them. Holy jumpin' buckets, I could knock them over with a stick. Our incendiaries have already set a lot of their planes afire far ahead of us, and our bullets are cutting them down by the hundreds. Their planes are exploding forward and our bombs are tearing them apart behind. The sky is alive with tracers and they are arching away from us which makes them ours.

We caught them asleep on the job. They fall before our

awesome firepower and we have no opposition so far. Our guns turn hot while we zoom over the far end of their field to a clearing, then out to sea.

They finally start shooting at us as we zip across the water. Some of our planes take a little flak, but no one is hit seriously. We look back to see an air base on fire with explosions shooting a thousand feet in the sky. All their airplanes are destroyed, hundreds of Japs killed and wounded, buildings and tents afire, equipment burning, and ammo and fuel is exploding a thousand feet in the air.

There were about 75 P-38's up there chasing the Zeros. The heavies dropped about 200 tons of bombs on the other air fields, but we lost four B-24's. The B-25's at Borum destroyed 60 bombers on the ground. They were all lined up with their engines turning over like the ones we destroyed at Wewak. The Grim Reaper outfit took credit for 36 aircraft destroyed, several fuel and ammo dumps, about 150 killed, and all the buildings and equipment above ground destroyed. The Grim Reaper lost no airplanes or men.

We learned later that the Japs were ready to take off from all four air fields to bomb our base at Marilinan. Had we been five or ten minutes later we would have missed them.

Two B-25's were lost belonging to another outfit, and we lost the four B-24's. No other planes were lost.

We stayed in tight formation while heading home and watched the P-38's knock Zeros out of the sky. Zeros were falling earthward in all directions. This was what we had hoped for all the time. To have P-38 escort and watch those beautiful pursuits dominate the sky, and to see them chasing the Zeros and killing them.

We destroyed everything at Wewak, but could have done more. There were several ships near the shore anchored out. But we did not have a single 500 pounder to sink them. The next day we went back with 500 pounders to sink them.

As we head south along the coast we see a torpedo boat, then three more. While strafing them they explode just like bombs. Evidently our bullets found their torpedos.

We followed the coast almost to Alexhaven, then out over the Bismarck Sea to avoid Madang and Saidor, then through the Vidiaz Straights to the Solomon Sea. Here we changed our course to head straight into Buna. After our victory buzz we settled down one by one and were home again from our biggest mission yet except for the big ones in the Bismarck Sea Battle.

At our briefing we were told of the success of the other squadrons and the damage they had done to the other bases near Wewak. At Borum our other B-25's destroyed one Jap bomber while it was taking off. It blocked the runway so others could not take off and they destroyed 59 other Jap bombers there that were all lined up ready for take off.

Our plans for tomorrow are to fly right back and hit them again. Someone said: "It's a pity we can't go back today. By tomorrow the convoy may be gone." But it is too late to get back up there before dark.

At our briefing the next day we were disappointed to learn that we would hit Wewak again with para frags and another squadron of B-25's would sink the ships. We did not think much of attacking Wewak again so soon. They should have time to re-build. But you don't argue with your orders.

Our flight this day was a duplication of the day before.

One plane had to turn back because of the drop tank. The heavies dropped another 100 tons of bombs in the area and 53 B-25's swept over the four bases cutting down everything that might have escaped yesterdays raid. Other B-25's sank four big cargo ships anchored out. About 40 Zeros at different times attacked our B-25's, our gunners were on the ball and shot down 19 of them. The P-38's shot down 14 more without any losses. A B-25 was attacked by four Zeros and was knocked down. The pilot tried to ditch in the ocean, but the plane exploded before it reached the water. All four crew members were killed. They all got the Congressional Medal of Honor posthumously.

After our two day attack on Wewak, it was estimated the Japs could not put more that 10 planes in the air out of a total of 200 they had before the attack. And we destroyed thousands of barrels of oil, many ammo dumps, buildings, destroyed untold millions of dollars of equipment, killed thousands of their men, sank four big ships loaded with supplies, and the heavies with their big bombs destroyed their airstrips at all four bases.

We all come back to Buna tired and with a few holes in our airplanes, but with no real damage. It is time for a much needed rest. We will let the Japs re-build Wewak, then we will go up there and wipe them out again. Our job now is to attack their shipping again. We'll strike at some of their other bases, and most dreaded of all, hit Rabaul.

Widowmaker II is assigned to transport a high ranking civilian official to an undisclosed base in New Guinea. We prepared to go as if it was a combat mission, sans bombs. There was no seat for the man, so he agreed to stand behind the pilot. This put him directly half way between the props. We zoomed down the runway and began to lift off.

Suddenly the plane began to vibrate violently. It dropped to the runway and spun and skidded all the way to a grove of trees before we stopped. After I gathered myself up I crawled out and jerked open the forward hatch to find our Aussie diplomat in a pool of blood. The tip of one prop blade broke off and flew through the fuselage. The blade struck him in the temple and killed him instantly. Widowmaker was not damaged except for the prop.

The allies now have air superiority over the Southwest Pacific. We have blasted every one of their bases except Rabaul. We can pulverize their bases whenever we desire. Mostly it is our strategy to let them re-build, then we hit them again. Their ships and barges are doomed if they send them south. It is not done without a few losses, but they have 50 times more losses.

The word is that two more destroyers and a troopship are heading south again through their Vidiaz Straits. So we are alerted to go up and sink them. This time we will go alone and will have no escort.

It is the crack of dawn and we are loaded with 500 pounders. The weather is good again, with visibility about 20 miles, which is what we need to find the convoy. Our course is straight north which will take us to the exact spot that the convoy was last seen. They are trying desperately to get to Lae again to try to save it. Regardless of the odds against them they don't give up.

After checking our guns I have nothing to do but wonder about the war and my chances of getting home. Of all the places I could have been sent in the world this is the worst. The kids in Europe have access to all the famous places and we are isolated in the unbearable jungle. It is a fact that the worst that can happen to the kids in Europe when they get shot down is to be placed in a German prison camp. When we get hit and are forced down it is almost certain death. If the Japs capture us it is either death, torture, or both. And if we go down in the jungle or the sea there is almost no chance of surviving. None of our outfit have ever come back. The men in Europe live in a tolerable climate also and are not forced to eat powdered food. To top it all off, they can go home after 25 combat missions and we have to fly 50. The thinking of a majority of the top brass is that the missions in Europe are rougher. Well, we wonder if those guys have ever flown broadside into a Japanese warship at mast height.

We gain altitude for a better view, then, on the horizon we see smoke. Quickly we drop down to the water again to be out of reach of their radar. In minutes the three ships are visible.

Like a panther stalking its prey we move in for the kill, hoping they don't see us 'til we open up on them. Our speed is maximum while the ships zoom toward us. Widowmaker II groans in agony under the strain of too much pressure and too much speed. Now we are in range and so far they have not fired on us. Our guns burst into flame to hose down one destroyer, and our bomb bay doors open to let out our first bomb which bounces off the water and right back at us. It lags behind and gets lower and lower to skip right into the belly of the big ship. All our guns are raking the deck as we bank to the right and away, all the time spraying the deck with the turret and waist guns.

The bomb explodes under the water line and the ship rolls on her side exposing a roomsize hole in her side. Then the ship rolls back as another 500 pounder hits her from the portside.

After each plane makes a pass, each ship takes three 500 pound bombs. Then the Zero escort jumps on us from behind and showers a B-25 with machine gun and cannon fire. Our gunners concentrate on the enemy fighters and the sky is filled with arcing tracers. The fighters keep their distance and we make another run on the other destroyer. The Widowmaker is making this run with the help of another B-25. We are going in double. Our airplane takes the stern and the other plane takes the bow. We power in on the warship with all guns pouring out their message of death. Two big bombs drop simultaneously and ricochet across the water to smash into the hull. At the same time a huge geyser of water is thrown up by an enemy cannon. This is the death knell for those valiant kids who came to help. They smash into the geyser of water, break in two, and sink like a rock. It is instant death for the four guys on that B-25. We do not know who they are at the time, but when we get back to base we learn all we can. They were fresh from the States, and had been in New Guinea only two days. They were inexperienced and eager.

Since the Bismarck Sea Battle the Japs are using their big guns in a different way. Rather than try to hit us directly, they shoot in the water in front of us to throw up a huge water spout. If an airplane crashes into that geyser of water it's the same as hitting a mountain.

Both bombs exploded against the hull of the destroyer under the water line, and the great power rolled the ship over on its side. Everyone aboard fell or jumped into the water in an effort to save themselves. All ships are sinking now, but we have one more bomb so Connley attacks once more.

"Radio to pilot, did you drop the last bomb?"

"Yes, I did."

"It did not fall."

I look in the bomb bay to see the bomb on its nose and hanging by one end. I call the Major and tell him I will crawl in there and try to pry it loose.

I disconnect my headset, tie my safety strap around my waist, grab my pry bar, and proceed to inch my way into the open bay. Our co-pilot is watching me from the forward end of the bomb bay. This is something new to him and he can't believe what I am doing.

While I'm trying to release the bomb, we do a few circles around the sinking ships to see the thousands of Japs scramble for their lives. Then we make formation and the Zeros leave us alone. In formation, they are now afraid of us. Our reconnaissance verifies that all three of the ships went down. There were nearly 7,000 men on the ships.

I worked myself into position where I could get leverage on the bomb shackle. Then I strapped myself to some fuel and hydraulic lines. But when I got ready to spring the shackle I found that if the bomb fell it might swing toward me and take me with it. So I had to work from a new position higher up. After getting into this new position, I managed to get my bar into the hook of the shackle and twist it far enough to free the bomb. It dropped to the water and bounced as if we were skip bombing. It sank and didn't explode. The fuses are three second delay and if they don't come in contact with a solid object they will not explode.

I called the Major and asked him if a message had been sent to our base. He told me to go relax and forget about it.

We had planned to go barge hunting, but the Major said we had had enough for one day. So we flew the water route back to our base, gave it a super buzz and landed.

249

In about four hours we had sunk three ships and all supplies. There were about 4,000 troops on the troopship, and about 1,500 on each destroyer. We lost four men and a B-25.

# CHAPTER 21

## WEWAK, BORUM, BUT, DAGUA

The Japs were bringing supplies to Wewak now via ships. Reconnaissance reported seeing several ships there on 1 September. Our next mission was cut out for us.

That evening we loaded all planes with five hundred pounders and filled all ammo containers. The next morning we all took off and headed for Wewak without escort. Our mission was to "sink those ships", and our plan was to stay in formation as much as possible so we could help each other fight off the Zeros. As usual, we planned to surprise them at least on the first attack.

It was tree top all the way straight as the crow flies. Then Widowmaker II hit the top of a tree and shook us up, but we didn't slow down. The baffles on one cylinder were jammed with leaves and wood pulp and this caused the cylinder head temperature to mount on number 1 engine, but we kept going. It took more than a little thing like a tree to stop our B-25's.

After we crossed the Sepic River we got rid of our drop tanks, and we all got rid of them.

As usual, we hope to sneak up on them using the jungle for cover, then, just before we get to Wewak we'll swoop out to sea to hit them if they are still there. If they are not there we will gain altitude and bomb the airdrome. It is not safe to drop these big bombs at low altitude. We would blow ourselves up. Also, if the ships are not there we will not break our formation for protection against the Zeros.

Our big worry is their ack-ack. The first of our missions there we lost a B-25 and also four B-24's. Their flak gunners seem to be extremely accurate in the Wewak area.

"Connley to crew, we'll be in the Wewak area in four minutes. Is everybody ready?"

"Roger. Roger."

I double check my equipment and look out the window. All I can see is the same old jungle. We turn right to avoid the airdrome and point to sea. The ships are still there and we can see a lot of activity. Several barges are shuttling cargo from the ships to the shore. Then we see something we have never seen before. Each ship has a huge barrage balloon tied to it. Do those Japs think those balloons will scare us away? We laugh to see this device.

Tension mounts as we brace ourselves and zip straight at them at full throttle and a speed unheard of for a medium bomber. Then most aircraft in our flight turn and bank away from the ships. We can't all go in at the same time. Widowmaker II and five other planes pick a ship. As the bottom doors open we let go with all we can muster. They are firing at us which means it is not a total surprise. One airplane on our right is already hit, and smoking. Six airplanes drop six bombs that skip on the water and smash into the hulls of six ships. The fantastic power of our bombs cause one ship to roll on its side.

"Jacobs to Connley, we're hit bad. We will head for home."

"Connley to Jacobs, maintain 190 degrees."

Their Zeros attack us from above and pour a lot of lead into a lone B-25, as we circle and watch, six other planes make their attack on the ships. We now are scattered and this gives them an opportunity. Ships gunners are giving us one hell of a time, and the Zeros are hitting every plane from behind. One makes a pass at us while Nelson and I follow it with our tracers. To my left is a Zero on fire and spinning toward the water. Three Zeros are chasing a B-25 and smoke trails from one engine. Then it bursts into a ball of fire and crashes in the water. They are clobbering us. All ships are on fire and one is sinking.

"Connley to Grim Reaper. Make formation. We are getting out of here."

They clobbered two of our planes. It's a bad deal. We are not used to such losses. We get the hell out of there.

After making our formation the Zeros back off. Our course back home is 190 degrees and we hope to spot Jacobs's plane if it went down. If they are in the water we can at least see them. But it's worse to see them than not when it is impossible to help them.

In about ten minutes we saw debris in the water, and two yellow specks. They had ditched and their plane had sunk. Two men were in the water wearing Mae Wests. Evidently the others had been killed or drowned.

We circle and waved at them and they waved back. We dropped a parachute to them which had a survival kit packed inside. But when it gets soaked it will sink, so that won't help. They had one chance. The coast of New Guinea is in sight. If they can swim that far maybe they'll make it. Also, the Japs have not sighted them, so they won't be shot in the water. However, we never heard from them. If they made it to the beach it would take them many months and maybe years to get to our lines.

We followed the coast to just north of Madang, then straight ahead out over the Bismarck Sea to the Vidiaz Straits, and over the familiar Solomon Sea to Buna.

None of us were proud of this mission. All we sank was one ship, and probably sank five more, but we lost two precious B-25's with all crew members. These losses are much bigger than we are used to now.

That was the last of the barrage balloons. We supposed the stupid Japs learned something for a change—that they were worthless.

The next day we attacked Lae for the last time. Our ground troops and the Aussie Diggers were waiting for our last attack before they went in to kill the diehards. We hoped we had the power to reduce the resistance there to a minimum so the infantry could take them without too much hand to hand fighting. The Aussie Diggers were tough soldiers. They were dubbed the "Rats of Tobruk", and it was the same outfit that acquired the name in North Africa.

Our attack on Lae was very successful. Our losses were nil and we leveled everything in our wake. They didn't touch us with one piece of shrapnel or bullet. The Aussies and Yanks moved in for the kill. It took several bloody days to send the remaining Japs to their ancestors, and a lot of them took to the jungle to become snipers.

As soon as the troops had filled in all of the craters on the runway at Lae, we flew in there and landed. We were anxious to see what we had done to them. It was a sight to behold. The whole area was a junkyard of wrecked airplanes and equipment. Their airplanes were a big attraction, and we immediately ran to see and inspect them. We were a bunch of kids in glory taking pictures of each other inside a Japanese airplane. Their bombers were what we called "Betties." They were of medium size to compare with our B-25's, but they were build very light and flimsy. The wrecked Zeros were built the same way and resembled our advanced trainers. Their wrecked airplanes had been an asset to them like ours. They had been cannibalized for parts just like ours. We photographed all their planes and equipment before our bulldozers pushed them into a trench and buried them. What do we want with them? They were copied after our planes, and inferior. I felt sorry for the poor dead Japs. They were killed with our much superior weapons, and had been brainwashed to believe in a lost cause.

Reconnaissance reports great activity in the area of Cape Gloucester. This base has been bombed by our heavies many times, but we haven't hit it yet with our flying battleships. While we are waiting for the Japs to re-build Wewak we are to hit Gloucester. Like all our other successful attacks we'll try to sneak in on them when it is expected the least, and destroy their airplanes and equipment on the ground.

On the morning of September 3, 1943, we thundered off the Buna runway and headed straight for New Britain Island. This will be our first time to attack the island itself, but soon we will be attacking Rabaul, their strongest fortification in the Southwest Pacific. Cape Gloucester is on the north side of the west tip of the island and our plan is to fly directly to their base, which will mean we will attack them from the jungle. We will make only one pass over their base, but we can drop all our para frags in the 13 seconds we will be over the runway.

Visibility is very good to about 20 miles. It will be easy for us to find the base. As we approach the island we run into three barges heading west. This is their doom. Our pay load is a bomb bay full of para frags, and they aren't big enough to sink barges, but no matter, we'll sink them

255

with our firepower. Three airplanes attack them with their guns and cannons, and we leave them sinking. We circle around them, watching as they sink, then go on our way to the big island. We drop all our tanks on the island so they will not be a shipping menace. Then it is straight on across the island to Cape Gloucester.

The fighters are not with us on this one, but we plan to keep in formation all the time coming and going. The P-38's are covering the Lae invasion. We learned later that Jap bombers tried, over the weekend to bomb Lae, and the P-38's knocked a lot of them down, and the rest turned tail toward Rabaul and jettisoned their bombs in the Solomon Sea.

"Connley to crew, we'll be there in one minute. Is everybody ready?"

"Roger." "Roger."

I check my guns and gear. Then our guns in unison, jolt the airplane so hard I thought we crashed. I begin to fire my guns forward and down, and as I flip my switches I see airplanes lined up on the ground and Japs running again in panic. We caught them with their pants down. Our incendiaries reach out like giant flame throwers to start the planes burning long before we get a chance to blow them up with our bombs. Then our little deadly para frags follow each other from the bomb bay and pop into their little chutes. In a start of excitement the gunners concentrate on the running men and the pilots hold down all gun buttons to saturate the whole base with hot lead and steel. The Japs have not fired a shot at us yet as we zoom to the far side of their base. Now the bombs are exploding behind us in straight as an arrow rows to cover every foot of the area. In a flash the airfield is behind us and we drop to the water

256

and are over the Bismarck Sea. Bombs, ammo, and fuel, is blasting black smoke high in the air, and the field behind us is an inferno.

They did not shoot at us. No flak or machine gun fire, or Zeros, and now we are out of range of their guns.

The Grim Reaper Squadron under the able leadership of Major Connley points north, then turns to port at minimum altitude toward the entrance to the Vidiaz Straits looking for ships, or any barges with crews stupid enough to expose themselves to us. But we don't want to see ships at this time without big bombs. We cannot sink the ships with our guns alone. Pappy Gunn tried it a month ago on a destroyer and the warship did not even slow down. Another B-25 skipped a big 1,000 pounder into it and cut it right in two.

Now we are barreling down through the Vidiaz Straights about four feet off the water and congratulating ourselves on our good luck when one of our airplanes hit the top of a wave and plowed into the sea. We couldn't believe it. It was something we never thought about. There we were, a cocky bunch of daredevils, completely unaware that such a thing could happen. One pilot got a little too close to the water, hit the wave, and bounced into the air, came down and hit again to break in two. And there we were circling around them and could do nothing to help. One man in a Mae West was floating, so apparently the rest of them were killed in the crash. Again we dropped a parachute to him with a built-in survival kit, but that would sink when it got soaked. We flew around him for a while, then had to leave him.

That day we learned something but soon forgot it. We had hit many tree tops and kept going, but the water was something else. The whirling props jerk the plane down. We flew a little higher for a while but it was soon forgotten.

After the accident barge hunting was not of much interest, so we flew directly back home.

Our photos showed the destruction of 14 airplanes, hundreds of barrels of oil, several ammo dumps, about 150 Japs killed or wounded, and the barges loaded with Japs and supplies. Our losses were three and probably four men and a brand new airplane.

Reconnaissance told us Wewak had more airplanes, so we were gonna get 'em. Armament cleaned and loaded all the fixed guns, and Nelson and I cleaned and loaded our own guns. Maintenance did all their work including fueling. We were loaded with para frags and all ready to go the evening before. We hit the sack early and the O.D. poked us out of the sack at 0100 hours. Beginning at a very early 0230 hours we thundered down the runway, burning our running lights so each airplane could follow the one in front. We flew at 290mph which put us over Wewak at 0500 hours, and at the break of day.

After we are settled and check our guns I tune my liaison receiver and we live it up with our music. There's another new co-pilot with us and he can't believe the luxury of music on a combat mission. It's a long way to Wewak and the music helps pass the time.

This is my 36th mission, and after a few more, I'll be going on my last leave to Australia if my luck holds. I am counting with my fingers crossed, hoping and praying my luck will hold to 50. There are about six in the outfit with that many missions, so it appears I'll be among the first to go back home.

Our stone monument that lists all those in our outfit who

have been killed or missing is over half filled now. It looks like we'll get another plaque. We are losing about 40 people every month which is not good. Our stone monument is in our tent area and when we all go the jungle growth will cover it completely. We should have built it near the beach where it would not be covered with growth.

The moon is about one quarter and some of the stars are out which gives us some light. Because it is night we are flying a little on the safe side—not quite so low. All the running lights are out now, but the dim blackout lights on the instruments are on. It is hot and I'd like to get rid of that tank so some air would come through the plane.

"Radio to pilot, when can we drop the tank?"

"About ten minutes."

To keep awake and have something to do, I rig my safety strap and get ready to let it go. Nelson is konked out on the floor. He has not a care in the world for the moment. There will be no Zeros out here in the dark, and that is about all he has to worry about.

"Pilot to radio, drop the tank."

"Roger."

I yanked the lever and it went. The hot and humid air rushed through the fuselage, and now I could lay over the hole to let it whip over my hair. Nelson roused and looked at me.

"What kind of flowers do you want for your funeral?" I asked.

"I'm not going to have a funeral with all those silly rituals."

"I'm on your side," I told him. "I'm not going to have one either."

It's 0405 hours and about 25 minutes to the target. We

hope the little yellow monkeys are sleeping well this morning. We'll soon let the monkeys know we are not asleep. The minutes do slow motion on my watch dial. If you think we get used to this and are not scared anymore, it is not true. Anything can happen any time and every second is fear.

First light is breaking in the east so we drop closer to the trees.

"Pilot to crew, we'll be there in two more minutes."

We are too early. It is not light enough to find the Wewak strip. So the Major surges our airplane ahead of the rest and begins a slow turn. It was a very slow turn and when we got back to our heading of 44 degrees magnetic, we had killed several minutes and it was lighter, so we went in.

There's the tower that marks the west side of their base. We are off course slightly, and we turn to the left to compensate. It is our third time here so we recognize the base, and there it is.

As our guns explode into action the jungle is cut down at the near end of the runway. The little deadly frag bombs start following each other out the bay, and our 208 machine guns in unison, with 16 cannons, level and ignite all that is in front of us. There are airplanes on the ground. They are scattered this time in an effort to save them. But we will destroy them anyway in one pass. Nothing above ground will escape us. Our guns get hot. They can't stand the tremendous heat generated for many seconds before they turn red. We have no opposition so far which means the Japs must still be in bed.

As we zoom away from their base our guns swing aft to fire back and the last of our parachute bombs leave the

260

bomb bay. Then it is away, and out to sea. I turn off the tail gun and camera and look back. Their base, in the semi-dark, looks like a flaming hades. Now we bunch together in tight formation and hug the water. Then a slow turn to starboard until the coastline appears, then southeast toward home.

On the way back we found two barges close to shore. We took turns filling them with big holes until they began to sink, then we headed straight for our base.

"Grim Reaper to (call sign Buna) Saturated Wewak. No opposition. Sank two barges. Coming home.

Call sign/time date

Our photos showed the destruction of 16 airplanes on the ground, hundreds of gas barrels, three ammo dumps shooting explosives high in the sky, and many fires burning.

The enemy cannot stop us. They can kill a few of us, but they cannot stop us. They will be annihilated.

# CHAPTER 22

## HOLLANDIA AND DEATH AT SEA

In modern warfare it seems war correspondents are important. The folks back home need to know about the successes and failures of the boys at the front. And what the reporters feed them sometimes carries a lot of weight.

So when Lee Van Atta, (a close friend of the famous Ernie Pyle) of the International News Service, showed up at Buna to fly combat with us, we were glad to take him aboard. We wanted to show him how to really kill Japs. He didn't know what skip bombing was, and he didn't know a lot about parachute fragmentation bombs, but he wanted to learn. One of our troops told him: "Do you want to learn how we kill Japs? When we sink them on the water, which is very often, we kill them at the rate of 10,000 at a time."

The big news was skip bombing. This type of warfare demanded the utmost in guts and skill in both men and machines. Not all the inventiveness and innovations took place on the drawing boards in the airplane factories. The technique of skip bombing and the conversion of our B-25's into a fleet of flying battleships was our own "on the job" development. The whole 5th Air Force had to try it. Even the cumbersome heavy bombers tried it at times. They couldn't hit the ships from a high altitude, so they would come down to try a little skip bombing. And even the heavies did a lot better that way. But it was dangerous.

The Japs are feverishly re-inforcing at Wewak. We deliberately let them do it so when we hit them again, we could destroy as much as possible. This time we'll put on a show to write a letter about.

One hundred B-25's and crews are just straining to be off. We carry enough explosive and incendiary fire power to level Tokyo. One hundred and thirty P-38's umbrella the sky above us, and 20 other B-24's will lay their big eggs from high above. After the B-24's drop their bombs, we will sweep in at mast height and rip their bellies open with our 500 pounders. The Grim Reaper Squadron will reap a grim harvest once more today. When we get through with them all their ships will be resting on the bottom at Wewak.

Our confidence is high this time with all these airplanes. The Zeros will not give any of us much trouble, but flying tree top puts a strain on the pilots. Automatic pilots can not be used at such a low altitude because it is so bumpy over the trees. The elevators, rudders, and ailerons, must constantly be corrected to keep from hitting the trees. The vegetation affects the air temperature which moves the air currents.

The P-38's are glistening in the sky over us. What a beautiful sight. They are the monarchs of the heavens, as far as we can see. The Zero pilots know that now and they are afraid of them. They are afraid of our gunners also when we are in formation.

Those high flying protectors of ours are now dropping their wing tip tanks. Those tear drop shaped tanks come tumbling down from 20,000 feet, spinning, turning, wobbling, glistening like confetti. They come straight down at us, and it seems we cannot avoid hitting a bunch of them. But when they get down to our level, they are far behind us as they bounce on the water.

I am concerned about the Japs finding the P-38's on their

radar screens, but after they drop their tanks they ease throttle and I see them fade from sight far behind us.

Then other squadrons of B-25's draw up to us on our port side. Then more squadrons appear on the starboard side. We have never seen so many B-25's.

Mr. Van Atta is standing behind the Major. I am concerned about him. I don't think he knows about that Aussie diplomat who got killed there with the prop blade.

We have the utmost confidence in the Major. I have been tempted to tell him that when I make my fortune I'm going to put him in my will. He always makes the most dangerous attacks. But of course he is the squadron commander and he must lead us. He sometimes scares us half to death.

Most of the other B-25's are loaded with the para frags, but we are going to sink ships and kill Japs by the thousands, so our load is 500 pounders.

While still hugging the trees we slowly turn to the right. In a few minutes the Bismarck Sea is in sight, and there are the ships. "Glory Halleluja." Six, seven, eight of them, and some are big. Three are tankers. We haven't had a chance at tankers before. Boy, are we going to pollute the Bismarck Sea with oil today. Oil is the one thing that keeps them going. We will let go the lifeblood of their whole war machine. To spill all that airplane and ship fuel in the sea is more than we dreamed of.

The ships are anchored out from Wewak. There is no activity around them. The Nips are having their tea and fish heads we assume.

The Major picks a tanker. I know he cannot resist spilling all that oil. It sits low so we know it is loaded. At 330 mph we scream in on them, making our evasive action, fantailing, and pointing directly at the big ship. As it looms up our guns roar out a rain of bullets and projectiles up and down her deck, and our big bomb bounces off the water. It ricochets back at us then skips three more times into the hull. As we are pulling away, a geyser of water climbs into the air to 300 feet then turns into a ball of red flame that drops to cover the ship with fire. A house size hole in her side gushes oil and fire into the sea and flames burst over the ship. As we re-position for another attack, the oil with the flames, spread over the water, and the smoke covers the ship so completely we can't see it.

Bombs are exploding under all the ships as all have been attacked by the Grim Reaper. There are smaller vessels nearby and some planes are going after them. We skip another bomb into another tanker with devastating results, and one more into a motor torpedo boat, then circle out of range to give Mr. Van Atta a good view so he can take pictures. He doesn't believe it.

The biggest ship is a transport and it has been hit too, but it is still high in the water, so we attack it with all guns blazing and skip a bomb into her belly. The deck of the ship is full of people and we cut them down with every gun aboard. Some are firing rifles at us and a few are manning deck guns. We take a few rounds in the bottom but no one is hit. Their ack-ack is minimal and the Zeros are not here which we take advantage of and make it a turkey shoot.

One tanker is sinking, two are very low in the water, and men are being burned alive in an attempt to swim through the burning fuel. Some of the smaller vessels have sunk and all those afloat are burning. Then we see another tanker settle into the sea stern first and the troopship rolls over on her side like a big mammoth.

From the shore black smoke is rising above the horizon

about 10,000 feet so we know those planes hitting the bases have struck something big. We later learned that a B-24 dropped a big bomb from 13,000 feet which hit an ammo dump. It, the ammo dump, gave them such a jolt they nearly bailed out. They thought they had been hit. The smoke from our bombing strike could be seen by all of us for 50 miles while flying home.

Before leaving we counted our kill. All the ships would sink in time. There were three tankers, one large troopship, two tenders, and about 23 barges of different types. The other B-25's and B-24's destroyed 40 airplanes on the ground, and with the help of the P-38's, shot down ten more, and destroyed two huge ammo dumps and several fuel storage areas.

As we watched the P-38's knock the Zeros out of the sky, we hugged the water and headed home.

"Pilot to radio, give 'em the good news."

I got on the liaison transmitter and sent a message to our base to let them know the good news and that we were on our way home.

Apparently we suffered no losses. I counted 95 B-25's around us, and the upper sky was full of P-38's and P-47's. This was a dream we had been waiting for. I knew what the might of America could be, and now we had come to realize it. We had come to what General Kenney had told us old timers: "We must have air superiority."

Now we are looking forward to hitting their big base at Rabaul, the Gibraltar of the South Pacific. Our reconnaissance reports the harbor at Rabaul is filled with 50 ships. They have a total of 367 gun emplacements on the land with over 400 anti-aircraft guns, and when we are in the right position, we'll go up there and annihilate them.

When we got back to base we learned that two B-25's from other squadrons had been lost over Wewak.

The tremendous production power of America was at last turning the tide. We now had ground, air, and sea superiority. In the long haul from the States to Australia, our shipping had been able to carry the great amount of war materiels that made the difference. But in all of my missions I had never seen a U.S. warship. They were someplace over here, but we never once saw any. And this was where the Japs were halted.

Now we have hundreds of airplanes and our fighter escort. Also, at our last briefing we were told we have air rescue. When we get shot down now a radio operator can immediately call for rescue and they can take off as soon as they get the message.

For the next three days after our big raid on Wewak it rained. This gave us a little rest, but the mosquitos almost ate us alive. They are worse when it rains. One would think with wet wings they couldn't fly. They are even meaner when it rains.

The night it quit raining 14 Jap bombers in formation, tried to bomb Oro Bay. Our fighters shot five of them down and the rest went back to Rabaul and dropped their bombs in the sea.

Orders have been cut to attack Hollandia. It is so far up the coast we can't believe it. It is the very limit of our range. It's so far we will have to conserve gas to get back. Our plan is to follow the same pattern we have used in our other successful raids. Our success is in coming in at tree top level and surprise, and to hit them so quick they won't know what hit them until it is all over.

Because of the distance we will have to go it alone. The

P-38's can't fly that far, so we hope they will meet us on the way back in case the Zeros are on our tails. We'll make only a para frag strafing pass of 12 seconds, then out to sea and home.

As usual, our preparation for the long trip is careful and minute. We spent one whole day inspecting our planes and equipment. Our briefing is thorough this time because navigation must be faultless. There will be no gas for a search for the base if we don't find it on the first attempt. There are no skyscrapers in the jungle to guide us in. We also have photos of the place, which will help.

It is a dawn take off. After clipping the tops of the trees we make our formation above the Solomon Sea, and throttle back to save a little gas. We were told at briefing that at a slow speed of 250 mph we would use 8% less gas, and this should give us enough to get back. The 90th Squadron is with us this time and we can see them off to our right.

Our photographs tell us what Hollandia and the area around it looks like from the air, but from where we fly it won't look the same. Without wind we know exactly how long it will take to get there, but we've got to do some navigating besides just follow the compass, so I will have to shoot a few bearings.

My mind is on the end of this mission. This will be my 38th and we are promised our leave to Australia when we get back. The city we will go to this time is called Cairns. There are a dozen people in the Grim Reaper Squadron that are eligible to go.

"Radio to pilot, are the P-38's meeting us on the way back?"

"Not as far as I know."

I am flying again with the Major and our co-pilot is

another new one directly from flying school with no experience. It seems we always have a new co-pilot and we never get to know their names. After they fly a few missions a majority of them become pilots.

"Radio to pilot, what about our tank?"

"A few more minutes."

To have something to do I get ready. Then I get the word to let her go. Caspar, our upper gunner is watching me, and hoping he will not have to help me, because it is dangerous. When I pull the lever the tank drops like a rock. A rush of hot air fills the fuselage as the tank spins and crashes into the trees. Now I can be at ease and cool off a bit while watching the trees flash by. This is new to Caspar and as I get relaxed he gives me a poke and asks me why I am doing that.

"How can you relax when we are so near to combat?" he asks.

"Well, maybe I am not relaxing. Maybe I'm just kidding myself."

"Pilot to crew. The target should be within sight, but I can't see it."

"Caspar to pilot, I see what looks like a water tower at 2 o'clock."

Sure enough, there it is. We missed the target by about three miles, but that's not bad for all this distance, considering we have no landmarks. We turn about 110 degrees to our target dead ahead.

"O.K. men, we're going in."

Our engines rev to full throttle and begin to throb. Tension mounts and our guns explode to shake the plane violently as the bomb bay doors open to let out our lethal little bombs. As the bombs begin to explode my guns find the target and I see Jap airplanes just sitting on the runway which means we have surprised them. Their planes are dispersed, but no matter, they will be destroyed. Our machine guns, bombs, and cannons cover their base like a blanket. Japs are running for their foxholes and we are toppling them over like tenpins. Our incendiaries cause a big explosion in our path and we plow right through the smoke and junk in the air to come out the other side and see more Japs running away from their airplanes. Those Nips cannot believe what we are doing to them. We are ripping their base and their airplanes to junk.

Another group of Japs are running to avoid us and I swing my guns to hose them down as we zip to the end of their runway. Then all gunners turn their guns aft and continue while we get out of their range and zoom out to sea. It is all over, and we look back to see clouds of smoke from the burning planes, ammunition and fuel storage areas, and warehouses.

There are ships anchored out, but we keep out of their range because we have no bombs. As our speed is reduced again, we stay in a tight formation and very near the water. On the way back we'll have to follow the compass and take it easy to conserve fuel.

"Pilot to crew, any damage back there?"

"Not a scratch."

I got on the key and told our base that we destroyed about 20 airplanes, killed about 100 Japs, and blew up a lot of ammo and fuel.

The Major snapped over the command set, "follow me." He slammed his throttles forward and surged ahead of the flight, then slowly turned to port and pointed at the beach.

This means we are going barge hunting. Evidently the gas supply looked good enough that we could afford to knock out a few barges on the way back.

The shoreline came into view and we began a new course along the beach. We didn't find any barges and to avoid Wewak, and the flak, and any fighters they might have there, we swung back out to sea. Then a whole bunch of barges came into view on the horizon. They were heading toward Wewak and appeared to have come from Rabaul. The Japs were trying to re-supply Wewak from Rabaul, and we just happened to be out here at the right time.

"O.K. you guys, pick a barge and have fun."

We broke formation and each plane pounced on a barge like a cat after a mouse. Hot lead and steel, and three inch explosive shells began to smash into the barges. Some of them, in a flash, began to smoke, others exploded, and some caught fire. Then we banked around to hit more barges over and over again.

A voice came over the radio: "You'll stab us in the back at Pearl, you little monkeys."

We used up all our ammo on the barges, so we again made formation and went home with a tally of 27 barges and hundreds of Japs.

# CHAPTER 23

## STRIKE RABAUL! STRIKE RABAUL!

My last combat leave from New Guinea—I hope.

Just 12 more missions and the war will be in the past for me.

The envious troops are eager for us to go on this leave because we promised to bring back a full load of booze. For some of the guys in New Guinea, booze makes life tolerable. It dulls the senses and relieves the fears and worries.

Widowmaker II was converted into a transport by our over-willing ground crews. They worked a big part of the night installing wooded timbers in the bottom of the bomb bay. We'll have a bomb bay full of liquor on the way back. Some of the men had been drinking "jungle juice" made from a concoction of any kind of grain or fruit available. Some men, especially those from the South, had their own stills in the boonies and had been making their own. But they were all anxious for some store bought stuff from Australia. So our leave went with the blessings of the whole camp.

We climbed into Widowmaker II with our parachutes and b-4 bags full of cigarettes. Our plane was overloaded and we all crossed our fingers. I knew those powerful engines would get us up and over the trees. We cleared the trees by only a few inches and turned to the mountains. Usually we climb fast enough to clear them the first approach, but this time we had to circle once. Those props were churning the thin air with everything they had to lift us over those 13,000 foot crags that we knew were down there under the soft and downy cover of the rain clouds. After our pass over the mountains, we pointed to Australia, then descended to 8,000 feet where the temperature was just right.

Flying over the beautiful Coral Sea and the Great Barrier Reef to the little coastal city of Cairns made us feel the whole thing was worth while. It was heavenly and I was drinking the beauty of it. I shall never forget the excitement and anticipation we had of spending seven whole days away from the hell of war. Time now suddenly became more precious and the minutes and hours took wings.

The city of Cairns is English, and much to our surprise, almost exactly like Mackay. The Aussies don't want to be called English, they would prefer America, but they cannot deny their ancestry. Australia hasn't obliterated the customs and the dialect.

We have just received our citations from a presidential order. For the Battle of the Bismarck Sea the President has awarded us the Presidential Unit Citation. The Grim Reaper Squadron just got another Presidential Unit for our daring raids on Wewak. They are worn on the uniform above the left pocket. Additional medals are shown with a star in the blue background.

We got settled in our hotel rooms and began to look for excitement. Priority one was fresh food and a close second was young people wearing dresses. They knew we were there and they were out in numbers showing us they were available. We were not the first Yanks in town, but we were the first on combat leave. We had come to town to spend and the people had both their hands out.

Our first stop was a milk bar. We ate their ice cream 'til it ran out our ears. After the ice cream bust we strolled around just to give the girls a break, as Hartman used to say. The girls were real and alive and wore the cutest dresses. We saw no sheilas wearing baggy pants. After the ice cream and novelty wore off most of us went to a restaurant and had roast beef. Roast beef? That was really a treat. Ice cream and roast beef could have been sold for a lot of money where we came from.

A poster caught our eye:

"In honor of the men from New Guinea we are inviting you to a beach party. There will be food and dancing."

That's for us. Every one of us will be at the beach party, you can depend on that. Planks were brought by the townspeople for the dance floor. They brought food and served it western, or chuck wagon style. A lot of the Yanks came with liquor they had bought from cab drivers. A few brought Aussie beer. Liquor was hard to acquire, but beer was easy at certain hours.

The girls came in droves. There were a lot of girls—more than enough to go around. Some of the smart among us took our time and took our pick, rather than grab the first girl.

The people had also brought wood for a fire to make it more romantic. The setting was near perfect and it did not take long until all of us had a girl and were having a ball.

The dance went on and we had a great time. As time went on the older people went home and soon there were just couples. Some just stayed around the fire, some disappeared, and a lot went skinny dipping in the warm Coral Sea.

It was a full week of fun that left many memories of a little beach town on the Coral Sea within a stones throw of

274

the Great Barrier Reef and in the heart of paradise.

It's time to go back to war.

When we got back we learned that a man by the name of Bob Hope and a group of starlets from Hollywood were going to give us a show in the jungle. We could hardly believe these show people would take the risks of Jap bombs right in the combat zone. If the Japs ever found out that thousands of people would be congregated in one spot, the whole Jap air force would be there.

Bob got up on a truck bed with thousands of GI's sitting on the ground and told silly jokes. But we didn't come to see him. We came to see those classy girls in bathing suits.

"Strike Rabaul!" "Strike Rabaul!"

This has been our ultimate objective for a long time, and our dread. We are now strong in a big way, and ready to hit the strongest base they have in the Southwest Pacific. It will be the first time for our skip bombers to hit the big fortress. The heavies have been bombing it for some time, but they could bomb it forever and the Japs would still be there. Now the B-25's, B-26's, A-20's, and a few Beaufighters are going to strike en masse. The P-38's, the P-47's, P-39's, and a few P-40's, will be above to knock the Zeros out of the sky. It will be the biggest concentration of air power so far in the Southwest Pacific. We will have a total of 350 planes over Rabaul at the same time. In this raid we will have about 125 B-25's, about 90 heavies, 130 pursuits, and a few Aussie Beaufighters.

We'll have plenty of targets. The harbor at Rabaul is huge, and constantly full of the Jap navy. They have the best defenses of any base we have ever attacked. Besides all the guns on their ships, they have well over 400 ack-ack guns on land. They have four big airdromes in the area with hundreds of bombers and fighters stationed there. Our B-25's are going to attack their airdromes called Vanakanaua, Rapopo, and Tobera. The heavies will bomb them from up high, and a few seconds later when their siren for all clear sounds, and the Japs come out of their foxholes, we will pounce on them at tree top level and saturate them with our guns and para frags.

It was 12, October, 1943. All day the day before, we prepared to go. Widowmaker II was in perfect shape. I worked with the mechanics all day making certain every inch of her was perfect. I had overheard the crew chief say he didn't give a damn what happened to her as long as she got up off the ground, so I did not trust them. Some of the mechanics were lax and indifferent because it was a fact they were stuck in the jungle for the duration and six months.

I installed my precious armor plate aft of my guns. That piece of steel had saved me several times, and I'm not about to go to Rabaul without it. I cleaned and checked my guns, checked every component of my radio equipment, filled my ammo containers, and inspected the airplane from nose to cone and from wing tip to wing tip. The Major came out to help me, but it was in vain. Most of the people who drive airplanes don't know anything about them.

It was a sleepless night. All I could put in my mind was: How can we get through all those ack-ack guns? Even if we surprise them and they throw their firepower at us while we are leaving, it is like an impossibility. Their guns are placed all over the area on land, and their warships and all ships have thousands more guns. They have been on the alert and waiting for us to dare to even try to attack them.

I awoke the next morning feeling terrible. How could I realize what I had to face today? Can we ever get used to it? The job had to be done. The General had been a man of his word so far, so we can't let him down today. Nobody refuses to go in view of everyone else. To be a coward in front of the whole squadron is unthinkable. The only way a complete annihilation of Rabaul can be done is if we do it.

The weather is with us. At our morning briefing we are told our fighter escort would be with us until they dropped their tanks, then they must lag behind far enough to be out of radar range.

All B-25's will rendezvous over sea, north of Buna, and each squadron will fly abreast at ten feet off the water making formation and getting into position on the way to Rabaul. Ten minutes before target the squadrons will separate to go directly to their assigned targets and everyone will attack at the same time. We have never, in all our missions, been to Rabaul, but the maps or charts made by reconnaissance are vivid.

The Grim Reaper has been assigned Rapopo, an airdrome. Our mission is the usual, to kill the enemy, destroy airplanes on the ground, destroy fuel and ammo dumps, and destroy everything on top of the ground.

Our planes were loaded to capacity, and we thundered down the metal strip one by one in a military manner. Each plane lifted over the end of the runway and followed our crew in the Widowmaker. When we finally made formation we saw the largest number of B-25's any of us had ever seen. Without a sound over the radio every airplane found its position and continued on toward Rabaul. On each side of us and aft I saw B-25's that looked like forever. In two years I had seen our strength grow from a handful of ancient

A-17's to this giant fleet.

General Kenney's strategy for destroying a stubborn enemy on New Britain is the same as it was for New Guinea: To destroy them from above first so it will be easier for those guys down in the jungle to kill those remaining. "They are vermin that must be exterminated," he said.

Now comes the worst part of the mission. We have nothing to do but wait. Waiting is worse than the attack. You imagine the worst and you have to live through it in your mind. Death is not the worst. Being shot down and captured is by far the worst. We know the Japs do not abide by the Geneva Convention, and we know they kill, degrade, and torture prisoners. We know the Jap feels superior to us and has no mercy. We call them monkeys because we feel they have not progressed very far above them.

Everything is go as we zip across the beautiful Solomon Sea at fantastic speed. Our goal is to sneak, strike, and run—just like they did to us on Oahu. There is one difference, we have a reason to do it. How could they do what they did? How could they have been so utterly stupid?

The P-38's are appearing above us. They are so beautiful up there glistening in the sun in formation. We won't have to worry about Zeros today. Our worry is all those hundreds of guns within a few feet of us.

The P-38's are dropping their wing tanks. What a sight. Those kids flying them are unaware of the show they are putting on. We look up to see the tanks falling. Down they come in scatter—twisting, turning, twirling, wobbling, and spiraling to finally splash into the water far behind us.

Then the Lightnings throttle back and begin to lag. Soon they are out of sight, but we are not to worry. We know they are still coming to knock the Zeros out of the sky.

"Radio to pilot, what about the tank?"

"Almost empty."

Caspar overheard and crawled out of the upper turret to help if necessary.

"Let her go," the Major called.

I brace myself and yank the lever. Out it goes spinning like a top. It bounces three or four times then settles down far behind. Then I watch the other planes drop their tanks. It is a maze of spinning, bouncing tanks. Finally they all settled on the water far behind in a placid manner like a bunch of bee hives.

The hot blast of air coming through the big hole in the bottom is refreshing. Caspar and I are sweating from the heat and from fear. But we try to relax, and then it is time to double check our equipment and get ready. We look at each other, shake hands, and he crawls in his turret. Then a dark line appears on the horizon that grows rapidly into the big island, and in a moment we are bouncing over the trees. The squadrons of B-25's remind me of a fleet of combines sweeping over a Kansas wheat field. We are getting close to our targets and the squadrons slowly separate and head for their respective targets. The Grim Reaper Squadron points at Rapopo, a place we have never seen, but our compass will find it. We even know the locations of the gun emplacements there, but we are to fly straight across the base, and the position of their guns is disregarded. Our mission is not to try to destroy their guns. They are protected with concrete, steel, and sand bags.

"Pilot to crew, we'll attack in two minutes."

The planes of the Grim Reaper are all in an abreast formation with Widowmaker II right in the center. Suddenly our guns explode and cut a swath in the trees ahead of us.

The bomb bay doors fly open and a steady stream of bombs in their little chutes follow each other to wipe the earth clean. The cameras are all switched on and we are over the target. There are a few airplanes on the ground, and some Japs are running for cover. Our incendiaries start explosions and fires forward and gasoline fires are billowing in front of us. We have to fly into the flames. We can't bank to miss the flames. If we did we'd crash into one of our own airplanes. All guns are pouring out their deadly sting of death while we blast through the fire and out the other side into a wall of tracers and flak thrown at us by the Japs. Widowmaker II jumps with a jolt and I know we have taken a chunk of flak. We keep flying through the maze of tracers and feel their lead and steel splatter on our airplane, and the heavy boom boom of our cannon. We are now in the thickest cobweb of tracers and flak we have ever seen. The tail section of our plane shudders as their bullets rip through it and my armor plate jumps at the same time, and I know my plate has stopped the jagged flak. I swing my guns around and fire a long burst at random in hopes of hitting some of their gunners. There is so much flak it is impossible to tell where any of it is originating. We zoom over an empty space and the flak and tracers are coming at us from both sides. One B-25 went down next to us and skidded what looked like a half mile leaving a wide path of flame on the ground. Widowmaker II keeps on a straight course hugging the ground for all the protection we can get, then the sea is in view, so we slowly turn and drop lower all the way to the water. The flak eases while we bunch closer together and fill up what appeared like two empty spaces where two lost planes had hit the ground back there.

Now we are far from their airdrome when another cluster

of shore batteries open up on us. In a flash we are out of their range so we get a chance to look back to see what we had done. Rapopo is a huge black cloud of smoke and fire shooting thousands of feet into the sky. Smoke is rising from the harbor too. The heavies are on the ball, and must have hit some of all the ships. There is other smoke in other places in the area which means the three bases have been hit by our other planes.

The sky above now is filled with our P-38's and other fighters drawing vapor trails in the blue sky. As the P-38's begin to chase the Jap Zeros, we set a course for home base. Then the Zeros begin to fall in flames. Some come spinning down toward us. Others go gliding off in the distance trailing smoke. No P-38's could be seen shot down. We watch the sky fighting for a few minutes 'til they fade from sight. When we get back to briefing we learn the elegant P-38's shot down 27 Zeros and lost none.

"Radio to pilot, I'm going back to see how much damage we have in the tail section. We took a clobbering back there."

I had to remove my armor plate to get past it. The plate had six indentations in the aft side. It stopped six bullets that were heading my way. The tail was full of holes, but all the control cables were o.k. I crawled back to my position, called the Major and told him not to worry, we only had a bunch of holes.

The Grim Reaper got back to Buna safely, but for one airplane and four crew members. They met a fiery death at Rapopo. Four other people were wounded. Two B-24's were lost with all crew members aboard. We had no other losses.

The B-25's destroyed 102 Jap planes on their airdromes,

many fuel dumps, several large ammo dumps, many buildings, much equipment, and many little Japs were killed. The B-24's and B-17's sank three freighters, 41 small merchant ships, about 60 small craft, and damaged many others.

The ice had been broken at Rabaul, and from now on we'll give them no quarter. This was our beginning to the total annihilation of the Japanese Gibraltar of the Southwest Pacific.

# CHAPTER 24

## STRIKE RABAUL! STRIKE RABAUL!

After our big raid on the heavily fortified Jap base at Rabaul the accolades were so numerous it seemed the whole 5th Air Force deserved honors. Distinguished Flying Crosses, Distinguished Service Crosses, Silver Stars, Air Medals, and Medals of Honor for those killed, were recommended and sent to Supreme Headquarters in Brisbane. Those wounded received the Purple Heart.

"Strike Rabaul!" "Strike Rabaul!"

The next day after our first attack we were feverishly getting ready for our second. The men in sheet metal had the worst job of repairing a multitude of holes. They worked night and day. The mechanics, armament, and radio, checked everything on the airplane. When they finished I got busy and double checked.

We had taken a clobbering on our first raid on Rabaul, but we felt they would get weaker on each raid like the other bases had. We felt it was a miracle that our planes could take so many holes and keep flying.

By midnight all planes were repaired, fueled, loaded, and ready to go. At 0200 the O.D. poked us out of the sack. At 0330 we were all on the flight line ready to go.

Widowmaker II cleared the trees, and all the other planes powered up to meet her one by one. As we circled, our running lights were softly in glow to guide each plane into position. This was to be another rendezvous of all the B-25 squadrons, but we were not losing any time in getting together. We all made formation and assembled on the way to Rabaul. The fighters were to escort us again which was a good feeling, but we couldn't see them yet in the dark.

This day again the Japs will feel the might of one of the greatest air attacks ever staged in the Southwest Pacific so far in the war. It will help put a stopper to the ambitious dreams of the Japanese war lords to conquer the world. The die is cast.

It is now light and we know we are getting a lot closer to the target. And with the light we get more heat and tension. The sweat runs down our faces. This is my 43rd mission and I should be used to it, but I'm not, and never will be. I have seven more to go and it appears they will all be over Rabaul. Will I make it?

"Pilot to crew, everybody ready?"

"Roger." "Roger."

Then our plane surges as the throttles push to the stops, and Connley's guns open up. We all hit triggers and gun buttons and jagged metalic junk cuts through trees, grass and anything in sight. Some Jap planes are on the ground again, and more men are running for foxholes. The airplanes explode and fires erupt as we sweep over their base in the greatest concentration of firepower ever known in the history of aerial warfare.

But the Japs are not all dead or hiding. The guns below are flashing at us and hitting some of us. Our plane gives a lurch from an ack-ack shell and more flying junk rains on the skin of our faithful airplane. We fly through the thousands of tracer arcs smashing them with all our guns, cannons, and bombs. Then another black explosion engulfs the sky before us and we are in a bind. It is impossible to veer away from the hidden junk inside the cloud for fear of our B-25's on our wingtips, so we are forced to keep on our course and fly through it. We rocket on through it with our guns still blasting to see the far end of the strip. A lone Zero got into the air and is right in front of our plane. The Major manages to get it in his sights and the Zero explodes into nothing but a ball of fire.

Our gun barrels turn red hot and fill Widowmaker with more stench of hot steel and burned gunpowder while we get another jolt with a ripping sound. We are hit again. The last of our bombs go out and we zoom away from their base but still in the path of their guns. Flak and tracers continue to follow while our own gunners swing aft and try to keep the lead down. It is impossible to get to their gunners. They are behind their bunkers of concrete, sand bags, and steel.

We stay in tight formation, drop even lower, and head for the sea. Their guns pour more at us and one airplane starts to smoke, but up to now our plane is not smoking. When we reach a most welcomed sea they fire into the water in our path. Then it is all over as we are out of their range. As we turn to avoid their ships I scan the skies for Zeros and our fighters.

"Pilot to gunners, how bad are we hit?"

"Radio to pilot, I don't see any damage."

"Pilot to crew, there's got to be damage."

"Caspar, watch for Zeros, I'll look."

I peeked around my armor plate, but could see no damage. Then I came back to my position and crawled over the big tank hole to the bomb bay. One bomb bay door was hanging down not in a closed position like it should be. The actuating cylinder that controls the door was hit with a shell and there was a hole in the fuselage forward of the wing butt. I went back to my headset, called the Major and asked him if his bomb bay door warning light was on. I told him the problem, and also told him that there was nothing to worry about, but he would have to land the plane with the door open.

We watched the dog fights again. Once more the P-38's were knocking the Zeros out of the sky as if they were shooting clay pigeons. The Nip kids were good too, but they were out manned and out gunned, and they faced a superior weapon. When the Jap designers came out with a light and maneuverable fighter, copied from us, they thought they had the ultimate. But the P-38 was on the drawing boards about the same time. It turned out to be far superior.

After watching a few Zeros go down we went on with our problems. I called the Major again and told him that nothing could be done with the bay door in flight, and with the gear down it would not scrape the metal strip, so we continued on.

I switched to command to listen to the other guys in the squadron. The smoking airplane continued to smoke for a while, then the crew managed to put it out. We got back to Buna in good shape thanks to good airplanes. The fire trucks and "meat wagons" were out on the runway to meet us, but we didn't need them.

At our briefing we recalled our exciting experiences and assayed the results of our raid. A total of three were wounded, but none killed. We had five damaged airplanes including Widowmaker II. Our films showed 16 enemy airplanes burning on the ground, and 12 damaged. Our squadron got credit for three planes shot down, and we destroyed two ammo dumps and two fuel dumps. There were many unidentifiable fires. The other B-25's in other squadrons had great success also. Without any losses the P-

38's shot down 21 Zeros.

The 3rd Attack Group is going right back to Rabaul. October 15th, 1943 was spent in preparation. By late afternoon all airplanes were back in shape and ready to be loaded. Fuel, ammo, and para frags were loaded to capacity. By midnight every plane in the Grim Reaper Squadron was on the line and waiting.

"Strike Rabaul." "Strike Rabaul."

It is out of the sack at daybreak for a lot of weary flyers. After we choke down breakfast, we drag ourselves into our planes, then check our systems and start the engines. With Widowmaker leading, we roll down the runway one at a time with our third load of death for the Nips at Rabaul. Only the 3rd Group will fly this mission, but with 45 P-38's to sweep the skies of Jap Zeros. All of us are loaded to the hilt with para frags again and leave their shipping alone. The idea is to wear them down at their land bases first and lead them to believe we're afraid to go in on all those ships.

After making rendezvous with the other Attack squadrons north of Buna we settle down and try to relax. On this mission the Grim Reaper is assigned the airdrome called Tobera, and our strategy of attack is the same. We will hit the base quick as lightning and run.

The P-38's appear overhead and begin to let go their tanks. They always put on a good show. The tanks tumble and sparkle in the sky and set to rest on the water far behind. Then we pass over the south coast of New Britain and begin bouncing over the trees. It is always hotter over those trees than over the water and always bumpy also.

We drop our tanks over the land with no problems and I try to cool off a little over the gaping hole in the wind.

"Jap fighters above us," cracks loud over the interphone.

287

I look up through my side window, but see nothing.

"Caspar, do you see them?"

"Yes, they are diving on us."

"Fire on them Caspar."

"They are diving behind us."

I could see them now. There are about ten and they dive to tree top level, straighten up and come directly at us from behind.

"There they are behind us."

"Fire on them Caspar."

The command set rings with: "P-38's, we are under attack. Where are you?"

The Jap fighters closed in on us with every one of their guns blasting us when all our gunners did the same and three Zeros exploded into balls of fire. The rest banked away from us. We continued straight ahead still in formation and still just above the trees.

The P-38's were far behind us and at 20,000 feet, but in a power glide it didn't take them long to get to us. Another flight of Zeros dove down out of the sky and came up from behind us with all their guns rattling and pointing at us. All our upper gunners and most of our lower gunners sprayed them like with fire hoses, and four more Zeros burst into flames and crashed on the trees. The rest veered off and were knocked out of the sky by our P-38's.

Don't mess with us, was our attitude. There isn't much we can do about your ack-ack, but you don't stand a chance with us in the air.

During these attacks the Grim Reaper didn't slow up, change direction, or break formation.

Tobera is dead ahead and we know now that a bunch of gunners there know we are coming. This will be no surprise attack. It might be a good idea to turn around and go home, but no, not the Major. He has never aborted a mission. We know what our reception will be. There won't be any airplanes on the ground and their gunners will have their fingers on their triggers. But we are going in anyway.

All throttles are against their stops and the bomb doors are open, the guns pour out a stream of hot lead and steel to level all things above ground. But this time the streams of death are coming our way too. There are no airplanes anywhere on the ground and there are no Japs to be seen. Their airplanes are in the air trying to stop us, but they can't stop us.

We swept through their base, through a hail of bullets, and came out the other side on the winning side again. It is unbelievable. With 195 machine guns and 15 cannons we saturated their base again, when they knew we were coming, only to be attacked again by Zeros that got through our P-38's. They came from the rear again three at a time, and then six at a time, but our gunners shot most of them down. The ones that got away from us were shot down by our P-38's.

When we got back to our base we learned that we had destroyed only four Zeros on the ground, but we had helped the P-38's shoot down 38 more. We were used to much bigger successes on these missions. It was because the Japs knew we were coming that we did not do so well on the ground. We lost no airplanes.

Japanese dive bombers attacked Oro Bay. It was the first time they used dive bombers here in this area, and we thought it was because of an airplane shortage, and they were scrapping everything they had together to throw at us. Fifty dive bombers were met by 47 P-38's over Oro Bay and 25 bombers were shot down. The rest turned tail and ran without dropping their bombs. None of the P-38's were lost.

This attack was reminiscent of our dive bombing attacks in the beginning of our raids. Dive bombing is obsolete. We knew that long ago, but it seemed the Japs were slow to learn. The real truth was that they probably did not have planes of other types in numbers to throw at us.

After chow that night we took a dip in the murky and fungus filled waters of the stream by our camp. This stream was alive with jungle rot and other kinds of microscopic crawling things, but we needed a way to cool off and have a bit of recreation, so we took a chance. Then it was time to watch the giant bats fly south again. It was also time to listen to Tokyo Rose tell her lies about the successes of the little men from heaven. She told the same old lies every night. That night she said the brave Japanese pilots shot down 23 B-25's over Rabaul. She said the American cowards turned around and went back to their bases when the Japanese stopped them. She said the Japanese did not lose any planes. Most evenings we listened to her just for kicks. But we knew she said what she was told to say. We also knew that now we were killing Japs at the ratio of about 100 to one, and destroying their property at about 10,000 to one.

"Strike Rabaul!" "Strike Rabaul!"

The 3rd Attack Group is going back again tomorrow to strike the same targets with our devastating para frags and gunfire. The other B-25 outfits are not going again. It seems that General Kenney thinks the men in the 3rd are super-men and don't need any rest. But there is a bit of good about flying a mission every day. If it keeps up and my luck holds I'll be going to the States in a week, and the war will be over for me.

Our attack this day was routine. We follow the same plan every day. Our briefing is always the same, our take off the same, and our rendezvous likewise. We are in the trucking business hauling bombs and ammo to Rabaul. A load a day will soon make Rabaul the desert we are going to make it.

Caspar, instead of sitting alert, is asleep on the floor. Oh well, let him sleep. His duties are about nil unless there are Zeros around. And likewise the co-pilot. He has no duties at all. The pilot and radio gunner do all the labor around here.

Little Dick Bong and his buddies are above us in their P-38's. That kid is making himself famous. He will go home the ace of aces in the Pacific. He will have shot down 40 Jap planes. These kills are all photographed or witnessed. He is not the only one. Many P-38 pilots shot down close to 40. The B-25's destroy many times more than the fighters, but we will never be heroes because we destroy the Jap war machine as a unit.

Now the P-38's begin to drop their wobbly gas tanks which means they will be easing off behind us. Then I get ready to drop our tank. Caspar, get out of my way. He drags himself, in half slumber, to his turret. I drop it in the same spot as yesterday and the day before.

The dark line of New Britain looms on the horizon and soon we are bouncing over the jungle again. The Major always knows when the old tank goes. He can feel it jerk the plane when the slip stream hits it.

We are going to hit Rapopo again today the Major informs us. He tells us to get ready and to watch for Zeros. I'm so sleepy I could not tell a Zero from a New Guinea mosquito.

I feel the airplane surge ahead, and now I know the target is near. Once again we tear up the landscape and Japanese war equipment as we rip across their base trailing our bombs while we cut everything down with our guns. All guns spring into action and we spew destruction out on this doomed airfield. They didn't expect us back so soon. A plane is setting, waiting for my incendiaries. I hose it down using my tracers for sights. It explodes into a ball of red flames. There is another plane and I swing my guns on it, and it too explodes. But we see no Japs. They probably had enough warning for a dive into their foxholes. Then they begin to shoot at us again and tracers arc our way with the usual black puffs of ack-ack. Once again a splatter of shrapnel drowns out the noise made by our guns. We plow through the hail of flying lead and steel to the open area where they have a clear shot at us. Our fixed guns switch off while the doors close and all gunners turn aft to continue hosing them down. The coastline zooms to meet us and another B-25 trails smoke. Then one more B-25 takes a splattering from the guns on shore, and two of our planes are in trouble.

We drop to the white caps and head for home again avoiding the ships. The two pilots driving the shot-up planes call the Major and tell him of their plight. One can make it home. But the other one had to ditch on the way home in the sea. I called Buna and gave the location of the ditching. An Air Sea Rescue PBY plane came out and landed on the water and saved the crew. This was the first time we had been able to save any downed crew members. It gave us a good feeling to know that now we might be rescued at sea if we go down.

Even though we suffered more damage on this raid than

usual, the enemy was getting weak. The Japs were in a desperate situation. They were now fighting for their very existence.

# CHAPTER 25

## STRIKE RABAUL SHIPPING!

Only three more missions to go and I'll have done my fifty, but they will probably be tougher than any. If I can make it I'll be free to leave green hell and go back to the peaceful climes of the States. There isn't one of the ground troops who wouldn't mortgage the rest of his life to be in my shoes. They call me "lucky", but they are the lucky ones. Most of them came over here when we had something to fight with, but for most of the time I've been here, the Japs have had it the way they wanted it.

Caspar calls me lucky, but you are the lucky one, I tell him. You are now flying with the best and biggest fleet of air battleships ever assembled. When we get through sinking those ships at Rabaul Harbor, it'll be downhill all the way to Tokyo. These raids coming up will climax all previous raids of the Papuan Campaign. This is the big one and tomorrow is the day.

Rabaul Harbor is the center of all Japanese shipping in the Southwest Pacific. The Nips do not think we have the guts to fly down their gun barrels where they have so many ships in a protected area. But, whether we like it or not, our orders are to do just that.

Our reconnaissance has been taking pictures up there for months, and they always show about 50 ships of all classes plus many smaller craft. The big difference at Rabaul is that the ships are concentrated, and there are so many of them. They are in a position to turn the guns of up to 20 ships on

## PICTURE TELLS GRAPHIC STORY OF STRIKE AT RABAUL

Huge
Swindle
In Coal
Alleged · 3

DOLLARS

one plane. How can we make it?

And we won't have the element of surprise, as the P-38's are going in at low altitude first, in an attempt to cloud the air with phosphorus. The phosphorus will be dropped in smoke bombs to try to create a fog so their gunners can't get us in their sights. This is the first time for this tactic and we are not sure how effective it will be. Common sense tells us that if the wind blows, the smoke will blow away with the wind. Prior to our attack, the P-38's will fan over the harbor at mast height and drop their smoke bombs, as we have been doing all this time. We think it is a bad idea, and after all, we should know more concerning this than a general who has never flown a skip bombing mission.

So many things could go wrong. Wind would be a problem. Our pilots could be blinded with the smoke, and not see the ships. We could crash into a ship, or the plane next to us, or the water. We will also be forced to throw away our biggest weapon—the element of surprise. The P-38's, in their smoke bomb pass will let the Japs know we are coming. But we don't question orders, even if they are stupid orders.

November 1, 1943. We spent the whole day in preparation. Our planes and equipment must be in perfect shape. I spent the day going over Widowmaker II. When the ground crews finished, I went back and inspected everything they had done. The Major came out to check also. I told him not to worry, that I would double check everything. He said, "Widowmaker must be the best airplane."

There will be about 90 B-25's in this strike. That is enough. If there were any more we would be crashing into each other. After the fighters drop their smoke bombs they will climb high to fight off the Zeros. The heavies will not be on this mission.

At daybreak on November 2, the Grim Reaper roars over the tree tops to make rendezvous out over the Solomon Sea with the rest of the squadrons. We are loaded with 500 pounders and ready at last to attack the biggest concentration yet, of Japanese shipping. Our mission is to smash as many of our bombs as possible into the hulls of as many ships as possible, and empty all our cannons and guns into the decks of the ships.

As we skim along over the waves of the Solomon Sea we can see the P-38's high above us. They will stay there until they have dropped their auxiliary wing tip tanks, then they are to dive down ahead of us and skim the tops of the waves, just like we do, until they get to the target. When they reach the target it is the plan for them to spread out to cover the whole harbor and drop their smoke bombs. When we get there we'll dive straight down through the smoke screen to the ships. Our flight and other flights will disperse to cover the area of the harbor and attack every ship in sight, or in the flight path without turning. After all airplanes are on the far side of the bay each plane will turn 180 degrees and do the whole thing over again.

The Japs will have the advantage because they will know we are coming and they will be scattered all over the harbor. It is a mission poorly planned, and we have a sick feeling about it, but nobody backs down.

Negative thoughts go through my mind as we speed along. I try to relax. But how can one relax when you have an uncanny sensation that it is not right. The General should ask us if it is a good plan.

The P-38's start dropping their tanks. It lets us know that it won't be long now. They fall in splendor as usual and we watch them settle on the placid water.

Our tank dropping operation was routine and with no problems. The other planes were in luck also.

"Pilot to crew, this is probably the mission most dreaded and the most dangerous one we will ever fly. I want you guys to know I appreciate what you are doing. I also meant to tell you that we are not going to get killed today. We will all come back alive."

The P-38's have moved ahead of us and have dropped down to tree top level, and are out of sight. New Britain is below us so now we count the minutes. Caspar has crawled back into his turret. "Watch for Zeros," comes over the headset. We are trained to spot Zeros, but we see only trees flashing by. In a few minutes smoke is visible ahead and we point straight at it. All our airplanes are strung out abreast. I can see B-25's on both sides forever. In just one minute we will launch the most deadly air attack ever on a Japanese harbor.

Then we get a glimpse of the harbor. Holy jumpin' buckets! Look at that! Look at all the ships! We have never seen so many ships all in one area. There must be twice as many as the Bismarck Sea Battle. And there are hundreds of small craft scattered around and tied to docks. Some of the big ships are docked also. The area along the shore is covered with smoke from the smoke bombs. The P-38's have done their job. I hope now they keep the Zeros away from us.

Each pilot of the Grim Reaper selects one ship in the flight path. The Major selects a heavy cruiser when there are plenty troopships and freighters. As we bear down on the ship I am trying to think about what I'm supposed to do. I'm so scared my thinker won't work.

The huge warship zooms to meet us while a 500 pounder leaves the bay and we all saturate the decks. Thousands of tracers are zipping at us from all directions and the sky darkens in a flash from clouds of flak puffs. I glance out the window to see the sky completely full of B-25's, flak, tracers, and the water full of ships.

"We're hit." "We're hit." Screams over the radio. This has to be a B-25. A P-38 pilot is alone. He would not say "we".

Our bomb smashes into the huge ship as we pull up over the superstructure and line up to the next target in our path. The warships now are firing their big guns into the water again creating giant water spouts. A tanker is ahead of us and I breathe a sigh of relief. We stand a much better chance with a tanker.

Out my port window I see a B-25 crash into the side of a ship. They are murdering us. It was stupid to have the P-38's come in first to warn them.

The ack-ack is so thick we could open the hatch and get out and walk on it. The air about us is clogged with exploding shells. How are we ever going to get through this?

The ripping sound of bullets tearing at our airplane drowns out the noise of our guns and engines as we barrel on the tanker at unheard of speed. Our rattling B-25 hoses the deck of the ship as our bomb bounces into its bowels and a geyser of water and oil shoots 400 feet into the sky. The oil turns to flame and the tanker disappears in the fire.

Widowmaker II drops to the water again and the Major looks for the next target. The sky above us is full of P-38's chasing Zeros and I see three Zeros spinning to the water. The far side of the harbor is covered with smoke which means the fighters have done a good job in the effort to cloud the area.

A P-38 is falling. For the first time ever we see a P-38 being shot down by Zeros. It is diving in a slow spin with a long trail behind it. The kid driving that P-38 must have fallen asleep to let the Zeros shoot him down. All he would have to do would be to slam forward his throttles to run away from the enemy.

Our plane has been hit but we are still flying and the next ship in our path is a warship. It is a smaller destroyer and the Major bears down on it with all the firepower we have. Both Caspar and myself help as much as we can. Our airplane is at full throttle and our guns are hot, but as long as the barrels don't melt we will pour out the lead and steel. The destroyer is firing at us with all her deck guns as the Major fantails the full length of the deck and Caspar a. ⁴ I do all we can to help. We are twenty feet from the Japs on deck when our bomb hits its belly and we run for safety. When it explodes under the water the ship rolls on its side and the Japs on deck fall into the water. The ship rolls back to the normal position and thousands of tons of water gush into the ship through the house size hole.

I turn off my tail gun because I know it is red hot, but leave my camera on to catch every scene of burning and sinking ships. Our plane is still flying, but I see another B-25 afire through my window. They are clobbering us. We are sinking their ships, but they are knocking the hell out of us too.

"We are hit. We are going down."

This means we have lost another B-25. There is nothing we can do to help here. They will be tortured and killed if the crash doesn't kill them. Air Sea Rescue can't help them here.

We have scored three direct hits on three ships. If the

other planes have done that well, there won't be a ship in the harbor without a house size hole in it. We fly through the fog bank on the far side of the harbor and look to our right and left. Then we keep going to make certain all airplanes are on this side. We must avoid smashing into our own planes in the turn.

"Connley to Grim Reaper, everybody o.k.?"

"This is Mary Jane, Jack the Ripper is in the bay."

"This is Hells Angels, we are wounded, and others are wounded."

Again we circle and line up all abreast to head back toward the bay. Then it is blind flying through the smoke and back at the ships. We pick the first destroyer in sight and barrel in at her with all our guns blasting and let go a bomb. They blast us too with all their guns and guns from other ships. As our bomb crashes into the hull of the ship, another B-25 hits the bay and bounces back into the air in two pieces. We have lost another airplane. There's no doubt we are destroying the enemy, but we're paying more than we had planned.

There are so many Zeros the P-38's are outnumbered and can't handle them all. The sky is full of them. We thought we had destroyed most of them, but they must have been shipped in. We see at least 200 Zeros. Four are attacking one B-25 and two are on our tail. Caspar knocks one down and I bring smoke to the other one. Three are in front of us and the Major gets one. We push across the harbor raking every ship in our path. The radio is a mess of garbled Yank voices.

"There goes another B-25" comes over the set.

This is the worst yet. Then another Zero is behind us and blasts my armor plate. Caspar hits it and draws smoke. The

300

sky is now full of Zeros as well as flak and tracers. Our P-38's are in there doing a magnificent job, and many of the Zeros are falling into the bay, but there are a much larger number of Zeros than P-38's. We are still flying and not trailing smoke yet. As we near the other side a blast jolts us again and shrapnel cuts more holes in our faithful plane.

"This is Connley, get together, make formation, let's get out of here."

Our only chance to survive the Zeros, is to make formation. Two more Zeros attack us, but now we are near another B-25 and both upper gunners knock one down, and the other runs away. Most of our airplanes are scattered, but slowly we get together and make formation. There are four missing, but one more shows up which leaves us three missing. There are three missing until we get back to Buna, then one more comes limping in.

On the way back to Buna I inspected the aft end for damage and found plenty. We had taken an unbelievable amount of flak and bullets. I could not however, find damage to vital parts. One engine had been hit and was misfiring, but it did not stop all the way back to Buna.

I called Buna and told them that we had attacked about 45 ships and many small craft, and we had three airplanes missing and much damage.

When we got back and added up the score, the results were: Six B-25's were shot down and all crew members could be counted as dead. The Grim Reaper lost two airplanes and crews. Many crew members had been wounded but none killed besides those who went down. Two P-38's were shot down with both pilots. There were over 150 Zeros in the fight. The B-25's shot down 28 of them and damaged 9. The P-38's shot down 42 Zeros. We sank or damaged 19 warships and 20 merchant ships, and damaged or sank many smaller vessels. About 300,000 tons of supplies were destroyed, and 120,000 tons of shipping.

Our roughest and toughest mission was over and we were all shot up and dead tired. But we were going right back as soon as our planes were repaired.

For the almost impossible accomplishment of this daring raid on November 2, 1943, more decorations were recommended and sent to Supreme Headquarters in Brisbane. The Yank heroism and dauntless ingenuity had been proven once more. The Japanese didn't have a chance. Their pride was bleeding and had received a mortal blow. We had proved that their men and materiels, in our area, were highly vulnerable and expendable. It must have been a sad tale the high brass received in Tokyo after this memorable day.

If medals can assuage the fear and death of such a titanic human struggle for survival, then we received all that a grateful government had to bestow on us. Our personnel were awarded the Congressional Medal of Honor, Distinguished Flying Crosses, Distinguished Service Crosses, Air Medals, Silver Stars, and Purple Hearts, for the attack on Rabaul shipping November 2, 1943. The crew members killed or missing were all awarded the Medal of Honor which is the highest decoration possible.

For the past two weeks we have been flying a combat mission almost every day, but we cannot go back tomorrow because our planes are so shot up it will require two days and nights to get them back in shape. So it is two days of rest, but I am back out on the line to make certain Widowmaker II gets all the attention she needs. Major Connley comes out to pat her on the back also.

Late the second night all repairs had been made, so the armament people went to work loading bombs and ammo.

"Strike Rabaul shipping!"

At the crack of dawn the next morning once again we take flight for Rabaul Harbor. All flyable B-25's in the 5th Air Force will be with us, and this time we are going to get smart. We will attack first and the P-38's will come from above later like we usually do. In two days the Nips have probably had time to repair a few of their losses, and we hope to catch them unaware.

Our bearing is straight as the crows fly to the target, and all squadrons of the 5th meet a few miles north of Buna to gradually move into an abreast line as we get closer and closer to the prey. We don't know how many planes we have, but there are enough. If there were any more we would be crashing into each other over the bay.

The P-38's drop their tanks again, and it is time to watch the spectacle. The Lightnings lag aft, so we get rid of our tanks and shake some more with fear.

"Pilot to crew, we have a good chance to do our old thing today and catch them flatfooted. I'll try to drop all bombs on one pass across the harbor, so we won't have to expose our airplane twice to them. Now I want to tell all of you again, we are not going to die today."

The harbor is full of ships again, but not as many as before. Some ships are half beneath the waves, and some bows and sterns are above the water line. A freighter is in our path so we rake it and skip a bomb into it, then continue to a destroyer. The destroyer is waiting for us and fires its big guns forward of our plane into the water. The Major is quick as a cat, and dodges the water spouts. Boy, did he shake us up doing it. We shatter the deck as we skip a bomb into its belly and continue on. Now a troopship is in our way so we blow a hole as big as a house in it under the water line. Then thousands of deck guns and shore batteries hit their triggers and open up on all of us. Their tracers cover the whole harbor and look like a giant cobweb. Our faithful airplane takes more splattering as we dive for the next ship. This one looks like some kind of a landing ship. We rake the deck with our guns and plant another bomb in its bowels. There are two more medium size vessels ahead so we attack them and there is the shore. As we cross the shore line both Caspar and I zero in on the source of all the tracers that are coming our way. Then, like a flash, they are behind us and it appears as if we made it.

"Watch for Zeros."

We search the sky for Zeros, but so far it looks like they have not broken through the P-38 cover.

The harbor is a black cloud of smoke spiraling thousands of feet high, and tracers fill the air completely. The tracers we see are a small part of the lead and steel in the air. Every seventh round in an ammo belt is tracer, so there is seven times as much lead and steel in the air as we can see.

"This is Connley, get into formation."

We watch for Zeros, make formation, check on the dogfights above, and head for home. It is time to take in the show above. The P-38's and Zeros are painting vapor trails high in the sky. Once again they are proving how superior they are compared to the Zeke. Then four Zekes break through and come at us from aft. They haven't got a chance. Our gunners focus on them and rip them apart.

Widowmaker II had left six gaping holes in six ships—all as big as a house. If the other planes have done half as well, all the ships in their harbor are sinking.

The next day our reconn revealed that we had sunk 15 ships and damaged 18 more. One B-25 was lost with four crew members. The Grim Reaper lost no airplanes, but four were damaged, and one gunner was wounded. The B-25's shot down 17 Zeros and damaged 6. The P-38's shot down 23 and damaged 2. The P-38's lost no airplanes.

Thus ended my 49th mission. I have one more to go. Rabaul is so badly wounded she is in her death throes. She will need a few more raids, but the one more I have to fly should pretty much knock her out of the war.

# CHAPTER 26
## STRIKE RABAUL SHIPPING!

For my 50th and last mission, and the third raid on Rabaul shipping, we spent one day plus the next night repairing airplanes and loading them. We had the Nips on the run and we had no idea of relenting. Much time had been spent in inspecting our airplanes and checking guns. With their load of 500 pounders and ammo, they were ready to go. I was straining at the bit to get it over.

We knew there was danger, plenty of it, but a lot of their strength had already been knocked out. I just knew I'd get through this one.

At 0330 hours the next morning we were zooming down the Buna runway, one at a time, rocketing over the trees. Each plane followed running lights until daybreak. Then we strung out in a straight line and dropped down to the water. It took a while for the other squadrons to get up to us, but in time we were all abreast. By that time the P-38's were dropping their tanks. The south coast of New Britain came up and we were soon bouncing over the trees and getting rid of our tanks.

Once again we don't know how many B-25's we have on this raid, but all that can fly are out there. When we flew our biggest raid on Rabaul airdromes we had 125, but we have lost quite a few since then, and replacements are slowing up. I can count about 85 and there may be more.

The heavies have been bombing Rabaul ships also, but they can't do a fraction of the damage we can unless they come down and skip bomb. They have been known to do that too, and they have had pretty good luck. But they are really too big for skip bombing. The B-25 is only half the size of the heavies, but we can do probably twenty times the damage to a ship or airdrome.

The trees are flashing by now and our airplane is bucking like a buckboard on a country dirt road. Our target is getting nearer as my watch ticks away, and I'm really sweatin' this one out. Will it be like my friend Kerstetter who was killed on take off on his way home?

"Caspar, you'd better not let the Zeros get us today. You know I'm going home tomorrow."

Then the Major calls:

"Hey, you guys, knock it off, we are all in the same ship, and we're all coming back today."

"Thanks Major, you're the boss."

We hug the trees as the target gets closer and closer. The water comes into view and the harbor is right before us. Our planes are all spread out in a straight line so we'll be able to hit all the ships in the huge harbor. There are less ships than on our last strike. Some of our planes are banking away because there are not enough ships for everyone to go in at the same time. When the first bombs explode those other planes will attack.

We select a cargo ship that is anchored in our path. An easy one for a change. The ships deck guns begin to fire at us and we rake the deck like with a giant fire hose. Their gunners quit firing at us when we drop the deadly bomb. They know what's in store for them and are trying to save themselves. The bomb explodes and rolls the ship on its side and a geyser of water engulfs the ship, then falls back to rush through the huge hole. There is nothing they can do to stop her from sinking.

We attack a small tanker in the same way and skip a bomb into it. The huge water spout turns to oil and flame and the water becomes an inferno around the ship. Then we head for a destroyer and give it the same treatment. I see the decks alive with white flashes. They are doing everything possible to keep us away from their ship, but we barrel on in just the same and give her a 500 pounder. One flak burst is too close and it splatters us with shrapnel. The Major banks to miss the superstructure and our bomb finds her amidships. The ship rolls to the side and struggles back to a sitting position, but the wound in her side will open up the sea to her innards. She'll soon be on the harbor bottom resting with the scores of the other ships we have sent there. Some of them are showing above the surface.

There are no more ships in our flight path but we spy a motor torpedo boat and plant a big one inside its hull. The bomb penetrates its wooden hull and explodes inside. The boat disintegrates into small pieces. Another small boat is in our way so we make a sieve out of it. Then our incendiaries turn it to a ball of fire.

Now we face the shore batteries. The Major dives on one gun emplacement to pour lead into it. It stops firing, but we doubt if we blew up the guns there. They are behind concrete and steel bunkers.

Somebody screams, "we're on fire."

We can't see any burning B-25's. It must be one of the other squadrons. One suicidal enemy fighter pilot gets through the P-38 cover to hit us from the rear. Our gunners all funnel into it and it explodes.

The Grim Reaper makes formation and we head for Buna. Smoke is billowing thousands of feet into the sky, and each ship has taken at least two 500 pounders under the water line. Some have taken four. They will all sink eventually.

I got on the key and told Buna that all our bombs found the target, and the Grim Reaper has lost no airplanes.

When we got back to our base we learned that two more B-25's went down. They belonged to the other squadrons. We sank or damaged all of the ships and most of the small craft in the harbor. None escaped our deadly onslaught.

And this is the end of my part in helping to stop the Japanese war machine. My job now is finished according to the word of the General, and the General is a man of his word. My orders are cut to send me back to the States. Now I have to find a hop to Australia, and it will be four days until I can get a flight to Brisbane. Meanwhile the war goes on. The Major is taking the Grim Reaper right back to Rabaul Harbor in the morning. He doesn't have a radio gunner yet. Will I go?

"O.K.," I tell him, "if you give me your word that we will come back alive."

"You have my word," he says. That is good as gold to me.

It was a routine mission. There was about ten floating ships in the harbor this time and some of those were sinking. We blew big holes in their bellies and smashed them with our cannons and machine guns, then left them to sink. Their once powerful harbor was now full of the junk we made of their ships. The bows and the sterns were protruding above the water on some. The heavies had blasted their gun batteries on shore which had cut way down on the ack-ack hazard.

I don't know how many ships we sank at the big base at Rabaul, but there were not many of them left when I went home. The 5th Air Force and the 13th Air Force continued to smash the area until there was nothing left there but a lot of debris. The town of Rabaul, all the airdromes, nearly 400 gun emplacements, the docks, all the buildings, all the ships, and the many small boats, were so completely destroyed that Supreme Headquarters decided it was not worth taking by the ground forces. They by-passed it. What had been Japan's "Gibraltar of the Southwest Pacific" was now just a huge pile of junk. And still, with all this evidence, the Japanese refused to admit defeat.

Back at Buna we mourned the kids who were killed in the C-47 crash on take-off. They had all completed their 50 missions and were on a C-47 at Buna taking off for their first leg of the long trip home. Many were my friends. Some I had known since radio school. What kind of a reward is this? After flying 50 skip bombing and strafing missions and facing death on all of them, they get killed on their way home. I wrote to some parents and wives, but what can you say?

There was no celebration or farewell party on my leaving. Some of the kids gathered round and someone said, "well, I guess most of the Grim Reaper owe our lives to each other." Hands were extended to friends I would never come in contact with again. No hero could be seen, and this is what made each one of us indispensable.

Saying goodbye to the Major was not an easy task. He had taken me into the very thick of the fighting, seeking out the most risky missions. He was the leader and commander, always saying "follow me." His was always the strong, quiet courage that inspired confidence. It was usual for the Grim Reaper to have fewer casualties, yet Major Connley always picked the hardest and toughest enemy ships. Connley believed in what we were doing, and he made all of us believers. When he said, "this is going to be the toughest raid we've ever been on," he was not fooling anybody. But then he added, "but no one is going to get killed today," and he was right.

Yes, Major Connley brought us home, day in day out. What could I say in farewell? It was a handshake, and he looked me in the eye. "Good luck," he said, "and thanks."

"You'll be going home soon," I told him. "The Japs are whipped. Now it's downhill all the way to Tokyo. I'll be looking for you back home."

My flight back to Australia was a dream. As we lifted over the rain clouds for the final time, and out across the beautiful Coral Sea and the Great Barrier Reef, I had a hard time believing that this was for real. So many memories came back to me. I could not help think that the wings that had carried me safely so many times into combat, had been given a kind of special blessing. Somebody had been doing a little praying, and I knew it was my mother.

The C-47 took me on the first and shortest leg of the long trip back to the States. The first stop was my old base at Amberly Field. From there I had orders to report to Supreme Headquarters in Brisbane. A staff car took us there along the winding road and the tracks of the little train with the high screeching whistle. How well I remember that. All in our party were given a suite of rooms in the best hotel in Brisbane for the night. My immediate orders were to report to General Kenney's old headquarters in the Lennon Hotel in the morning. But tonight we'll celebrate.

It's hard to believe that in three days I will be living in the Mark Hopkins Hotel way back in San Francisco, and in a week I'll be living in the Hollywood Canteen and doing

311

the rumba with movie stars there. And my friends back in the sweaty jungle have over two and a half more years to sweat it out.

Brisbane is still crammed with Yanks. How is it possible to win a war when there are so many men not fighting? What wasteful blundering inefficiency.

When I awoke the next morning I could not understand what my dread was this day. I had no combat to worry about, then I remembered. I had to report to General Kenney's office. This was worse than combat.

When I walked through the door to his big office I was frozen with fear. General MacArthur was there, but he immediately left like the good actor he was. Then General Kenney introduced himself as if I didn't know who lead the 5th Air Force. He said, "try to relax, I am not here to scare you. I know you kids by now. You would rather face the enemy than your commanding general." "Sit on my desk," the General said.

I sat on his desk and I couldn't believe it. Me, sitting on the General's desk? He was only trying to make me feel more comfortable.

"Where are you from?" he asked.

"From a little one-horse town in Utah."

"I see where you have flown over 50 combat missions in my commerce destroyers," he said.

"Yes, I have flown 51 combat missions, but some were in the old Douglas Dauntless divers."

"Oh yes," he replied, "they were something out of the first war."

"I don't know how old they were, but we had a bad experience with them, and lost them with all crews."

"How did you like the B-25?" he asked.

312

"Well, I owe North American Aviation for my life many times over. They will take a lot of punishment in combat and keep flying."

"Why do you call them commerce destroyers?" I asked.

"Well, my idea was to convert them to skip bombers and strafers to destroy Jap commercial shipping. I didn't realize then that you eager kids would have the guts to attack their warships with them."

"General, all the kids in the B-25 outfits believe that "Pappy Gunn" conceived the skip bombing strafing idea."

"No," he said, "it was my idea, but that does not matter, you were the ones who proved it."

"I helped "Pappy" test the B-25 when he had them converted, and he just about scared me to death. He must be the most daring pilot in the Army Air Corps."

"General, you'd never believe what we did with those B-25's. Not a ship escaped us. We never failed to plant our 500 pounders under the water line next to their hulls. We ripped them to ribbons with all those guns. We laid waste their airdromes and even blasted their fighters from the sky."

"Yes, I know what's been going on up there. I know about Major Connley and Colonel Davies of the 3rd Attack Group. Did you fly the Bismarck Sea Battle?" he asked.

"Yes sir," I said, "all three days."

"Yes, that was a bloody mess." "Did you fly Wewak?"

"Yes sir, my outfit destroyed 36 airplanes in 12 seconds, plus ammo dumps and fuel dumps on the first day."

"Well, I don't have to ask you if you did Rabaul. You wouldn't be on your way home if you hadn't."

I can't believe it. Why should a general who commands the whole 5th Air Force spend so much time with me?

313

"I am going to award you two crosses," the General said. "They are Distinguished Flying Crosses. There will also be some lesser decorations you will receive."

He shook my hand and wished me well on my way home.

Medals? They don't mean much to me. But I will take the Distinguished Flying Crosses. It pays a pension, and is like money in the bank. In the British and Aussie Air Forces it is a title and printed after your name and carried for life. But not in the States.

The General told me he was going to write a letter to my father to tell him what I had done. I told him my father had been dead for three years. "Then I'll write to your mother," he said.

The next morning I caught a C-54 for Canton Island, Hickam Field, and San Francisco.